Anthologia Graeca. English. Selections

The Greek Anthology

AND OTHER ANCIENT GREEK
EPIGRAMS

A selection in modern verse translations,
edited with an
introduction by Peter Jay

NEW YORK
OXFORD UNIVERSITY PRESS
1973

ISBN 19 519 745-3

Library of Congress Catalog Card Number:

73-81114

Printed in Great Britain by
Hazell Watson & Viney Ltd
Aylesbury, Bucks
Set in Monotype Bembo

Contents

INTRODUCTION 9

EDITOR'S NOTE 27

ACKNOWLEDGEMENTS 31

1 *The Greek Period: Archilochos to Hegemon*
   (c. 700–350 B.C.) 33

Archilochos	Parrhasios
Kleoboulos	Thukydides
Phokylides	Plato
Anakreon	Demodokos
Simonides	Hegemon
Aischylos	Anonymous Inscriptions

2 *The Hellenistic Period: Menander to Meleager*
   (c. 350–90 B.C.) 53

Menander	Erinna
Perses	Moiro
Asklepiades	Nossis
Philitas	Theaitetos
Simias	Kallimachos
Phalaikos	Herakleitos
Alexander	Euphorion
Douris	Hegesippos
Poseidippos	Leonidas of Tarentum
Hedylos	Mnasalkes
Anyte	Theodoridas
Theokritos	Nikainetos
Nikias	Tymnes

Hermokreon
Thymokles
Aristodikos
Rhianos
Dioskorides
Damagetos

Alkaios
Philip V of Macedon
Artemidoros
Zenodotos
Antipater of Sidon
Meleager

3 *Other Hellenistic Poets* 149

Ariston
Chairemon
Dionysios
Diotimos
Glaukos

Karphyllides
Nikarchos
Pamphilos
Phanias
Anonymous Epigrams

4 *The Roman Period: Diodoros Zonas to Philip*
   (c. 90 B.C.–A.D. 50) 165

Diodoros Zonas
Philodemos
Krinagoras
Erucius
Antipater of Thessalonika
Marcus Argentarius
Statilius Flaccus
Apollonides

Bianor
Bassus
Pompeius
Thallos
Honestus
Antiphanes
Philip

5 *Other Poets of the Roman Period* 221

Adaios
Alpheios
Antimedon
Antistius
Archias
Automedon
Diodoros

Euenos
Gaetulicus
Isidoros
Julius Polyaenus
Maccius
Myrinos
Parmenion

CONTENTS

Pinytos
Serapion

Anonymous Epigrams

6 *The Roman Empire: Antiphilos to Julianus of Egypt*
   (c. A.D. 50–450)   243

Antiphilos
Lucilius
Nikarchos
Leonidas of Alexandria
Trajan
Ammianus
Asklepiodotos
Strato
Claudius Ptolemaeus
Lucian

Skythinos
Diogenes Laertios
Palladas
Gregory
Flavius Claudius Julianus
   (Julian the Apostate)
'The Delphic Oracle'
Rufinus
Theon
Julianus of Egypt

7 *Other Poets under the Empire*   315

Apollinarius
Capito
Cerealius
Cyrillus
Diophanes of Myrina
Euodos
Gauradas
Glykon
Herodikos
Killaktor
Plato

Satyros
Thyillos
Tryphon
Anonymous Epigrams
   Erotic
   Dedicatory
   Epitaphs
   The Famous Dead
   Gnomic
   Satirical
   Miscellaneous

8 *The Early Byzantine Period (c. A.D. 500–600)*   337

Marianos
Eratosthenes
Paulos

Agathias
Isidoros
Leontios

7

CONTENTS

Macedonius	Theaitetos
Johannes Barbukollas	Damocharis
Damaskios	Theophanes
Irenaios	

9   *Anonymous Byzantine Epigrams*   367

10   *The Later Byzantines*   371

Kometas
Kephalas

APPENDIX 1 – *The Proems*   375

Meleager – to the *Garland*	Agathias – to the *Cycle*
Philip – to the *Garland*	

APPENDIX 2 – *A Poem by Palladas*   379

NOTES   381

GLOSSARY   394

A SELECT BIBLIOGRAPHY   423

NOTES ON CONTRIBUTORS AND INDEX TO THE
    TRANSLATIONS   425

INDEX OF GREEK POETS   431

INDEX TO POEMS FROM THE PALATINE
    ANTHOLOGY   434

INDEX TO POEMS FROM OTHER SOURCES   440

MAPS   443

Introduction

I

Four thousand poems: half a dozen, at least, of the great names of Greek poetry: a poetic genre preserved in quantity, with a traceable history: poems which are much closer to the modern reader's poetic habits than any other classical verse, save perhaps Catullus and the Augustan elegists – and yet the compendium of epigrams which is The Greek Anthology remains largely unknown and little read.

To be sure, there have been many slim 'selections from The Greek Anthology' in English versions. And now the labours of A. S. F. Gow and Sir Denys Page have provided the student with critical texts and commentaries on the Hellenistic poets and the poets of Philip's *Garland*. Yet since the last edition of J. W. Mackail's *Select Epigrams from the Greek Anthology* (1911), there has been no useful selection of the texts in circulation. And not since 1833, and the last edition of Bland and Merivale's anthology, has there been anything like a representative selection in verse translation of the epigrammatists. I have attempted to fill this gap by providing versions of all the poems of living interest – to wrest them from the disorganized mass of the sixteen books which form The Greek Anthology, and to provide something of a historical framework in which all aspects of this astonishing range of poetry can be enjoyed.

2. GREEK EPIGRAM – A HISTORICAL OUTLINE

The reader must for the moment put aside his modern notion of 'epigram' as a short poem of pointed humour: throughout this book the term is used in its Greek senses – the development of which is of some importance in understanding the role of epigram in its later, more literary forms.

The primary meaning of 'epigram' is 'inscription'. The earliest metrical inscriptions appeared in Greece in about the seventh century B.C. Votive offerings and tombstones had a few lines of commemorative verse – hexameter, elegiac or iambic in metre – inscribed on them. At this stage the inscriptions simply recorded facts: the name of the dedicator, his family and town, and the name and title of the god, with perhaps the reason for the offering. Even the tombstone inscriptions were impersonal in nature, employing no phrases of personal regret. Wayside tombstones often bore a few lines addressing the passer-by, inviting him to meditate on the human condition as evinced by the circumstances of the life and death of the tomb's occupant. Most of these inscriptions came to be written in the elegiac couplet, a verse-form which developed in the late seventh and early sixth centuries, and which became the most common medium for formal inscriptions.

Elegiac verse★ seems originally to have been the metre of flute-songs. The root survives in the Armenian word for the flute, *elegn*. The metre itself is an extension of the hexameter, the metre of Homeric epic, to bring it closer to a lyric, non-narrative form.

The first line of the elegiac couplet is the hexameter, a line

★ Unless otherwise noted all the Greek originals of poems in this book were written in elegiac couplets. A very small number of poems employ hexameters, iambic trimeters (the metre of dialogue in tragedy), hendecasyllables (adopted so frequently by the Romans, Catullus and Martial) or other, mixed metres. The metres of these poems, which are marked with an asterisk against the reference to the Greek text, are given in the Notes.

One or two poets, such as Philip, seem to have been particularly interested in unusual metres to give a new twist to their epigrams.

of six feet with a caesura (pause) in the middle of the third foot. Each foot is either a dactyl (– ∪ ∪: a long and two short syllables), or a spondee (– –: two long syllables). The second line is the so-called pentameter – which is really two half-lines of 2½ feet, each half-line being metrically equivalent to the first part of the hexameter. There is a pronounced pause between the two halves of the pentameter.

$$\overline{As}teras \mid \overline{ei}sa\mid threis, \parallel \overline{A}\mid ster\ emos. \mid \overline{Ei}the\ ge\mid noimen$$

$$\overline{ou}ranos, \mid hos\ pol\mid lois \parallel ommasin \mid eis\ se\ ble\mid po.$$

(Plato: no. 27 here)

The scansion is quantitative, that is to say, determined by the length or duration of vowels – not by a count of stressed syllables. Despite this, both stress and pitch play a part in the metric. The nature of Greek pitch is now little understood, but the stress, in counterpoint to the length of syllables, creates the rhythmical tensions of Greek verse. A glance at the poem by Palladas printed in Appendix 2 will give a picture of what this means in practice.

The couplet has a tendency to end-stop; it is very rare that enjambement occurs between two couplets. It is therefore less suited to narrative poetry than the simple hexameter, and in the poets of the seventh century B.C. – Archilochos, Tyrtaios, Kallinos and Mimnermos – we find two main uses of it: both, as it happens, associated with flute-music. The first is basically military: exhortations, such as those of Tyrtaios, to soldiers to fight bravely. This was in the time of prolonged wars between Sparta and the Messenians, when every male citizen was also a soldier. Flute-music was used for marching, and also to accompany convivial songs sung over the wine. Archilochos' poems of life in the camp are of this second kind, as are Mimnermos' reflective poems. The poems of Kallinos are really a combination of the two types.

With the convivial elegiac we may include the historical and mythological poems – such as Mimnermos' lost *Smyrneis* – in which poets recounted their city's legends and past glories; and also poems commemorative of the dead. These were exemplary poems, holding up the virtues of a dead warrior, say, for emulation by young recruits, rather than elegies in the modern sense. The use of the elegiac couplet for epitaphic inscriptions probably derives from this, rather than from the almost unknown brand of elegiac lament which existed, and from which elegy got its reputation as a gloomy and mournful kind of poetry (*flebilis elegeia*, as Ovid calls it). Inscribed dedications may also be a development of the convivial type of elegiac poem – though the simple convenience of the form is an equally plausible explanation.

In the sixth and fifth centuries the elegiac couplet was mostly used for epitaphic inscriptions, and for longer reflective poems. The inscriptional epigram reached its peak of refinement with Simonides, who harnessed the form's brevity and impersonality for his art of concentrated intensity and pathos. No translation can give any sense of the qualities which raise

Ō xein' angellein ‖ Lakedaimoniois hoti tēde

keimetha, tois keinōn ‖ rhēmasi peithomenoi (no. 10)

to the highest level by exploiting all the qualities inherent in the language. No explanation of the subtle word-disposition, the assonances, the texture and shades of meaning of the eleven simple words can recreate this inaccessible art.

With Theognis, the sixth-century master of the reflective elegy, the seeds of the subjective epigram were sown. By 400 B.C. Plato was writing personal epigrams which foreshadow the direction epigram was to take in the Hellenistic period. This new direction becomes apparent with Asklepiades, and his associates Hedylos and Poseidippos. In their personal poems the emotional range associated with the reflective elegy and the drinking-song merge with the comparative brevity of the inscription. At the same time, the writing of artificial 'epideiptic' epigrams ('for display', because they were never intended to fulfil a truly inscriptional function) expanded the scope of epigram in another direction: poets now began to write pseudo-epitaphs, descriptive poems about works of art, places, historical events, poems commemorative of long-dead historical or legendary figures and early poets, etc. The epigram had now become a literary form.

In the third century two 'schools' of epigrammatists are thought to have existed. One is the 'Peloponnesian': poets like Anyte and Nossis, writing mainly in Doric dialect on themes of local and country life. Anyte introduced the pastoral element into epigram. Their poems were epideiptic, not subjective, and set the standards for the conventional themes so much imitated in the Graeco-Roman period.

The 'Ionian' school, led by Asklepiades, was centred not on mainland Greece but in the new Greek world of Alexandria and Samos. It was more cosmopolitan and sophisticated, concentrating on subjective poetry about love, wine, literature and art. The two schools can be contrasted in the work of the two major figures of the mid-third century, Leonidas and Kallimachos. The subjective epigram reaches its highest point of lyric (in the modern sense)* development later still, with Meleager.

* Today we use the term 'lyric' so loosely as to make it almost meaningless; it is applied to nearly all subjective poetry. No doubt we use it primarily of the kind of poetry which in Elizabethan or earlier times was actually sung, but the strict sense of lyric – 'for singing to the lyre'

The Alexandrian age explored the epigram's potential in almost every direction. Much of the poetry of the following period, however, is merely conventional, in the sense that the poems are literary exercises on now more-or-less standard themes. The greatest epigrammatist of the period between Meleager and Philip (roughly 100 B.C.–A.D. 50) is the Roman, Catullus (c. 84–54 B.C.) who, like the Alexandrians he so much admired, was not even primarily an epigrammatist.* On the whole the Graeco-Roman poets confined themselves to epigrams deliberately imitating their favourite Hellenistic poets, such as Leonidas. 'Originality' was not a highly-regarded quality, at least in the sense we use the term. Skill in adapting traditional themes, clever phrase-making and even a certain bizarreness of subject-matter were what these poets aimed at. This generalization is however quite unfair to poets like Philodemos, Krinagoras and Marcus Argentarius, who are far above the general level of undistinguished versifying. It is noticeable that these poets wrote mostly on convivial and erotic, rather than epideiptic, themes.

The invention of the humorous, pointed epigram must be credited to Lucilius and Nikarchos, in the time of Nero. It was an age of satire, and their light verse is an amusing

---

– is lost. The Greeks kept their poetic genres quite separate: poetry to be sung to the lyre evolved quite different metres, and largely different themes, from elegiac verse; and the Romans, on the whole, maintained the thematic distinctions. Subjective epigrams written in elegiacs are in no ancient sense 'lyric'; yet when we come to talk of the difference between the poems, say, of Kallimachos and Meleager, the modern sense of 'lyric' is useful to convey an impression of Meleager's unusual use of the medium. In any other age he would very likely have written in lyric forms.

*He wrote elegies, lyric poems, satires, a small epic, and a miscellany of occasional poems of all kinds. On the relationship between his epigrams and lyrics see 'Ezra Pound and Catullus' by Peter Whigham in *Perspectives*, ed. Noel Stock, Regnery, 1965.

counterpart to the masterpieces of the fifties and sixties A.D. –
Persius' *Satires* and the *Satyricon* of Petronius. The Greek
poets display little of the real poetic talent and wide interests
of the Roman epigrammatist Martial (*c*. A.D. 40–104), who
was at least their equal as a humorist; but they undoubtedly
extended the meaning of 'epigram' in the direction which is
familiar to us.

The next three centuries provide little that is new, until we
come to the bitter Palladas, whose mordant genius harks back
to the gnomic style of Theognis, yet seems to exist in a literary
and cultural vacuum.

The last burst of activity in epigram comes with the early
Byzantines at Constantinople, under Justinian. Theirs was a
conscious attempt to revive classical Greek literature in the
new capital of the Roman empire; they wrote in the now
archaic, elegiac metre, and the old literary language, which
had long since lost its spoken currency. This in itself is not
surprising; they were highly educated men, conscious of the
Greek heritage which gave the city its character. Agathias
tends to write rather verbose, elegiac-descriptive poems, many
of which cannot be called epigrams; but Paulos and Mace-
donius both give a personal stamp to their poetry, and are at
their best in convivial and erotic poetry, rather than in the
more stylized epideiptic modes.

3. THE NATURE OF GREEK EPIGRAM

This summary historical account of epigram will, I hope,
enable the reader to distinguish the basic types of epigram as he
meets them. The first general observation to be made is on the
range of subject-matter available to the epigrammatist, and
the considerable flexibility of the medium. Each new poet of
any talent extended the form in one way or another for his own
purposes; it would be tedious to categorize the distinctions

which may be drawn at every point. The epigram was an ideal form both for the subjective and personal, and for the more formal, rhetorical poem. At the same time it had severe limitations. The Greeks did not expect epigram to compete with lyric, epic, elegiac, tragic or comic verse – though subject-matter was occasionally borrowed from these genres. Epigram survived after the demise of these other poetic forms partly because of its status as a genre of 'occasional' poetry. This allowed the poet to write either in an accepted style on general subjects – with as much latitude as his verbal ingenuity permitted – or to write in a personal vein without any sense of constraint, anachronism or artificiality. Epigram continued to be written for the same reason that any poetry ever continues to be written, after the major forms seem to have been perfected and exhausted. It was an inclusive, eclectic form, in which any talented poet could write distinctively.

The question may be asked: is not the epigram, by its own nature, a minor genre? Pressed, one would admit that 'the Greek genius' – if there was anything as all-embracing as that – found its fullest expression elsewhere: in the Homeric epics and the Attic tragedies. But this is not the point. Except for purposes of tracing a brief history of a literary form's uses, one cannot speak of 'the epigram' as a composite genre with any uniformity. It is sentimental and facile to view The Greek Anthology as the 'record of a civilization' – as if the poems in it, taken together, somehow make up a unit which has a composite spirit. The poets are so very different from each other. Part of the difficulty has lain in the present arrangement of texts of the Anthology, which group the poems by subject-matter and type, not by their authors: an arrangement which encourages both random reading of the epigrams and anti-critical, generalized ideas about what Greek epigram is. 'If we really love poetry, then we know and must know all its degrees.'* For this reason the poets are presented here individually, in as near a chronological sequence as can be attained, in the hope that they may be read and appreciated for their individual qualities.

It ought not to be necessary to apologize for the presence of so much occasional and light verse in this collection. The core of *essential* poetry could perhaps be narrowed down to a hundred or so pieces; but to demand only those pieces would be to ignore an enjoyable variety of lesser material – which is valuable also because it provides a context in which the best poetry can emerge in its fullest perspective. There is no real divorce between 'poetry' and 'occasional verse' here, because in the true sense almost all Greek epigrams are 'occasional' – composed for or on specific occasions, private or public. The lighter forms of verse are much maligned nowadays; it is thought to be condescending, or a sign of failure of talent, for poets to write epigrammatic or light verse: as if poets should be restricted to 'serious' poetry, whatever that might be, the whole time. Exceptions to the rule, to name two only, are Ezra Pound and W. H. Auden – disparate figures whom I link only to point to their professionalism and craft, which are manifested as much in their epigrams as in their other poetry.

English epigrams are for the most part in the Latin tradition of Martial. One thinks of Ben Jonson, the Cavalier poets and the Augustans: a poetry of wit, exploiting the effects of rhyme as a clinching device to point the poem. By contrast, the qualities of tone and texture which make the best Hellenistic

---

*T. S. Eliot in his Introduction to the *Selected Poems of Ezra Pound* (1928), where he points out that if nothing but the very best poetry were admitted 'the result would be to censor a larger part of the published work of most of the accepted poets. It might also expunge several excellent poets altogether. ... If we only knew "perfect" poetry we should know very little about poetry.'

epigrams so memorable are extremely difficult to charac-
terize, and there is very little in English poetry which has a
comparable 'feel'. *The* tone, *the* texture of a good Greek
epigram is barely appreciable even by those who have long
studied the language. As anyone with an experience of con-
temporary poetry in his own language will attest, only the
most intimate acquaintance with the spoken language can
provide the feel for linguistic nuance in which the poetry
resides – and in this sense Greek epigram is truly dead.
Nevertheless, enough of its qualities can be sensed to form an
opinion of what is good in Greek epigram – and in what
respects it is unlike anything English.

The best description of the general qualities of Greek
epigram that I have found was in the *Times Literary Supple-
ment*'s review (17 September 1971) of Robin Skelton's recent
selection of epigrams. It is worth quoting an extract:

> What exhausts the imagination is the minute range of the effective
> variations of tone, of rhythm, and of theme on which all these poems
> depend ... the names and props of an Anthology poem were often
> meant to be formal, or in some subtle contrast to an expected for-
> mality; it was a matter of exact usage and resonance, a different kind
> of poetry from anything in English ... the exact rhymes and clear,
> sharp rhythms of Gravesian English verse knock the humour and
> the pathos flat: the elegiac couplet was not built to withstand accentual
> climax, and the climax that the rhythm of English verse imposes on
> a short epigram is the bump of a hammer where the poem was con-
> ceived as the dying notes of a guitar.

The modern poems which come nearest to this are a few of
Pound's epigrams – though he most nearly approaches the
satirical and gnomic style of the later epigrammatists, such as
Lucilius or Palladas; Eliot's 'Death by Water' from *The Waste
Land*, and a few poems by Edgar Lee Masters from *The Spoon
River Anthology*, which borrows some of the formal devices

of Greek epigram (e.g. epitaphs in which the dead person is supposed to speak, as in the beautiful poem 'Anne Rutledge').

In a more 'lyric' vein, poets like Ian Hamilton and even Robert Creeley often seem to be aiming at a resonance akin to that of Greek epigrams – though with an increased self-consciousness. There is very little in current poetry that is at all like Greek epigram – which is a very good reason for reading the Greek poems in modern verse translation.

4. THE GREEK ANTHOLOGY

The Greek Anthology is the name generally given to the combined resources of two anthologies of epigram – that of Maximus Planudes, and The Palatine Anthology, so-called because the manuscript was rediscovered in 1606 in the Count Palatine's library at Heidelberg.

The earliest collections of epigrams were made in the Alexandrian age. Papyrus fragments* of one or two of these have been found; but the most important was the *Garland*, edited by Meleager sometime between 100 and 90 B.C. It is now lost, but much of it has been absorbed into The Greek Anthology. Meleager's book included the work of at least forty-seven poets named in his Proem (see Appendix 1), from Archilochos to himself, but was especially rich in Hellenistic epigrams of the third and second century.

Philip of Thessalonika compiled in about A.D. 40 his *Garland*, which was expressly designed as a supplement to Meleager's anthology, covering the intervening period (see

---

*One of the Berlin Papyri consists of a papyrus roll containing, on one side, some Greek lyric verse, and on the other a selection of Greek epigrams. With characteristic humour, Wilamowitz notes that the size of the roll was such that it could neatly have been lodged in the décolletage of a fashionable Roman lady's dress.

Appendix 1 for his Proem). Strato made an anthology of homosexual verse in the second century A.D., and Agathias compiled his *Cycle* of contemporary poets in about A.D. 570 (see also Appendix 1).

The Anthology as we have it retains strong traces of these old collections. Kephalas in the tenth century made his anthology by distributing the poems of Meleager's, Philip's and Agathias' anthologies under headings of their subject-matter, so that all the erotic poems, all the dedicatory poems, etc., are grouped together in separate books. He also added Strato's collection, the Christian epigrams mainly from Byzantine churches (Book 1), Christodoros' description of the statues in a Byzantine gymnasium (Book 2), and the inscriptions from the temple of Apollonis at Kyzikos (Book 3). Kephalas' anthology forms the first fifteen books of modern editions of the Anthology.

The polymath Byzantine scholar Maximus Planudes (*c.* A.D. 1255–1305) made another anthology, based on that of Kephalas, but with many alterations – mostly omissions – and some additions. Planudes' anthology, first printed in 1484, replaced Kephalas', which had completely disappeared from view: fortunately it was rediscovered at Heidelberg. The additional material which Planudes included is now added as the 'Planudean Appendix'; it forms the last book of modern editions of the Anthology, and is here referred to as Book 16.

Kephalas was not very consistent in his redistribution of the poems by subject-matter. Book 12, based largely on Strato's *Mousa Paidiké* (Pederastic Poems), has a number of hetero-sexual poems in it; Book 5, the other collection of erotic poems, likewise has some homosexual poems. A great deal of scholarly energy has gone into efforts to reconstitute the contents of Meleager's and Philip's anthologies, or at least to determine which parts of Kephalas' book can be said to be

'Meleagrian' or 'Philippan'.* Certain sections have plainly been directly copied by Kephalas from his sources. Meleager and Philip arranged their collections not by authors, but partly by subject-matter – poems on similar themes grouped together, a Leonidas poem, for example, with imitations of the poem by later writers following the 'original' – and partly alphabetically, by the first lines. Occasionally the context of an anonymous poem in the Anthology enables the scholar to assign it with some certainty to Meleager's *Garland*.

My selection of poems is not entirely restricted to poems from The Palatine Anthology and the Planudean Appendix. There are three other sources of epigrams which I have drawn on: inscriptions carved on stones, of which several modern collections have been made, notably Kaibel's; epigrams quoted by writers such as Athenaios, who has a number of poems by Hedylos and Poseidippos; and finally, a few genuine epigrams by poets such as Archilochos, which are to be found in modern editions of the early poets.†

5. THE TRANSLATIONS

Translation is an art of fiction. There is the fiction of the translator, who pretends to be another poet at another time, writing in a language that men had not yet begun to speak. And there is the fiction demanded of the reader, who must believe that the poem he is reading is at the same time an ancient poem and a modern one. When translation is success-

---

*Excellent work in this highly complex field has been done by A. S. F. Gow, in 'The Greek Anthology: Sources and Ascriptions' (1958).

† The Palatine Anthology includes a few poems, such as the pattern-poems by Simias and others, and some other pieces which are in no sense epigrams, which I have omitted. The epigrams said to be 'by Sappho' are certainly not hers, and many of those 'by Simonides' are not his.

ful, the translator and reader conspire to have their cake and eat it. The purist demand – that poetry should never be translated, but must be read in the original – is salutary at times when it seems easier to use a respectable translation than to wrestle with a difficult original. This does not, however, explain the urge of poets to confront a text with the best of their literary experience, to translate it. The only reason for it is the sense the translator has, that his original has qualities peculiar to its own language and culture, which seem to him worth sharing, worth trying to recreate, because there is nothing quite like it in English.

Translation is thus important not just as a lazy way for the reader to get near a linguistically inaccessible poem – but as an act of imaginative, creative criticism. No scholar who respects the language and life of his own society as much as that of his subject would deny that this function of translation can be illuminating, both of the past and the present. It can expose neglected elements in an ancient poet which have a modern – even a permanent – relevance. Propertius is a case in point: whatever one thinks of Pound's poem, one cannot read the Latin poet again without an increased awareness of the qualities brought to the fore in *Homage to Sextus Propertius*.

It hardly needs stressing that Greek culture of the period which this book spans is an alien culture; the reader who does not want to enter into something different, who is immune to the shock of cultural dislocation, had better stick to contemporary English poetry (which he probably thinks is 'better' anyway). There is, of course, common ground between the two cultures – and it is this that the modern poet attempts to exploit in his translation, as he tries to produce a poem which is most fully expressive of what the original means for him.

'A poem for a poem', though, is too simple a recipe. There are poems and poems: what does 'a poem' mean? It is more to the point to ask that a translation be, at the very least, composed in recognizable modern verse (at all costs not in some special imaginary language which one can only call 'translationese').

We tend, unfortunately, to grant less 'originality' to the strict verse-translator – however proficient a poet he is – than to the bold spirit who is prepared to raid ancient poetry and steal what he wants, in order to write what can then be called 'new poems of his own'. And there are good reasons for this: the ransacking of ancient poetry does sometimes provide very exciting new poetry, and it must be admitted that much classical verse-translation of the orthodox kind has been hopelessly dull and inert. We are right to refuse to believe that Vergil or Sophokles could have been as boring or irrelevant as they appear to be in most versions.

With epigrams, however, we are not likely to need drastic rehandlings, and there should be no temptation to write off fairly direct transpositions of poems with the idea that the translator has not 'done anything new' with his original. At any rate, the narrow compass of an epigram demands that the translator should have very good reasons for altering or omitting details, or changing the context, of the original.

There is no standard approach which a translator can apply to all Greek epigrams. The poems are too various in kind, and each poem presents its own problems. The same text, indeed, will provide different poets with different stimuli – compare, for example, the versions of the Palladas poem given in Appendix 2. If there is a lesson to be drawn from this, it is that good translation is as dependent on inventive skill, on fortunate turns of phrase in its composition, as any new poetry. The translator must draw on all the resources of poetic experience available to him as a poet, to make poems in which he can convincingly carry off the illusion of an ancient poem speaking again.

The old theory of the 'equivalent line' for translation – an

English metre for a Greek metre – may be tenable, if not much to modern taste, for some longer poems, but with short pieces it is a non-starter. The associations of the heroic couplet run counter to nearly everything the Greek elegiac couplet aims at in epigram. Most traditional English metres with rhyme tread heavily over any semblance of the Greek style. Rhyme as a technical device obviously has its uses as one element in verse-making available to the contemporary poet, but constant use of it tends to drag the Greek epigrams down to the level of a sub-Augustan light verse.

The modern poet has a much wider armoury for creating genuinely new poems from the Greek, and for assimilating the distinct modes of epigram in forms which give a closer sense of the originals, with the modern forms of free verse. With these, too, he can if he wishes imitate the rhetorical structure of the originals more fully.

This book contains examples of every type of translation, from straight verse renderings to outright imitation. The brevity of most of the poems, their narrow compass, generally provides a firm enough framework for the translator to recreate a poem without having to resort to radical dislocation of the poem's trappings.*

*Robin Skelton will, I trust, forgive me for taking issue with him here on the matter of modernization of proper names. In the Introduction to his recent *Two Hundred Poems from The Greek Anthology* he writes, 'When we read a delightful little love-poem addressed to a girl by a young man in a fit of affection and exuberance, the whole spontaneity is lost if the name of the girl is given as Rhodope. The poem becomes immediately a piece of antiquity instead of a part of our own existence.' This is altogether too simplistic. Quite apart from the dubious conception of poetic 'spontaneity', he seems to assume that the reader has no imaginative historical sense at all. As a piece of antiquity, which it undoubtedly is, the poem is still part of 'our existence' the moment we choose to read it. Of course I am deliberately missing his point, because it seems to imply, if not that all pieces of antiquity are outmoded, that we cannot enter into their spirit until

With Greek poets as various as Simonides and Strato, there are greatly varying degrees of 'translatability'. No doubt some of the more minor figures will seem more attractive, in translation, than their betters. In the case of Simonides, translation in any helpful sense is more or less impossible, because the whole ethos which informed his manner has no modern parallel. Strato has, if anything, too much that is modishly 'contemporary' in his favour. There is nothing that can be done about this. The reader must acclimatize himself as best he can to the different sorts of effort required of him to enter into the poems' lost occasions.

For the most part I have avoided the kind of version which completely alters the context of the original poem. I have, however, made some attempt to signify that some versions are more in the nature of adaptations than others, by stating at the foot of a poem that the translation is 'after' a Greek original. My purpose in this has not been to draw a hard-and-fast line between translations and imitations – such a line does not exist – but simply to indicate cases where the reader would be more than usually unjustified in drawing conclusions on the evidence of the version printed, about the form or precise content of the original.

Occasionally I have given two versions of the same epigram, for the pleasure of comparison, when both versions have merits which seem worth displaying.

At the outset I had hoped to represent the work of each Greek poet in translations by the same hand, to give some impression of a consistent original oeuvre, and of a consistent

---

they are processed into some easily digestible form. It seems to me that translation puts a barrier between the reader and the idea of an authentic original which he must derive from the version, if an ancient poet called, say, Meleager, appears to be addressing amorous verses to Gloria and Janet, not to mention Gerald and Julian – with the improbable connotations such names evoke.

approach in translation. It was not possible to maintain this ambition in the long run, although most of the major poets do have a single main translator.

The majority of the translations have been specially made for this edition since 1970. I had hoped to find more poems in modern versions by earlier poets, and have been disappointed at the lack of lively material: more than compensated for, I hope, by the new versions. I have drawn on printed collections for versions made before 1950 by John Peale Bishop, Edmund Blunden, Robert Bridges, Dudley Fitts and Ezra Pound; versions by Willis Barnstone, Richmond Lattimore, Kenneth Rexroth and Clive Sansom are from volumes published in the late fifties and early sixties.

With more than 850 poems out of some 4,000, this book has grown into the largest selection of Greek epigrams in verse translation ever assembled. All the important poems, I believe, are included. 'The time of life does not exist when it is impossible to discover in it [The Greek Anthology] a masterly poem one had never seen before', as the T.L.S. reviewer quoted above put it; if the reader feels any comparable sense of excitement in the discovery of new poems, this anthology will have served its purpose.

PETER JAY

Editor's Note

The poems are arranged according to their authors, who are placed, as far as possible, in chronological order. This order must be regarded as approximate only; in the Hellenistic and Graeco-Roman periods especially, there is a profusion of nearly contemporary poets whose exact dates are rarely known. Even this slightly chancy order makes, I think, more sense than the alternatives which have generally been employed – alphabetical arrangement of the poets, or thematic grouping of the poems.

In each period there are a number of completely undatable minor figures and anonymous poems. These are grouped together in Sections 3, 5 and 7, with the poets in alphabetical order.

The headnotes are intended to give the Greekless reader a sense of the poet's milieu, and to summarize what is known of his life and work, without entering into detailed controversy. All too often the poet is no more than a name, and there is little or no information to give.

Each author's poems are arranged roughly by subject-matter in the genres of the Byzantine editors: poems erotic, dedicatory, sepulchral, epideiptic, hortatory, convivial and satirical, to give them their traditional names. Where a poet is included in either Gow and Page's *Hellenistic Epigrams* or *The Garland of Philip*, I have put his selection in the order of Gow and Page. In a few cases, such as Paulos and Rufinus, the poems are in the order preferred by their translator.

Few of the poems can be dated, but occasionally the subject-matter provides a definite terminus post, or ante, quem; and these are indicated either in the explanatory titles or Notes.

The convention of using titles as an integral part of a poem is modern, and the only 'titles' we find in the Greek texts are in the form of explanatory notes by the copyists, or information on the occasion of a particular poem given by other Greek authors. The titles of poems translated here are generally those of the translator; occasionally I have added a purely descriptive title to obviate the need for a note.

An asterisk against the reference at the foot of a poem indicates that the original is in a metre other than the elegiac couplet; the metres of these poems are given in the Notes.

References to the Greek texts are, unless otherwise stated, to The Palatine Anthology (*AP*), with the Planudean Appendix as Book 16. For poems taken from other sources, references in the text and index are as follows:

CIG – Boeckh's *Corpus Inscriptionum Graecarum* (1828–77)

D – E. Diehl's *Anthologia Lyrica Graeca* (3rd edition, 1952)

E – J. M. Edmonds' *Elegy & Iambus* (1931)

G – J. Geffcken's *Griechische Epigramme* (1916)

HE – A. S. F. Gow and D. L. Page's *Hellenistic Epigrams* (1965)

K – G. Kaibel's *Epigrammata Graeca ex lapidibus conlecta* (1878)

M – J. W. Mackail's *Select Epigrams from the Greek Anthology* (3rd edition, 1911 – the numbering of poems in earlier editions varies slightly)

OBGV – *The Oxford Book of Greek Verse* (1930)

P – W. Peek's *Griechischen Vers-Inschriften,* Band I, Grab-Epigramme (1955)

The Palatine Anthology gives a number of poems with either plainly false or double ascriptions (e.g. 'by Poseidippos or Asklepiades'). Plato and Simonides are notable recipients of poems which are undoubtedly not their work. I have followed the opinions of Gow and Page in dividing poems 'by

Antipater' between the two poets of the name, and in deciding between rival claimants to poems of double ascription. Obviously falsely ascribed poems will be found here as anonymous; some uncertain poems are given at the end of the section by the poet to whom they are ascribed, or are otherwise tentatively ascribed to probable authors. The reader who has trouble in locating a poem he has known as 'by Plato', etc., should use the index provided.

A word about the style adopted for transliteration of Greek proper names. I have tried to distinguish between genuinely 'Greek' poets – poets with Greek names, usually living in the Greek-speaking, culturally Greek world – and poets, usually of Roman origin and with Roman names, who wrote in Greek. Thus I write *Kallimachos*, though the name has almost been naturalized in the Latin form *Callimachus*; but *Lucilius* not *Loukillios* – the name was never Greek. It seems a useful distinction to make, though I am aware that consistency is impossible. I have not thought it reasonable to assert my preference in this matter on the contributors, some of whom prefer the traditional Latinized forms. The Glossary seeks to alleviate any possible confusion by giving cross-references when two or more forms of a name occur in the text.

Some names are too familiar in their Latinized forms, and it would seem perverse to insist on Platon, Meleagros, Antipatros, etc.; the familiar forms Plato, Meleager and Antipater have been retained.

The distinction between Greek and Latin forms for names breaks down with the early Byzantines. One cannot know for certain whether Paulos was originally of Greek or Roman extraction. He would have been bilingual from birth. Since Justinian gradually abandoned speaking and writing Latin in favour of Greek at Constantinople, I have generally plumped for the Greek forms as more reflective of the culture of the early Byzantine age – despite the fact that the official titles *'silentiarius'*, *'referendarius'* etc., are Latin.

There is little to be gained from detailed instructions for pronunciation of proper names. The reader should in general remember that *all* syllables – including final *es* – are sounded: so that Meleager is four syllables, and Anyte three. Occasionally I have used accents (e.g. Danaé) to signify a diaeresis, where it is not too obvious to the eye.

Finally, it is a pleasure to acknowledge the cooperation of the many people who have helped make this volume possible. To Jeremy Trafford, Julia Vellacott and Betty Radice my thanks for their interest in and support of the project; to Alison Wade for reading the manuscript, and to Peter Whigham for various chores in the final stages of organizing the book. To Professor Sir Denys Page and A. S. F. Gow, whose published work has been invaluable: without it, indeed, the job would have been impossible. To all the correspondents who have offered ideas and suggestions, many of which have helped the book on its way. But most of all, to the many poets on both sides of the Atlantic who have undertaken the better part of the translations specially for this edition. Without their enthusiasm in tackling the most seemingly intractable material, the book would not exist.

PETER JAY
London, November 1971

Acknowledgements

Grateful thanks are due to a number of publishers for permission to reproduce poems by the following translators:

Willis Barnstone, *Greek Lyric Poetry*, Schocken Books Inc.

John Peale Bishop, 'To a Swallow' from *Selected Poems*, Charles Scribner's Sons, copyright 1941, renewal copyright 1969 Margaret G. H. Bronson.

Edmund Blunden, *Halfway House*, A. D. Peters & Co.

Robert Bridges, *The Poetical Works of Robert Bridges*, The Clarendon Press, Oxford.

J. V. Cunningham, *Collected Poems and Epigrams*, Faber and Faber Ltd, The Swallow Press, Chicago.

Guy Davenport, *Carmina Archilochi*, University of California Press.

Dudley Fitts, *Poems from the Greek Anthology*, New Directions Publishing Corporation.

Richmond Lattimore, *Greek Lyrics*, The University of Chicago Press.

André Lefevere, *Classical Epigrams*, Studio Vista Publishers.

William J. Philbin, *To You Simonides*, The Dolmen Press.

Ezra Pound, *Collected Shorter Poems*, Faber and Faber Ltd, New Directions Publishing Corporation.

Kenneth Rexroth, *Poems from the Greek Anthology*, The University of Michigan Press.

Andrew Sinclair, *Selections from The Greek Anthology*, George Weidenfeld and Nicholson Ltd.

Robin Skelton, *Two Hundred Poems from The Greek Anthology*, Methuen & Co. Ltd, University of Washington Press, McClelland & Stewart.

Stephen Spender, *The Generous Days*, Faber and Faber Ltd, Random House Inc.

I

THE GREEK PERIOD
c. 700–350 B.C.

ARCHILOCHOS

Archilochos of Paros lived early in the seventh century. He
was a mercenary soldier and fought with the Parian colonists
to establish Thasos. Some fragments of his verse describe these
events. The most famous event in his life, and the one which
earned him his reputation for savage invective, was his quarrel
with Lykambes, whose daughter Neoboulé he hoped to
marry. Lykambes broke off the engagement; the legend of
Archilochos' poetic revenge is described by Gaetulicus (see
no. 498 below). Nothing else is known of him except that
he died in battle.

The first poet of the lyric age, Archilochos was a great
innovator in metre, language and subject-matter. His material
was drawn from his immediate experience, and he wrote
mainly in the language of everyday speech. His work had a
lasting influence on poets as diverse as Kallimachos, Catullus
and Horace. The last poem given here is only doubtfully
his.

1

> Sergeant to Enyalios,
> The great god War,
> I practise double labor.
> With poetry, that lover's gift,
> I serve the lady Muses.

GUY DAVENPORT *E*1

2

> My ash spear is my barley bread,
> My ash spear is my Ismarian wine.
> I lean on my spear and drink.

GUY DAVENPORT *E*2

35

3

I don't give a damn if some Thracian ape strut
Proud of that first-rate shield the bushes got.
Leaving it was hell, but in a tricky spot
I kept my hide intact. Good shields can be bought.

STUART SILVERMAN *E6*

4

When Alkibié married,
She made of her copious hair
A holy gift to Hera.

GUY DAVENPORT 6.133

KLEOBOULOS

Kleoboulos, son of Euagoras, was tyrant of Lindos, and was
numbered among the legendary 'Seven Sages'. He died in
the mid-sixth century.

5

I am the maiden in bronze set over the tomb of Midas.
As long as water runs from wellsprings, and tall trees burgeon,
and the sun goes up the sky to shine, and the moon is brilliant,
as long as rivers shall flow and the wash of the sea's breakers,
so long remaining in my place on this tomb where the tears fall
I shall tell those who pass that Midas lies here buried.

RICHMOND LATTIMORE 7.153*

PHOKYLIDES

Phokylides of Miletos was writing in the mid-sixth century
B.C. Among the few remains of his elegiac and hexameter

verse are these two poems. His work is gnomic, and is charac-
terized by the formulaic use of his own name as a trademark.

6

> Phokylides says this: Lerians bad men. Not
> This one bad, that not – but all.
> Except Prokles. And Prokles? He's Lerian.

PETER JAY *E*1

7

> Phokylides says this: what's the use of blue blood
> In people whose talk and opinions lack all grace?

PETER JAY *E*4*

ANAKREON

Born in Teos, about 570, Anakreon was famous as a lyric
poet. As a young man when Teos was threatened by the Per-
sians, he left with the colonists bound for Abdéra. The power-
ful tyrant Polykrates invited him to Samos, and became his
friend and patron at the brilliant court where the poet Ibykos
was also resident. After the fall of Polykrates, Anakreon went
to Athens and later to Thessaly before finally returning to
Athens. His poems were edited in six books by the Alexandrian
scholar Aristarchos. Anakreon is almost proverbial for
hedonistic love-poetry and drinking songs, but he also wrote
bitter satirical invectives and varied elegiac verse. These two
epitaphs both refer to the fighting of the Abdéran colonists
against the Thracians.

8

> Timokritos was bold in war. This is his grave.
> Arês the war-god spares the coward, not the brave.

PETER JAY 7.160

9

> All Abdéra mourned at the funeral pyre
> Of Agathias the strong, who died for them.
> Bloodloving Arês in the vile whirlwind of warfare
> Killed no other young townsman such as him.

PETER JAY 7.226

SIMONIDES

Simonides was born in Keos in about 556. As a young man he went to Athens at the invitation of the tyrant Hipparchos. When the tyranny fell, he went to Thessaly, but returned to Athens in 490, where he became nationally known for his poems written in commemoration of the great events of the Persian War. He was a friend of Themistokles, the Athenian statesman. About 476 he went to Sicily; his nephew the poet Bakchylides joined him there, and Bakchylides' great rival Pindar was also at the court of Hieron. Simonides died in Akragas in about 468.

Most of the choral lyric poetry for which he was famous is lost. He wrote hymns, dirges, epinikian odes (the genre made famous by Pindar) and elegies, as well as drinking songs and epigrams. Despite his early connection with the discredited Athenian regime, Simonides was a highly respected and popular poet throughout Greece. He had a great capacity for sympathy with the tastes and ideals of different Greek cities: the two poems on Plataia, one written for the Athenians, the other for the Spartans, show how subtly and tactfully he could match his poetry to its occasion. Above all, his conception of the Greek cause gave true expression to feelings and ideals which transcended political divisions between the city-states, and made him, in the time of his country's greatest danger, her first national poet.

Many epigrams are ascribed to Simonides, but it is clear that a good deal of later, inferior work has spuriously attached itself to his name. Apparently Simonides did not collect his epitaphs; and it was not till some fifty years after his death that Philochoros edited a collection of Attic inscriptional epigrams. The poems included here, however, are all well attested. They are only a small selection of the epigrams likely to be genuinely his, because his poetry almost completely defies translation in any important sense. The poetry is inseparable from the language, and his effects, so dependent on the capacity of an inflected language to admit skilful manipulation of word-order, are simply not available in English. The verse is restrained and harmonious, each word and image deployed to maximum effect. All that can be suggested, perhaps, is some shadow of the measured gravity which made the commemorative poems so famous.

10   *For the Spartan Dead at Thermopylai (480 B.C.)*

Inform the Lakedaimonians, friend – we rest
Here, understanding their orders to the last.

PETER JAY 7.249

11   *On His Friend Megistias, Who Died at Thermopylai*

This is the tomb of great Megistias.
The Persians killed him as they crossed the river
Spercheios: the seer knew that death was close,
But could never desert his Spartan lords.

PETER JAY 7.677

12   *For the Spartan Dead at Plataia (479 B.C.)*

These men clothed their land with incorruptible
Glory when they assumed death's misty cloak.
They are not dead in death; the memory
Lives with us, and their courage brings them back.

PETER JAY 7.251

13   *For the Athenian Dead at Plataia*

If to die honourably is the greatest
Part of virtue, for us fate's done her best.
Because we fought to crown Greece with freedom
We lie here enjoying timeless fame.

PETER JAY 7.253

14

Because of these men's courage, no smoke rose
Skyward from Tegea's burning. They chose
To leave their children the broad land's township green
With freedom, while in the front line they went down.

PETER JAY 7.512

15   *Cenotaph at the Isthmos*

We did not flinch but gave our lives to save
Greece when her fate hung on a razor's edge.

PETER JAY 7.250

16

While bringing Apollo the pick of the Etruscan plunder
One sea one night one ship sent these men under.

PETER JAY 7.270

17

No alien dust covers your tomb.
Death caught you, Kleisthenes,
Roving around the Hospitable Seas
And you have forfeited the sweet return
Back to Keos, your sea-circled home.

PETER JAY 7.510

18

The stone of Megakles who's dead:
Looking at it, I pity you,
Poor Kallias, for what you went through.

PETER JAY 7.511

19

I Brotachos of Gortyn lie here. This
Was not what I came for, but to do business.

PETER JAY 7.254

20

Drinker, glutton supreme,
Supreme defamer of men –
I, Timokreon
Of Rhodes, now lie down here.

PETER JAY 7.348

21   *On Theodoros*

Someone is glad that I, Theodoros, am dead
Another will be glad when that someone is dead
We are all in arrears to death.

PETER JAY 10.105

AISCHYLOS

The life of Aischylos (525/4–456 B.C.) spanned the period of Athens' growth to democracy after the overthrow of the Peisistratid tyranny in his youth (510 B.C.). He started entering his tragedies in competitions in the early fifth century, and his first victory was in 484 B.C. He wrote some eighty plays, of which only seven (including the *Oresteia* trilogy), selected by Alexandrian and Byzantine scholars, remain.

Aischylos fought at Marathon (490 B.C.) and probably also at Salamis (480 B.C.). He twice visited the court of Hieron at Syracuse, the cultural centre which attracted his contemporaries Pindar, Simonides and other leading Greek poets and artists. He died at Gela in Sicily. These epigrams are the only two by him which survive.

22 *On the Thessalians who Fought at Marathon*

> And black Fate took these stubborn spearmen
> guarding their sheep-rippling acres.
> They died but not their fame, their stubbornness.
> Clothed now in dust of Ossa.

EDWIN MORGAN 7.255

23

This mountain's secret is the son of Euphorion of Athens –
Aischylos. He died by Gela's wheatfields.
But a wood in Marathon could speak of his famous strength,
 and so could the thick-haired Mede who felt it.

EDWIN MORGAN E4

PARRHASIOS

Parrhasios, the greatest painter of his time, was born in Ephesos but lived and worked in Athens. He was active in the mid-fifth century. He was noted for his subtlety of outline and his skill in depicting details of facial expression. His handling of the human figure in paintings of gods and heroes set the style for later artists. He also wrote on painting; and two complete epigrams by him are extant. They are noteworthy at least for their sublime arrogance: the second was actually inscribed on his painting of Herakles at Lindos.

24
I tell you (you needn't believe it) – I have found now
   clearly with my hand the limits of art.
The boundary has been set now which none may pass over.
   But no human deed has been blameless.

RICHARD EVANS E2

25   *Herakles*

    Now you can see him, exactly as he came
    To me Parrhasios often in my dream.

PETER JAY E3

THUKYDIDES

Thukydides was born in about 460 B.C. An Athenian with Thracian family connections, he was a strong supporter of Perikles. In 424 Thukydides was elected general, but his failure to save the Athenian colony of Amphipolis from the Spartan

Brasidas led to his exile. He returned to Athens in 404, and died about 400. His great history of the Peloponnesian War is incomplete; he intended to end with the capture of Athens in 404, but the work breaks off in 411/10. The following epigram by him survives.

26   *Euripides*

All Greece is his monument, though his grave
Lies in Macedon, refuge of his last days.
Hellas of Hellas, Athens his land, who gave
So much joy by his art, whom so many praise.

PETER JAY 7.45

PLATO

The great Athenian philosopher and prose-writer (*c.* 429–347 B.C.) is traditionally supposed to have written poetry as a young man. I include here only the best-attested poems; a few which are definitely not his work are to be found amongst the anonymous poems. His poetry reveals the same clarity and polished elegance as his prose. In the two poems on the boy Aster (the name means 'star') he attains Simonidean heights of wit and poignant simplicity. Shelley thought the second the most perfect of epigrams and used it as an epigraph for his *Adonais*. The poem on Dion of Syracuse, if by Plato, was a very late work – Dion was murdered only a few years before Plato's own death.

27 *Aster*

My star, star-gazing? – If only I could be
The sky, with all those eyes to stare at you!

PETER JAY 7.669

28 *Aster*

You were the morning star among the living:
But now in death your evening lights the dead.

PETER JAY 7.670

29 *Dion*

For Hekabé and the women of Ilion
Tears were fated from the day of their birth.
But in your moment of glorious triumph, Dion,
The Gods spilt all your far-flung hopes. Now earth
Cloaks you with civic honour in your hometown,
You who maddened my heart with love, my Dion!

PETER JAY 7.99

30 *Alexis*

All I said was – Alexis is gorgeous. Now
Everyone stares, ogles him everywhere.
Dear heart, why show the dogs a bone? You'll care
Later. Remember? Phaidros went that way too.

PETER JAY 7.100

45

31 *Sokrates to Agathon*

Kissing Agathon, I found
My soul at my lips. Poor thing!
– It went there, hoping
To slip across.

PETER JAY 5.78

32 *Sokrates to Xanthippé*

I am an apple, tossed
By one who loves you. Say
Yes, Xanthippé. We both go to waste.

PETER JAY 5.80

*Two Poems on the Eretrians Taken Prisoner by the
Persians (490 B.C.)*

33 (1)
We are Eretrians from Euboia. We lie
Near Susa, alas how far from our own country.

PETER JAY 7.259

34 (2)
Leaving behind for ever the thundering Aegean,
Finding in Ecbatana these midland graves,
We take our farewell of all things Eretrian –
Of Athens, Euboea, and the encircling waves.

CLIVE SANSOM 7.256

35 *Pindar*

This man charmed newcomers, and he was dear
To his own townsmen: the Muses' servant, Pindar.

PETER JAY 7.35

36 *Sappho*

Some say there are nine Muses: but they're wrong.
Look at Sappho of Lesbos; she makes ten.

PETER JAY 9.506

37 *Aristophanes*

Looking for a shrine that would not fall
The Graces found Aristophanes' soul.

PETER JAY *E*18

DEMODOKOS

Demodokos is most probably a fourth-century poet – he is certainly before Aristotle, who quotes him. He came from the island of Leros, but nothing else is known of him.

38

All the Cilicians are bad.
    Listen, I'm telling you:
The only good one's Kinyres –
    And he's Cilician too.

ALISTAIR ELLIOT 11.236

39

A nasty snake once bit a Cappadocian,
but died itself, having tasted his blood's poison.

PETER JAY 11.237

HEGEMON

Probably to be identified with an epic poet called Hegemon
of Alexandria, who was writing about 370 B.C. This is his
only epigram.

40   *Thermopylai*

Passing this tomb without a smile on his face
Some traveller might say, 'Here a thousand brave Spartans
Held the myriad hordes of Persians, and died
Facing the enemy. That is Dorian discipline.'

PETER JAY 7.436

ANONYMOUS INSCRIPTIONS

41   *Epitaph from Athens*

Whether you are a citizen or a stranger coming from
    elsewhere,
    take pity on Tettichos as you pass by: a brave man
killed in battle, who there lost the pride of his fresh youth.
    Mourn for him a while, and go on. May your fortune be
    good.

RICHMOND LATTIMORE K1

42 *Epitaph from Athens*

When you look at Kleoitas' memorial,
Menaichmos's son who was lost in boyhood,
pity him for dying so beautiful.

PETER JAY *K* ADD. 1a

43 *Epitaph of a Girl*

The monument of Phrasikleia:

For ever shall I be called virgin,
The gods having granted me this instead of marriage.

DUDLEY FITTS *K*6

44 *Epitaph from Athens*

As you walk on your way thinking of other things
Stop, man, and have pity when you see Thrason's tomb.

PETER JAY *G*41

45 *On the Athenians Who Died at the Hellespont,*
440–39 B.C.

Death took these early, to our land's great honour,
Trapped at the Hellespont. The enemy
Fought them all summer, learning to curse the war.
Deathless their courage, and this its memory.

PETER JAY *G*86

46   *After the Inscription on a Greek Stele of a*
        Woman Holding Her Grandchild on Her Knees

My daughter's dear child here I hold on my lap: so
I used to hold him of old in those days
When with living eyes we both looked on the sun:
Now that he's dead, I still hold him: for I
Am dead too.

STEPHEN SPENDER *P*I600*

47   *Epitaph from a Tomb in Asia Minor*

Death is not harsh: Death is our lot: but harsh
To die before our parents die, as one
Sans bride-rite, -hymn, -bed, lov'd of the Living,
Lov'd, in this tomb, of the millennial Dead.

PETER WHIGHAM *K*373

48   *Epitaph from Piraeus*

Earth wraps your body, Kallisto, in its lap
But you left your friends the memory of your goodness.

PETER JAY *K*56

49   *On the Statue of Epaminondas in Thebes* (c. *360* B.C.)

This came from my counsel:
Sparta has cut off the hair of her glory;
Messene takes her children in:
a wreath of the spears of Thebe
has crowned Megalopolis:
   Greece is free.

PETER LEVI *E*33

ANONYMOUS INSCRIPTIONS
On Plato's Grave

Asclepius cured the body: to make men whole
Phoebus sent Plato, healer of the soul.

WILLIAM J. PHILBIN 7.109, lines 1–2

2
THE HELLENISTIC PERIOD
c. 350–90 B.C.

MENANDER

The leading Athenian poet of the 'New Comedy', Menander (properly Menandros) lived about 342–290 B.C. He wrote more than a hundred plays; the only more or less complete play is *Dyskolos*, discovered in an Egyptian papyrus in 1958. His plays were adapted by Terence and Plautus, through whom his influence extended to Shakespeare; he is the father of the situation comedy. This single epigram is attributed to 'Menandros the comic writer'.

51   *On Epicurus and Themistokles*

Farewell, twin sons of Neokles.
One saved us from subjugation,
    the other from trash.

ALAN MARSHFIELD 7.72

PERSES

Nine poems by Perses remain; he is once called 'the Theban and once 'the Macedonian'. The poems are all genuine inscriptions. It seems probable that they are of the late fourth century B.C. 'They are in poetry what the beautifully restrained and impersonal Attic tombstones are in sculpture,' wrote Gilbert Highet.

52   Artemis,
This Zone, this Breastband & girlish frock
Take, votive, from her whom you delivered,
In her tenth month, of a most harsh childing,
                    Timaessa.

PETER WHIGHAM 6.272

53

    Lucina, Care
    Of child's coming,
    Accept, votive
    For your labour
    At her childbirth
    These bride-clothes,
    Bright-hair fillet,
    From Tisis
    Who remembers.

PETER WHIGHAM 6.274

54

Death came before Marriage, Philaenion.
Your Mother did not lead you to a bridegroom's bed
In season: She led you to the bed of Death,
With torn cheeks covered you here in this tomb:
            Aetatis 14

PETER WHIGHAM 7.487

55

Mnasylla, the daughter you lament,
    Neotima, dead in childbirth
In your arms, lies still in your arms
    On your tomb's pediment, the carved
Eyelids misty. Aristotle,
    Her Father, rests nearby his head
On his right hand. A stricken group:
    Whose grief, even in the relief
Of Death, in stone goes unrelieved.

PETER WHIGHAM 7.730

Time & prayer fitting, I, the god
Tychon, lowly among the lowliest
Have my *virtù*. It is not much.
But let the sharecropper stand needy –
That which he needs is in my gift.

PETER WHIGHAM 9.334

ASKLEPIADES

In Idyll 7, written at some time between 275 and 265 B.C.,
Theokritos speaks of Asklepiades (whom he calls 'Sikelidas')
and Philitas as poets of established reputation whom he would
like to emulate. Asklepiades came from Samos and was
probably born about 320 B.C. His poetry is important not only
for its intrinsic merit – the forty-odd remaining epigrams
reveal him as a highly imaginative and economical poet – but
for his introduction of new themes into epigram, and con-
sequent influence on later poets. Kallimachos and Dioskorides
are in his debt; so, too, are Hedylos and Poseidippos, his
closest literary friends and disciples. Asklepiades also wrote
lyric poetry which is now lost – two lyric metres are known
as Asklepiad. His epigrams combine the themes of the love
elegy and drinking song, transforming the epigram into a
vehicle for personal poetry.

56

Great is a drink of snow
                    to men parched by summer.
Great the spring breeze
              to a sailor when
winter's gone. But greater
                    is the one sheet on

57

two lovers as they
          venerate Venus.

             ALAN MARSHFIELD 5.169

58

    You're saving it? What for?
            In the underworld
you'll acquire no one
        to enjoy you, girl.
Lovemaking's for the living.
          Past Styx we shall
as bones and urn-meal,
        virgin, sprawl.

         ALAN MARSHFIELD 5.85

59

    Nikarete's face, sweetly moistened
            by her desires
and frequently shown
         at her gabled window,
was parched by Kleophon
          at her door below
and, dear Kypris, his eyes'
        sweet blue-bright lightning.

        ALAN MARSHFIELD 5.153

60

    I touched up sexy Hermione.
           She had on a belt
that had on it pied
         brilliances –
gold letters, Kypris: all told
         saying, 'Love me
and forget it hurts
       if another has me.'

       ALAN MARSHFIELD 5.158

61

Didyme waved her wand at me.
I am utterly enchanted.
The sight of her beauty makes me
Melt like wax before the fire. What
Is the difference if she is black?
So is coal, but alight, it shines like roses.

KENNETH REXROTH 5.210

62

The pampered Philainion stabbed me.

The wound might not
be plain, but the pain
sinks to my fingers.
I've had it, I'm gone, clean gone.

Nodding, I trod
on a *petite amie*
and I brushed death.

ALAN MARSHFIELD 5.162

63

To you, Kypris, Lysidike
has offered her spur,
gold prick once fixed
to a sweet leg's ankle.
Many inverted studs
were disciplined –
her own thighs never
reddening, she
so lightly rode. She finished
course without spur,
so this gold gear hangs
at your portico.

ALAN MARSHFIELD 5.203

64

Bitto and Nannion do not
              desire to come
to Aphrodite
              conventionally
but take themselves off
              another way, not nice.
Hate these swervers
              from your bed, Kypris.

ALAN MARSHFIELD 5.207

65

Dear Lamp, she swore by you
To come, and does not come.
Therefore, some future night
When she is at her sport
Wink once, and gutter out.

EDWARD LUCIE-SMITH 5.7

66

Snow, hail and smut the sky;
              dazzle and thunder;
toss over the country
              your smoky gloom.
Kill me and I'll give in;
              but let me breathe,
though through worse than this,
              and I'll have my fling.
I am goaded by the god
              who was your lord, golden
Zeus, when he thrust you
              in the brass cell.

ALAN MARSHFIELD 5.64

67

Stay, my tendrils, where hung
                    over these french doors.
Be in no hurry
                    to moult your leaves.
I have showered you with tears –
                    lovers' eyes are showers.
But when these doors swing
                    open and he
appears, rain me upon
                    his head, that my tears
may be drunk by at least
                    his yellow hair.

ALAN MARSHFIELD 5.145

68

Drink, Asklepiades.
What's happened? What tears are these?
You're not the only one
Tough Venus has undone.
For others too Love narrows
His eyes and aims his arrows.
What says that a live man must
Go on biting the dust?

ALISTAIR ELLIOT 12.50

69

Leave the rags, you tiny lusts,
                    of my heart whatever,
let rest these at least
                    for God's sake or
gash no more with arrows
                    but thunderclap:
So! make me utterly
                    clinker, ash.

So, so, you tiny lusts, gash me, withered
   with grief – if I
may have such a little,
   or any, gift.

   ALAN MARSHFIELD 12.166

70

Wine is love's test.
Nicagoras told us he had no lover,
but the toasts betrayed him.

Yes, his tears & unhappy eyes,
the tight wreath on his bent head
slips out of place.

   THOMAS MEYER 12.135

71

Although she's a girl, Dorkion
Is wise to the ways of the boys.
Like a chubby kid, she knows how
To throw over her shoulder, from
Under her broadbrimmed hat, the quick
Glance of Public Love, and let her
Cape show a glimpse of her bare butt.

   KENNETH REXROTH 12.161

72

Love has found out how to mix
Beauty with beauty. Not
Emerald with gold, which does not
Gleam and sparkle like these do,
Nor ivory with ebony,
Less dark and light than these are,
But Kleandros and Eubotis –
Flowers of Love and Persuasion.

   KENNETH REXROTH 12.163

73 *Colophon to a Roll of Erinna's Poems*

This is Erinna's sweet *oeuvre*, but small
(the girl was nineteen, after all):
yet stronger than many others. If death
had not appeared in youth's hot breath,
who would have had such a name?

LEE T. PEARCY 7.11

74 *A Tomb on the Shore*

Stay off from me, wild sea,
two coffins' lengths,
and seethe and whine
with all your power.
But if you do sack the grave
of Eumares, me,
you'll find nothing real:
just dirt and bone.

ALAN MARSHFIELD 7.284

75

When soft Irene like a
Holy flower came from the
Golden room of Cypris, her
White body seemed carved out of
Marble, and the Loves themselves
Escorted her, loosing from
Purple bowstrings arrows that
Found a mark in young men's hearts.

EDWARD LUCIE-SMITH 5.194

76 *Arkheanassa*

Here lies Arkheanassa of Kolophon,
Courtesan with sweet love scored on her face.
Lovers who had the pick of her youth's garden
In its first spring, through what a furnace you passed!

PETER JAY 7.217

77

Night long and wintry,
   the Pleiades half set.
Outside her door
   I pace, wet through,
seared by an agonizing
   white-hot prong –
not love but lust
   for her, deceiver.

ALAN MARSHFIELD 5.189

78 *On a Ring*

I am Drink, carved by a skilled
   hand, carved
amethyst, stone
   new to the image,
Cleopatra's object, sacred.
   On a queen's hand
even the goddess
   of drink should abstain.

ALAN MARSHFIELD 9.752

PHILITAS

It is uncertain whether 'Philitas of Samos' (author of two
epigrams) is the same man as the notable poet and scholar
Philitas of Kos (*c.* 330–270). The Koan poet certainly wrote
epigrams as well as elegiacs and other poetry, and was at the
centre of a literary school in Kos, where he was Theokritos'
tutor. Quintilian tells us that he was generally rated second
only to Kallimachos as an elegist; both Propertius and Ovid
speak of them in the same breath.

79

> Past fifty and cloyed at last,
> Nikias, who loved to love,
> Hangs up in the temple of
> Kypris her sandals, her long
> Uncoiled hair, her shining bronze
> Mirror that never lied to her,
> Her rich girdle, and the things
> Men never mention. Here you can
> See the whole panoply of love.

KENNETH REXROTH 6.210

80

This tombstone heavy with grief announces
'Death took little Theodota's tiny life',
And the little one says to her father, 'Don't be unhappy,
Theodotos. Men are always having bad luck.'

PETER JAY 7.481

SIMIAS

Also spelt Simmias, he was a Rhodian contemporary of Philitas of Kos and Theokritos, a scholar as well as a poet. He wrote three books of scholarly *Glosses* and four books of poems. Amongst his fragments are bits of a hexameter poem on Apollo, and some lyric pieces. The Palatine Anthology includes three interesting curiosities – the 'pattern-poems' *The Egg*, *The Axe* and *Wings of Eros*, written in the shape of the object they describe; they are however not epigrams, and may be found in Anthony Holden's *Greek Pastoral Poetry*. Seven epigrams appear under Simias' name; there is some doubt about the ascription of the second poem here to this Simias.

81   *A Decoy Partridge*

Your throat, my hunting partridge, will no longer
Send its cry echoing through the shady copses,
Chasing your spotted friends in their woodland pastures.
You have made your last journey, to Acheron.

PETER JAY 7.203

82   *At the Tomb of Sophokles*

Gently about this tomb wind gently O Ivy
where Sophokles lies

                        mingle your green with the rose
and the new tendrils of the gathering vine
soft-cluster

66

For his sake whose dark wise heart
shuddered with the glory of the Deathless Ones
who spoke through his fatal tongue.

DUDLEY FITTS 7.22

PHALAIKOS

Phalaikos was probably writing around 300 B.C. Five epi-
grams are his, and only two are in elegiac couplets: he seems
to have been interested in metrical variety. The hendeca-
syllable, adopted by the Roman Catullus, is often called
Phalaikean after him.

83

This gift, her gold-hemmed saffron gown, Kleo
gave to Dionysos, dressing his statue, because
she always outshone the company, and no man
could touch her when it came to hard drinking.

PETER JAY *HE*i

ALEXANDER

Alexander 'Aitolos' was born in Aitolia late in the fourth
century. He worked in the Library at Alexandria, and was
chief organizer from about 285 until 283 B.C. of the collection
of tragedy and satyric drama. A few years later he went to the
court of Antigonos Gonatas in Macedonia. He was best known
as a tragedian, though he also wrote epic and elegiac verse.
Three epigrams by him are extant; the poem printed here is
more likely to be his work than that of Automedon, to whom
there is an alternative ascription.

84 *Epitaph for Cleonicus*

You who will die, watch over your life; don't set sail
   at the wrong season, for at best no man lives long.
Poor Cleonicus, so impatient to reach
   bright Thasos, trading out of hollow Syria,
trading, Cleonicus, sailing just as the Pleiades
   were setting, so that you and the Pleiades sank together.

W. S. MERWIN 7.534

DOURIS

Nothing is known of Douris, except that he came from
Elaia, an Aiolian port about eighty miles north of Ephesos.
The destruction of Ephesos took place about 290 B.C.

85 *Ephesos*

Clouds of the heavens,
     where did the disastrous waters
you absorbed come from,
     which with unflinching night
flushed out everything?
     Not the Sahara desert.
These countless homes
     possessions of prosperous days
were Ephesos.
     Where were its guardian spirits
looking? It was the most
     hymned of Ionian cities.
Along with the rolling waves
     everything ran out to sea,
with the flooding rivers.

PETER JAY 9.424

POSEIDIPPOS

Poseidippos, born about 310 B.C. in Pella (Macedonia), was a close friend and younger contemporary of Asklepiades and Hedylos. About twenty of his poems remain. He is to be distinguished from the namesake of the same period who wrote comedies. By about 280 his poems were included in anthologies, and an inscription in Thermon (Aitolia) records that he was granted *proxenia* (equivalent to our 'freedom of the city') in 264/3. Poem 88 suggests that he visited Athens. He wrote poetry other than epigrams but none has survived except an elegy on old age which may be by a namesake of the first century A.D.

86

> If someone's with her, then
> I'll go, but if she sleeps
> Alone please let me in,
> And say that drunk I came
> Past brigands to this door,
> And bold Love guided me.

EDWARD LUCIE-SMITH 5.213

87

> On sea and land alike
> Direct your prayers towards
> This temple of the Queen
> Goddess Arsinoé.
> She gives safe passage, and
> In the mid-winter storms
> Pours oil upon the waves
> For those who pray to her.

It was Callicrates,
Her admiral, built it
Here – high, facing towards
The west wind on the cape.

EDWARD LUCIE-SMITH *HE*13

88

Here in this rough trench lies,
Wrapped in his shroud – the rags
Which served as his best coat –
One Phyromachus, the
Poor tattered glutton who,
Like a bedraggled crow,
Hung hopefully about
At midnight revels. Please
Anoint his stone and put
Some flowers there if you
Ever in the small hours
Were joined by such a one.
From the Lenaean games
He came, with broken teeth,
Black eyes, a bloody pate
(The oil-flask in his hand
Was everything he owned),
And, drunk, fell in this hole:
A tragi-comic fate.

EDWARD LUCIE-SMITH *HE*16

89

Doricha, your soft bones are
Asleep, your shawl of hair has
Breathed its perfume out, so too
The robe that wrapped Charaxus
Skin to skin with you, at dawn,

When, pressed together, you clinked
Cups of wine. But still it lasts
Upon the page: Sappho's ode
Which speaks your name. Naucratis
Will recall you now so long as
The sea-going ships shall come,
Finding their way to the Nile.

    EDWARD LUCIE-SMITH *HE*17

90

Three-year-old Archianax,
At play beside the well-head,
Saw his dumb double. Soon his
Mother dragged him dripping from
The water, wondering if
Some life was left. But the Nymphs
Were not defiled. Now in her
Lap he's sleeping, safe and sound.

    EDWARD LUCIE-SMITH 7.170

HEDYLOS

Hedylos was active perhaps about 270 B.C., and seems to have lived in Samos while having Athenian connections – his mother Hedylé also wrote poetry, and his grandmother Moschiné was 'an Attic iambic poetess' (Athenaios 7.297). He was a friend of Asklepiades and Poseidippos; probably rather younger than Asklepiades. He may have visited Egypt (see no. 93). A dozen epigrams survive (mainly through Athenaios) but unfortunately most are badly mutilated. He is an interesting and lively poet.

91

The wine, the toasts that could not be refused,
    her drowsy, trusting love for him,
lulled Aglaonice to sleep. She gives
    to Venus tokens of her first
surrender – dripping still with scent, and won
    with ease, her sandals and the band
that yielded her breasts – as witnesses
    of how she slept, and what he took from her.

ADRIAN WRIGHT 5.199

92   *A Dedication to Aphrodite*

Drinking against men, Kallistion
(a fantastic feat, no question) downed
eighteen pints before dinner-time.
This – scented with the lees of wine –
this *lesbion*, goblet of purple glass,
is her present for you, Paphian queen.
If you see to her safety in all things,
stolen shipments of sweet beverage
will come *your* way in its hold.

WILLIAM MOEBIUS *HE*3

93   *A Musical Wine-Jar*

Now winedrinkers, this way to an airy shrine
to see a *rhyton*, august Arsinoé's:
Bes, of Egypt, dancing, toots his high-pitched horn
as the run-off duct below him is turned on –
no appeal for war – his golden clarion

calls us to celebrate a new lease on life,
just like the valiant tune his majesty
the Nile from elevated waters airs,
the one religious processionals prefer.
So revere the 'erudition' of Ktesibios:
this way, boys, to the shrine of Arsinoé.

WILLIAM MOEBIUS *HE4*

94

Let's drink up: with wine, what original,
what nuanced, what sweet fancy speech
I might hit on! Soak me with a jug of Chian,
and say, 'Have fun, Hedylus.' For I hate
wasting time unless I'm high.

WILLIAM MOEBIUS *HE5*

95

From dawn to dark, and back from dark to dawn,
Sokles downs it from the three-gallon jugs
unless he has a sudden call somewhere.
But with his wine he makes much sweeter sense
than our man from Sicily: 'more solid is he.'
As the blessing shines upon you, friend,
just keep up the writing – and drink on!

WILLIAM MOEBIUS *HE6*

96

Our prize fish is done!
Now jam the doorpin in;
Proteus, I mean Agis
the fancier of dishes
might come in. He'll be
fire and water, anything

he wants. So lock it up ...
But maybe he'll arrive
turned into Zeus and shower gold
upon this Danaé of a dish!

WILLIAM MOEBIUS *HE*8

ANYTE

Anyte came from Tegea in Arkadia. Nineteen genuine epigrams by her survive; versions of all these are given here, together with two of the five others of disputed authorship (116 and 117). Anyte also wrote lyric poems, and probably hexameter verse as well. She is probably contemporary with Nikias, and a little earlier than Mnasalkes – the two poets with whom her work has most in common. Of the poems which are certainly hers, all but one (108) are in four lines, and all take the form of inscriptions – real or imaginary. She seems to be the first poet both to write epitaphs on animals, and to introduce bucolic themes into epigram.

97 *Dedication: A Spear*

Stand you here, murdering shaft, no longer
Dripping the enemy's spilt blood from your bronze claw;
But staying in Athena's tall-built house of marble,
Advertise the bravery of Echecratidas, the Cretan.

JOHN HEATH-STUBBS and CAROL A. WHITESIDE 6.123

98

Big enough for an ox, the cauldron. The gift
Of Cleobotus, Eriaspidas' son.
Wide-plazaed Tegea his city. The gift
To Athena. Aristoteles (of that ilk),
The Cleitorian, made it.

JOHN HEATH-STUBBS and CAROL A. WHITESIDE 6.153

99

To shock-haired Pan and the nymphs who protect the
   cow-byres
Theodotus the loner set up this his gift
Under the look-out peak. Because they gave him ease,
Worn out in the parching summer, protending,
In their hands, sweet water.

JOHN HEATH-STUBBS and CAROL A. WHITESIDE 16.291

100

Indeed then, it was your own courage
Destroyed you, Proarchus, in the battle –
Dead, you have put the house of your father Phidias
To murky sorrow. But this stone above you sings
A splendid tale: how you were slain while fighting
For the sake of your own dear country.

JOHN HEATH-STUBBS and CAROL A. WHITESIDE 7.724

101

On this her daughter's tomb
                Cleina could not stop
crying bitterly for her short-lived child,
calling to the soul of Philaenis, who crossed
Death's pale joyless river before her wedding day.

SALLY PURCELL 7.486

102

I mourn for Antibia the virgin,
the fame of whose modest beauty
drew many suitors to her father's house
– for Fate the destroyer whirled all their hopes away.

SALLY PURCELL 7.490

103

Throwing her arms around her father,
her eyes streaming with pale tears,
Erato spoke these last words:
'Oh father, I am leaving you; over my eyes
Death draws his darkness –
and I go into the dark.'

SALLY PURCELL 7.646

104

Instead of a solemn wedding and marriage-bed
your mother gave you a statue for your marble tomb,
Thersis. It stands life-sized, it has your beauty,
so, although you are dead, we can still speak to you.

SALLY PURCELL 7.649

105

Damis set this up, to commemorate
His steadfast horse, when dead:
The crimsoned War-god beset it, at the bare breastbone.
Through the tough hide the black blood seethed,
Making wet the soil in grim slaughter.

JOHN HEATH-STUBBS and CAROL A. WHITESIDE 7.208

106

And you too perished long ago, by a bush with matted roots,
Lokrian bitch, swiftest of whelps delighting to give tongue –
A speckled throated adder coiled about
Your light-moving limbs such a corroding poison.

JOHN HEATH-STUBBS and CAROL A. WHITESIDE *HE*10

107 *A Cock*

   Never again rising at dawn
   will you wake me from my bed,
   flapping your noisy wings;
   for while you slept, the Ripper sneaked up
   and sank his claws down swiftly in your throat.

SALLY PURCELL 7.202

108 *On a Dolphin*

No more in delightful chase through buoyant seas
Shall I toss up my throat from the depths, nor blow around
The ornamented beak of the ship, exulting
In the carved figure-head, my image. But the sea's
Glittering blue has thronged me out of the moist element:
I lie stretched out on a narrow space of dry land.

JOHN HEATH-STUBBS and CAROL A. WHITESIDE 7.215

109

The children have tied you, billy-goat, with bright
purple reins, and a band round your hairy mouth,
teaching you to race, like a horse, around the god's temple
that he may keep an eye on their games.

SALLY PURCELL 6.312

110

Look at the horned goat of Dionysus,
with what spirit he looks out proudly
from his shaggy face.
Often in the mountains a Naiad has stroked
his curly cheeks with a rosy hand
– and this has made him vain.

SALLY PURCELL 9.745

111

This place is the Cyprian's for she has ever the fancy
To be looking out across the bright sea,
Therefore the sailors are cheered, and the waves
Keep small with reverence, beholding her image.

EZRA POUND 9.144

112

Sit down in the shade of this fine spreading laurel,
draw a welcome drink from the sweet flowing stream,
and rest your breathless limbs from the harvesting
here, where the West wind blows over you.

SALLY PURCELL 9.313

113

I, Hermes, have been set up
Where three roads cross, by the windy
Orchard above the grey beach.
Here tired men may rest from travel,
By my cold, clean, whispering spring.

KENNETH REXROTH 9.314

114

Ease your weary limbs, stranger, under this elm –
Truly the soft breeze speaks through the green leaves.
Drink a cool draught from the fountain.

This is indeed a place to take your ease,
And dear to wayfarers in the intense heat.

JOHN HEATH-STUBBS and CAROL A. WHITESIDE 16.228

115

'Why, country Pan, sitting still
Among the lonely shades of the thick-set wood,
Do you shrill on your sweet reed?'
                              'So that the heifers
May pasture on these dewy mountains, cropping
The long-haired heads of the grass.'

JOHN HEATH-STUBBS and CAROL A. WHITESIDE 16.231

116

The child Myro made this tomb
for her grasshopper, a field-nightingale,
and her cicada that lived in the trees,
and she cried because pitiless Death
had taken both of her friends.

SALLY PURCELL 7.190

117

When this man, Manes, lived, he was a slave;
Dead, he is worth as much as Darius the Great.

SALLY PURCELL 7.538

THEOKRITOS

Theokritos (c. 310–250 B.C.) was born in Syracuse, but went
to Kos in about 275 B.C. where he was associated with Philitas
and the other poets connected with the Koan movement in
poetry. He was at Alexandria for some years around 270 B.C.,
but returned to Kos. His *Idylls* ('Little Portraits') contain his
popular and highly influential hexameter poems. He is

chiefly famous for his pastoral poems, but he is by no means limited to this genre: there are also hymns, mythological poems, panegyrics and court poems, the marvellous Idyll 2 on the love-charms, and the dialogue-portrait of two suburban housewives going to a festival (Idyll 15). I include here only eleven of the twenty-two epigrams which are certainly by Theokritos – Anthony Holden's complete version of the epigrams appears in his *Greek Pastoral Poetry*.

118

> Those dew-moist roses and that bushy thyme
> are sacred to the Muse of Helicon.
> But yours, Apollo, is the dark-leaved bay
> which sanctifies your shrine on Delphi's height;
> this horned white goat chewing the terebinth
> shall stain your holy altar with his blood.

ANTHONY HOLDEN 6.336

119

> Daphnis the fair-skinned, who plays pastoral songs
> upon his well-tuned pipe, now gives to Pan
> his flute, his staff, his javelin, a skin
> and this, the pouch in which he carries fruit.

ANTHONY HOLDEN 6.177

120

> You left behind, Eurymedon, an infant child
> when, in your prime, death took you to your grave.
> Now you are with the godly; but your son is shown
> respect, in memory of his father's name.

ANTHONY HOLDEN 7.659

121

This is the grave of Eusthenes the wise,
a physiognomist, whose eye could read
a man and know the nature of his mind.
His friends have buried him with honour here,
a foreigner in foreign soil, a poet
loved dearly by his fellow-men. The sage
died destitute, but now has all he should –
for such a man, help was not hard to find.

ANTHONY HOLDEN 7.661

122

Take, friend, Orthon of Syracuse' advice:
never sail on a stormy night when drunk.
I did; and now lie here abroad, short-changed,
deprived of richer burial at home.

ANTHONY HOLDEN 7.660

123

Look on this statue, traveller; look well,
and then, when back at home, 'In Teos', say,
'I saw an image of Anacreon,
the greatest of the songmakers of old.'
And, if you seek the essence of the man,
then say of him 'He gave joy to the young.'

ANTHONY HOLDEN 9.599*

124

The words are Doric, Doric too the man:
the poet Epicharmus, pioneer
of comedy. To honour you, Bacchus,
his fellow citizens have raised in bronze
what once was flesh and blood. Our debt is paid.
We men of Syracuse remember here

the wisdom of his words, the way of life
he taught our children. Here we offer thanks.

ANTHONY HOLDEN 9.600*

125

This bank makes welcome citizen and foreigner
alike. Deposits and withdrawals strictly depend
upon the state of your account. No haggling here.
Caicus will change your money even after dark.

ANTHONY HOLDEN 9.435

126

You sleep here, Daphnis, on the leafy ground,
resting your tired limbs, now your nets are staked
high on the hills. But Pan is after you;
and Priapus, too, with ivy-gilded brow . . .
together they approach your cave. Now run!
Shake off this drowsiness! Wake up and run!

ANTHONY HOLDEN 9.338

127

Along that footpath, shepherd, past the oaks,
you'll come across a statue newly carved
from fig, its bark still fresh. You'll see it's lost
its legs and ears, but still has all it needs
to procreate, to do great Cypris' work.
It's in a sacred grove, close by a spring
forever flowing from the rocks round bays
and myrtles and sweet-smelling cypresses.
A vine spreads out its tendrils there, and bears
its fruit; in spring, the clear-voiced blackbird sings
his lively tune and lilting nightingales
return the song in honeyed notes. Go there;
sit down, and pray to gracious Priapus

that I may lose my love for Daphnis. Say,
should he grant this, at once I'll offer him
a fine young goat. Should he refuse,
I'll make three offerings to win my love:
a goat, a heifer and a hand-reared lamb.
Now may the god receive and grant my prayer!

ANTHONY HOLDEN 9.437

128

What do you gain, poor Thyrsis, by these tears?
Why weep your eyes away? It's gone, your kid,
your pretty love, it's dead and gone, caught up
and savaged in the cruel jaws of the wolf.
Your dogs still bark; but when death comes, and bones
and ashes both are gone, what do you gain?

ANTHONY HOLDEN 9.432

NIKIAS

Nikias was a contemporary and close friend of Theokritos,
whose Idylls 11 and 13 are addressed to him; Idyll 28 was
written to accompany a present of a distaff to Nikias' wife
Theugenis. From this (and Theokritos' epigram on the statue
of Asklepios which Nikias commissioned from Eëtion) we
know that he was a doctor practising in Miletos. How he met
Theokritos is not known; possibly he was in Kos as a medical
student at the time of Theokritos' visit. Eight epigrams are
extant.

129

Spring blossoms, honey-bee, in the colours you parade,
exulting, yellow one, in her first flowers.
Fly to the fragrant fields, and set about your work:
your waxen honeycomb must be well filled.

ANTHONY HOLDEN 9.564

130

    I, Hermes, guard Cyllene's wooded slopes,
    keeping my watch on her handsome parklands here.
    Boys often crown me with fresh violets,
    lay marjoram and hyacinths at my feet.

ANTHONY HOLDEN 16.188

ERINNA

Erinna probably lived in the early third century as a contemporary of Theokritos, Anyte and Asklepiades. She came from the Dorian island of Telos, and died aged nineteen, as we know from Asklepiades' poem on her (no. 73 above). It has been inferred from the same poem that Asklepiades edited her collected poems after her death. Three epigrams survive, and sixty more or less decipherable hexameters of her 300-line poem *The Distaff* were discovered in a papyrus and published in 1929. In *The Distaff* Erinna describes girlhood experiences shared with her friend Baukis, whose early death she mourns. She was associated with the Koan literary movement and influenced by Theokritos, and probably also wrote lyric poetry. The epigram I have omitted (*AP* 7.710) is another epitaph for Baukis.

131   *On the Portrait of a Girl*

        This drawing
        came
        from subtle hands

        (Prometheus,
        there are men

84

with skill
equal to yours)

Yes,
he who
made this girl
had he but added voice
made Agatharchis.

LENORE MAYHEW 6.352

132 *Epitaph on a Betrothed Girl*

I am Baukis the bride's.
When you pass this bitter pillar
say to death
under the ground,
'You are envious, oh death';
for they who see
this monument
will know
that the father-in-law
burned the girl
on the pyre
with the unused torches
of the marriage train.
Oh Hymen
    you have changed the singable bride song
to a dirge.

LENORE MAYHEW 7.712

MOIRO

Two epigrams by Moiro survive. She was a Byzantine and according to the *Suda* 'wrote epic, elegiac and lyric verse; was the mother of Homer the tragedian, and wife of Andromachos the well-known philologist'. She was probably contemporary with Anyte. Fragments of her hexameter verse (ten lines on Zeus) are included in Powell's *Collectanea Alexandrina*.

133

> Now you lie – a grape-offering,
> A severed cluster, a bag of wine-juice –
> In Aphrodite's gilded porch.
> Never again will the vine your mother
> Curl her kindly branch about you
> Or spread over your head her scented leaves.

FLEUR ADCOCK 6.119

134

> Hail, forest nymphs, daughters of the river,
> Holy creatures who dance forever
> On the flowing surface with feet like flowers:
> Heal Cleomynus, I pray, who has given
> These pretty carvings to stand in your pine-grove.

FLEUR ADCOCK 6.189

NOSSIS

Nossis came from Lokroi – a town of the same name, Locri, is still there – on the south-eastern coast of the toe of Italy. She

was active in the first quarter of the third century B.C. A
dozen of her epigrams survive; she may also have written
lyric poetry.

135

> Most honoured Hera, who descends from heaven
> to look on this temple sweet with incense,
> accept this linen dress which Cleocha's daughter
> Theophilis, and her good child Nossis, have woven.

SALLY PURCELL 6.265

136

> Melinna herself! It *is* – see how kindly
> her gentle face looks down at me,
> & how like her mother she is!
> It's good when children look so like their parents.

SALLY PURCELL 6.353

137

> Let us go to the temple
> to see Aphrodite's image,
>   delicately worked in gold.
> It was put up by Polyarchis,
> who had become a person of substance
>   from her body's beauty.

SALLY PURCELL 9.332

138

> This is Thaumareta's picture, and how well it captures
> her elegance, her mild-eyed beauty!
> If your little watch-dog saw you here,
> she'd wag her tail, believing you were her mistress.

SALLY PURCELL 9.604

139

Laugh aloud, then pass by, with a kind
word at my tomb. I am Rhinthon of Syracuse,
a minor nightingale for the Muses, but
for my parodies of the tragic poets, collected
a special ivy-wreath, of my own.

PETER JAY 7.414

140

Nothing is sweeter than love, all other blessings
Come second to it. I have spat even honey
From my mouth – I, Nossis,
Say this is so. But one whom Kypris
Has not loved, will never know
What roses her flowers are.

PETER JAY 5.170

THEAITETOS

It is probable that this Theaitetos, author of six extant epi-
grams, is the third-century poet on whom Kallimachos wrote
his epigram (no. 160 here). Nothing else is known of him.

141   *Krantor*

he gave joy to men & more joy
still to the Muses but did not

live much into his age: o earth
in you this sacred man may be

folded by death or instead live
far into his joy there

DENNIS SCHMITZ *HE*2

KALLIMACHOS

Kallimachos (*c.* 300–240 B.C.), son of Battos, came from Kyrene. He lived in Alexandria, where he taught at a suburban school before taking up a post in the Library. There he worked on a vast catalogue project, to produce – in 120 books – what was effectively the first organized Greek literary history. Both as poet and prose-writer he was extraordinarily prolific. A few snippets of his scholarly, critical and encyclopaedic prose-writings survive; of his poetry – as well as sixty-odd epigrams – six hymns survive, and fragments of other works such as the *Lock of Bereniké* (translated by Catullus, poem 66), lyric poems, *Iambics* (occasional poems, some of them satirical), and epyllia (miniature epics) like *Hekalé*; and substantial fragments of his most famous work, the *Aitia* ('Causes'), a sequence of elegiac poems in four books on the origins of religious festivals and customs. It was first published about 270 B.C., and later reissued with a prefatory 'Reply to his Critics'.

Though he enjoyed favour at the court of Ptolemy Philadelphos, and late in life was accepted by Ptolemy Euergetes, Kallimachos' life was always involved in controversy. His critics were numerous, and included Asklepiades and Poseidippos. He was variously charged with inability to write sustained long poems; aridity; and too much variety in metre and dialect. The controversies may have started with his outspoken dislike of Antimachos' long poem *Lyde*. Kallimachos maintained that epics of the traditional structure were obsolete – 'big book, big bore,' he said. A bitter quarrel (both personal and literary) broke out when his former pupil Apollonios of Rhodes, who was Head Librarian at Alexandria from about 260–247, produced the *Argonautika* – a 6,000 line epic, which for all its Alexandrianism was too much in the grand manner for Kallimachos. Matters were doubtless not helped by the fact that Kallimachos was working under Apollonios at the Library. At all events, Apollonios was badly hurt by the whole business, and retired to Rhodes. Kallimachos wrote an obscure poem, the *Ibis*, which apparently attacked Apollonios.

These literary debates are touched on by Kallimachos in the epigrams, though his other fragments, and the ancient commentaries on the poems, provide most of our knowledge of them. Kallimachos was the most important figure of his time, and his influence was crucial not only for Greek poetry but for the Roman elegists and lyric poets. Both Catullus and Propertius were deeply indebted to him. Kallimachos' range was very wide; he was a bold experimentalist with the courage of his convictions. In the epigrams his erudition is lightly worn, and his subtle, ironic urbanity shows to good effect.

142

    I despise neo-epic verse sagas: I cannot
    Welcome trends which drag the populace
    This way and that. Peripatetic sex-partners
    Turn me off: I do not drink from the mains,
    Can't stomach anything public.

                       Lysanias,
    Yes, you're another who's beautiful, beautiful – and
    The words are hardly out of my mouth, when Echo
    Comes back with the response, 'Yes, you're another's.'

                       PETER JAY 12.43

143

    Something's there, by Pan there's something hidden
    By Dionysos, fire beneath the ashes!
    I've lost my nerve: don't get me involved. Quiet
    Rivers often gnaw at the wall secretly,

And Menexenos, I am afraid
This silent crawler will find a way into me,
And I will be in love.

PETER JAY 12.139

144

Kallignotos swore to Ionis – no one
(Boy or girl) would ever be dearer to him.
He swore! But the proverb is right – the gods have ears
Impervious to lovers' oaths. He's fired
With love now for a boy. As for her, poor girl –
One no more hears of her than of the Megarians.

PETER JAY 5.6

145

Our guest's wound went unnoticed. Didn't you see him
Dragging breath painfully from his lungs
As he drank the third cup? And the roses
Taking leave of his garland, dropping their petals
Over the floor? He's properly cooked. Good gods,
I'm not guessing wildly. Set a thief
Like me, who knows the clues which others leave.

PETER JAY 12.134

146   *A Statue of Bereniké*

There are four Graces. Beside the original three
Stands one newly translated, still dripping with scent
Blest and emulated by all – Bereniké,
Without whom the Graces themselves are no Graces.

PETER JAY 5.146

147

Kallistion the wife of Kritias
Gave me to Sarapis, a lamp with twenty wicks
Vowed for her child Apellis. See my lights
And say, 'Hesperos! how art thou fallen from heaven!'

PETER JAY 6.148

148

Menoitas of Lyktos
Gave Sarapis this kit,
Saying, 'I present you
With the bow and quiver:
The men of Hesperis
Still have all the arrows.'

PETER JAY 13.7*

149

Eileithyia, once more
Come at the call of Lykainis,
As you have helped her to a painless birth –
So that, while now she gives you
This for her daughter, your fragrant
Temple will have something else
Another time – for a boy.

PETER JAY 6.146

150   *On Himself*

You're walking by the tomb of Battiades,
Who knew well how to write poetry, and enjoy
Laughter at the right moment, over the wine.

PETER JAY 7.415

151

> *Does Charidas lie beneath you?* If you mean
> The son of Arimmas of Kyrene – yes.
> *Charidas, what's it like down there?* Great darkness.
> *And resurrection?* A lie. *And Pluto?*
> A fable. *Then we are finished....* What I'm saying
> Is the truth. If you want to hear something nice,
> The cost of living is low in Hades.

PETER JAY 7.524

152

Someone spoke of your death, Herakleitos. It brought me
Tears, and I remembered how often together
We ran the sun down with talk ... somewhere
You've long been dust, my Halikarnassian friend.
But your *Nightingales* live on. Though the Death-world
Claws at everything, it will not touch them.

PETER JAY 7.80

153

> The stranger was short: let my verse be such.
> *Theris from Crete, Aristaios' son* – too much.

PETER JAY 7.447

154

> Here Saon of Akanthos, Dikon's son
> Sleeps the sleep of the just.
> Don't say good men are dead.

PETER JAY 7.451

155

His twelve-year-old
son, Philip gave up
here: his one
great hope – Nikoteles.

PETER JAY 7.453

156

Who were you, shipwrecked stranger? Leontichos found
My body here on the beach, and buried it
In this tomb, bemoaning
His own life's hazards, since he cannot
Travel the high seas untroubled, like a gull.

PETER JAY 7.277

157

*Since you are dead, Timon, tell me which
You find more loathsome – darkness, or the light?*
Darkness. There are more of you down in Hades.

PETER JAY 7.317

158

'Goodbye Sun!' said the Ambracian
Kleombrotos, as he jumped
Off a high wall to Hades:
Not that he found any evil
Worthy of death, but he'd read
One of Plato's treatises – *On the Soul*.

PETER JAY 7.471

159   *Aratos'* Phainomena

Hesiod's style and themes: the poet from Soloi
Modelled his work not on the greatest of poets
But, I admit, on his finest moments. Welcome,
Verses of subtle refinement – tokens
Of all the nights which Aratos spent awake.

                              PETER JAY 9.507

160   *Theaitetos*

The road he took was virgin territory.
If different paths lead, Bakchos, to your ivy
Other names will be heralded for a while,
But Hellas will always know his skill.

                              PETER JAY 9.565

161

          Sleep cold at someone's
          Door as, shivering,
          I lie tonight at
          Yours. The neighbours weep
          To see me here, but
          Who will weep for you,
          Crouched on a doorstep
          When the grey hairs come?

     EDWARD LUCIE-SMITH 5.23

HERAKLEITOS

Herakleitos must be the friend for whom Kallimachos wrote
his famous poem (no. 152 above). Kallimachos' poem is
quoted by Diogenes Laertios who says Herakleitos was 'an

elegiac poet from Halikarnassos'; Strabo mentions him as a distinguished Halikarnassian together with the fifth-century B.C. historian Herodotos and the first-century B.C. critic and literary historian Dionysios, and refers to him as 'the friend of Kallimachos'. Gow and Page comment on his sole epigram, 'its quality is such as to make one regret the loss of his other *Nightingales*' (evidently the title of a collection of his poems).

162

> The soil is freshly dug, the half-faded wreaths of leaves
> droop across the face of the tombstone.
> What do the letters say, traveller? What can they tell you
> of the smooth bones the slab says it guards?
> 'Stranger, I am Aretemias of Cnidus. I was the wife
> of Euphro. Labour-pains were not withheld
> from me. I left one twin to guide my husband's old age,
> and took the other to remind me of him.'

EDWIN MORGAN 7.465

EUPHORION

Born in 275 B.C., according to the *Suda*, in Chalkis (Euboia), Euphorion studied poetry and philosophy in Athens before leaving to become Librarian to Antiochos the Great in Syria, where he lived the rest of his life. He was an epic poet and wrote mainly epyllia (mythological miniature epics of several hundred lines). Abstruse in subject matter, bizarre and obscure in language, he was nevertheless an important influence on later Roman poets – notably Catullus and the young Vergil. Cicero's off-hand jibe at the Roman neoteric poets as '*cantores Euphorionis*' (Euphorion's warblers) shows that his influence was not unanimously regarded as beneficial. Both his surviving epigrams are given here.

163

When first Eudoxos cut his lovely hair
   he gave this crown of childhood to Apollo.
For these locks, archer-god, let him have beauty,
   and the crown of Acharnian ivy that grows forever.

ALISTAIR ELLIOT 6.279

164

Not the wild olive, not the fatal stones
   that bear these letters cover up the bones.
No, the Icarian wave breaks them to pieces
   on the pebbles of Doliche under Mount Drakanos.
Not hospitality heaped for Polymedes
   but empty earth on the parched Dryopian fields.

ALISTAIR ELLIOT 7.651

HEGESIPPOS

Probably active about 250 B.C.; nothing is known of him.

165

Hang that day with black, that night, sinister, moonless,
   that fearful wind-whipped sea-howl
which threw on shore the ship of gentle Abderion
   as he made unheard vows to the gods.
For out of that utter shipwreck on the sharp rocks
   of Seriphus, all he got was fire
from the city's pious hosts, and a voyage home
   to Abdera, bound in a bronze urn.

EDWIN MORGAN 13.12*

LEONIDAS OF TARENTUM

Just over a hundred epigrams by Leonidas are preserved in the Anthology. We could guess from this alone that he was both a prolific and popular writer. He was much imitated by later epigrammatists and appreciated by the Romans; Propertius and Vergil both borrow from him. All that can be gleaned from the poems about his life is that he was poor, and travelled widely. A poem on a famous painting by Apelles in Kos suggests that he travelled there, but there is (surprisingly) no reference to Egypt or the Ptolemies, and nothing to suggest that he ever went to Alexandria.

Erotic and convivial epigrams are conspicuously absent from his extant work. The poems are mostly epitaphs or dedicatory poems; nearly all are concerned with the life of working-class people – farmers, fishermen, craftsmen, etc. (It should not be assumed from this that he regarded himself as a working-class poet, any more than Theokritos thought of himself as a shepherd.) Opinions differ greatly as to his merit: Gilbert Highet thought him 'one of the greatest Greek epigrammatists', while Gow and Page regard him as rather tedious. His style is rather elaborate and mannered – compound words and technical terms going side by side. Leonidas certainly enlarged the scope of the epigram in a different direction from that of his contemporaries.

His precise date is not ascertainable: one may guess that he was born early in the third century, and one poem suggests that he lived till old age. Edwyn Bevan's *The Poems of Leonidas of Tarentum* (1931) contains a good account of his work.

166

Atthis hung up the belt with the pompoms
and a loose dress over the virgin's door,
because you brought a child alive out of her labour
when her womb was heavy, Artemis.

PETER LEVI 6.202

167

The silver Eros the ankle bracelet
the Lesbian purple hair-band
crystal-skin breast-girdle, bronze mirror,
and the wide wooden hair-trawling comb:
Kallikleia has got what she wanted:
Cretan Kypris, she leaves them at your columns.

PETER LEVI 6.211*

168

Sheep-folds, holy spring of the Nymphs,
streams under the rock, fir tree by the water,
four-cornered Hermes, flock-god, son of Maia,
Pan, god of the goat-nibbled rock,
accept cakes and a jug filled with wine
from Neoptolemos Aiakides.

PETER LEVI 6.334

169

Theromachos of Crete came to hang up
his rabbit-stick to Lykaian Pan
on an Arkadian crag. Favour him
hunter god, make his hand shoot
the bow right in battle, and in valleys
stand beside him, give him best gain
from the hunt and from whoever he fights.

PETER LEVI 6.188

170

Cold water falling out of the split rock,
and herdmen's carvings of the nymphs,
rocks of the springs, figures of the virgins
water-sprinkled a hundred thousand times,
Aristokles who came by and washed
and lost his thirst has left this present.

PETER LEVI 9.326

171

Nymphs of water, daughters of Doros,
flow in to wet Timokles' garden,
because Timokles always gives you
fruit from this garden when it ripens.

PETER LEVI 9.329

172

Theris, whose hands were cunning,
Gives to Pallas, now the years
Of craftsmanship are over,
His stiff saw with curved handle,
His bright axe, his plane, and his
Revolving auger.

KENNETH REXROTH 6.204

173

Ambrosia, brought safe
Through the sharp pain of labour,
Lays at your glorious feet,
Eileithyia, her head bands,
And her gown, for in the tenth
Month she brought forth double fruit.

KENNETH REXROTH 6.200

174

Philokles offers his bouncing
Ball to Hermes, along
With the other toys of his
Boyhood, his boxwood rattle,
The knuckle bones he once was
So crazy about, and his
Spinning top.

KENNETH REXROTH 6.309

175

For that goatfucker, goatfooted
Pan, Teleso stretched this hide
On a plane tree, and in front
Of it hung up his well cut
Crook, smiter of bloody-eyed wolves,
His curdling buckets, and the leash
And collars of his keen-nosed pups.

KENNETH REXROTH 6.35

176

This beast which preyed on sheep
And cattle and herders alike, and
Which had no fear of barking dogs,
Eualkes of Crete killed in the night,
While guarding his herds, and hung up
For a trophy on this pine tree.

KENNETH REXROTH 6.262

177

A wallet, a rawhide goatskin, a cane,
A filthy oil flask, never cleaned out,
A penniless dog-skin purse,
The hat which covered his cynical head,

These are the mementoes of Sochares
Flung into the tamarisk bush
By famine when he died.

KENNETH REXROTH 6.298

178

Here is Klito's little shack.
Here is his little cornpatch.
Here is his tiny vineyard.
Here is his little woodlot.
Here Klito spent eighty years.

KENNETH REXROTH 6.226

179

Sōsos the cattleman slew the lion
that dismembered his burgeoning calf,
and flayed it. Flayed, it loped
from forest to fold, from fold
to forest no more. Stuck, it discharged
its bloody debt with its blood.

W. G. SHEPHERD 6.263

180

Antiginides' two daughters, Melo
and Satyra, are withered but
once did their bit for the arts. Now Melo
dedicates to the Muse of Glut
this well-tongued flute and its boxwood case; while
her nymphomaniac sister,
hostess for a night to men-about-town,
gives wax-welded pipes, sweet whistle
that she once played all night till dawn, not sore
that no man there would let her go.

ALAN MARSHFIELD 5.206

181

I am the tomb of Tellen, I contain
under this ground the first old man
who discovered the science of comic songs.

PETER LEVI 7.719

182

Night and mist, what bones you have eaten,
earth what a loved head you have covered:
Aristokrates friend of the fair-haired Graces
remembered with friendship by mankind.
He could speak and there was peace, he had never
any scowl in his words, among bottles
he held the rudder of the talk at peace.
Generous to strangers and to his people.
Lovely earth, this is the man you cover.

PETER LEVI 7.648

183

Eros taught Pratalidas his adolescent beauty,
Artemis hunting, a Muse dancing,
the god of war fighting, he should have been
immortal, prince of music, love, spears, the trap.

PETER LEVI 7.449

184

Give me one small smothering of earth,
the unhappy cemetery weight
of a heavy stone is to crush richer sleep.
If I am dead who cares I was Alkander.

PETER LEVI 7.655

185

You shepherds who wander this lonely mountainside
Taking your goats and fleecy sheep to pasture:
I ask a favour in the name of mother Earth
And Persephone, who shares our world below –
A slight enough thing, but one that means a lot
To a dead man: let me hear your sheep bleating
While one of you sits on a rough rock, softly
Playing the pipes to them; let a village man
Pick wild flowers in early spring
To decorate my grave; and let a shepherd
Raise the full udder of a nursing ewe
And squirt rich milk onto my tomb.
I, Cleitagoras, will remember you;
Even we dead can return favours.

FLEUR ADCOCK 7.657

186

Go softly past the graveyard where
Hipponax is asleep: take care!
Don't wake that spiteful wasp, who stung
Even his parents with his tongue.
In Hell itself, where now he lies,
His red-hot words can cauterize.

FLEUR ADCOCK 7.408

187

Remember Euboulos, who lived and died sober?
This is his grave. We might as well drink, then:
We'll all drop anchor in the same final harbour.

FLEUR ADCOCK 7.452

Who are you, whose pitiful bones
Lie bleakly naked by the roadway?
Your battered coffin is half-open;
The wheels and axles of passing wagons
Are steadily wearing your tomb away.
Soon they will actually scrape your ribs;
And not a tear will be shed for you.

FLEUR ADCOCK 7.478

189

Far from Italy, far from my native Tarentum
I lie; and this is the worst of it — worse than death.
An exile's life is no life. But the Muses loved me.
For my suffering they gave me a honeyed gift:
My name survives me. Thanks to the sweet Muses
Leonidas will echo throughout all time.

FLEUR ADCOCK 7.715

190

Theris, the old man who lived by his fish traps
And nets, more at home on the sea than a gull,
The terror of fishes, the net-hauler, the prober
Of sea caves, who never sailed on a many oared ship,
Died in spite of Arcturus. No storm shipwrecked
His many decades. He died in his reed hut,
And went out by himself like a lamp at the
End of his years. No wife or child set up this
Tomb, but his fisherman's union.

KENNETH REXROTH 7.295

191

Sudden strong squalls from the sou'-west,
Night, and the waves that dark Orion stirs
At his November setting — these were my fate.

And I, Callaeschrus, wrenched from life
As I sailed the mid-Lybian waters, my bones
Now thread the sea, as the fish and the tides turn them,
And this stone lies that says it lies on me.

CLIVE SANSOM 7.273

192

'I'm like a vine supported on a stick,
And death is calling me to underground:
– Gorgus, stop playing deaf. Are they so sweet,
Three or four summers more beneath the sun?'
The old man quietly put his life away
And moved house to the greater company.

ALISTAIR ELLIOT 7.731

193

Eurotas said to the goddess of love,
'Wear weapons or don't live in Sparta,
this city has gone weapon-crazy.'
She laughed nicely and said to the river,
'But I shall be weaponless for ever,
and I shall live in Sparta for ever.'
She is unarmed. It is blasphemous
to talk about the weapons of love.

PETER LEVI 9.320

194

Good hunting, rabbit-catcher and bird-catcher,
but under these rock-faces shout from the crag
to Pan who rules in the woods.
I hunt with you: I have dogs and reeds.

PETER LEVI 9.337

195

The sun whirls an axle on fire,
blackens stars and the moon's holy wheels:
Homer lifting the clear light of Muses
has darkened the hymnsellers in one crowd.

PETER LEVI 9.24

196

Don't waste yourself, dragging out the life of a vagrant
   wandering on from country to country; don't
Waste yourself. Take a rough cottage for shelter,
   a simple place warmed by a small fire;
Where in a hollow rock you can knead cheap pastry
   with your own hands, from common meal,
Where you have mint and thyme, and coarse
   salt that's tasty for flavouring what you eat.

PETER JAY 7.736

197   *Spring on the Coast*

The season of ships is here,
The west wind and the swallows;
Flowers in the fields appear,
And the ocean of hills and hollows
Has calmed its waves and is clear.

Free that anchor and chain!
Set your full canvas flying,
O men in the harbour-lane:
It is I, Priapus, crying.
Sail out on your trades again!

CLIVE SANSOM 10.1

MNASALKES

Mnasalkes of Sikyon in the Peloponnese was active in the middle or second half of the third century. His style and subject matter are indebted to Anyte and Asklepiades. Theodoridas, in a satirical pseudo-epitaph on him (*AP* 13.21), doubtless written in Mnasalkes' lifetime, accuses him of plagiarizing Simonides and of turgidity; he must have been referring to works by Mnasalkes that are now lost. Eighteen epigrams remain.

198

Promachus hangs here
As a gift to thee,
Apollo, his bow,
Also his quiver.
His arrows, given
As presents to his
Foes upon the field
Of battle, he left
Sticking in their hearts.

EDWARD LUCIE-SMITH 6.9

199

My fighting days are done;
I rest here now. I took
Them all – arrows and stones,
The probing thrust of spears –
Turning my back to save
My master. I've quit him,
But I never left his
Arm amid the battle.

EDWARD LUCIE-SMITH 6.125

200

Setting their country free,
They clothed their bones in dust.
Their prize is praise. And if
War comes may we be brave.

EDWARD LUCIE-SMITH 7.242

201

Aristocrateia,
You've crossed the dark stream
Young and unwed, alas!
Your mother's left with just
The tears she sheds, when
Often now she weeping lies
Prostrate upon your tomb.

EDWARD LUCIE-SMITH 7.488

202

No longer, cricket, sitting
In a furrow, will you sing
Out, delightful, nor lull me
With music from your wingbeat
As I lie beneath the vine.

EDWARD LUCIE-SMITH 7.192

203

I, wretched Virtue, sit
By Pleasure's tomb, my hair
Cut off, struck to the heart
To find the world so sure
That Sensuality
Must triumph over me.

EDWARD LUCIE-SMITH *HE*17

204

Broad-acred Ascra bore me, like
Its grain. And Orchomenus
Has what's left of me. My name
Is Hesiod, and I am
Dubbed the wisest of the wise.

EDWARD LUCIE-SMITH 7.54

THEODORIDAS

Theodoridas lived in the second half of the third century. He came from Syracuse but seems to have had connections with Thessaly. He wrote dithyrambs (one was called *The Centaurs*), iambic and hexameter poetry, but apart from very short quotations from these, only his nineteen epigrams survive.

205

To the triple goddess of Amarynthus
Charixenus made this threefold dedication
For the shorn-off locks he had in his youthful time,
Together with his beautiful cicada hair-slide;
An ox likewise sprinkled with lustral water.
The boy gleams like a star, having shed as a horse does
His downy foal's coat.

JOHN HEATH-STUBBS and CAROL A. WHITESIDE 6.156

206

Roused by November seas, wrecked on Italian rocks,
    a kraken squid was washed ashore:
The masters of the cattle-ships set up this,
    its huge rib, in homage to the Gods.

W. G. SHEPHERD 6.222

207

I am the tomb of a shipwrecked man. Sail on;
when we went down, the other ships went on.

PETER JAY 7.282

NIKAINETOS

Five epigrams by this poet, who lived probably in the second
half of the third century, are extant. He is connected both with
Samos and Abdéra; he also wrote epic verse, a *Catalogue of
Women* and an epyllion called *Lyrkos*.

208

Speaks Bito's tomb to whomsoever reads:
'If from Torone to Amphipolis you go,
Give Nicagoras this message: his one son
Died in storm, in early winter, before sunrise.'

PETER WHIGHAM 7.502

209

Not in the city, Philoterus, but
Al fresco, under west wind,
With Carian willows for couch,
Withies binding our glad heads . . .

And music sounding, wine playing,
That, toasting with song
Hera, Queen of our island,
Her may we celebrate.

PETER WHIGHAM *HE*4

TYMNES

The name is Karian rather than Greek; he is perhaps of the third century B.C., and is certainly post-Leonidas since he imitates him in a poem not included here. The poem on the Maltese dog is well-known, and there are also nice versions of it by Fitts and Rexroth. Seven of his epigrams survive.

210

> Dear little bird, the Graces' favourite,
> Your warbling-voice rivalled the halcyons.
> Now you're dead, night's paths of silence
> Hold your sweet character, and your breath.

PETER JAY 7.199

211 *The Dog from Malta*

> He came from Malta, and Eumelus says
> He had no dog like him in all his days;
> We called him Bull; he went into the dark;
> Along those roads we cannot hear him bark.

EDMUND BLUNDEN 7.211

212

> Don't let it matter much, Philaenis –
> Not sharing earth beside the Nile,
> But lying here in Eleutherné. Think:
> Hades is just as far, anywhere.

ALISTAIR ELLIOT 7.477

HERMOKREON

There is some doubt whether the same poet is the author of these two poems ascribed to Hermokreon. In the case of no. 213, the name may have been extrapolated on the assumption that the dedicator is the poet.

Both poems, however, are doubtless Hellenistic and are typical of third-century poets.

213

    Nymphs of the surface, whom Hermokreon gave
      these presents when he found your lovely spring,
   welcome! and tread the water of your house here
      with charming feet, filling it with pure drink.

ALISTAIR ELLIOT 9.327

214   *Inscription on a Statue*

   Come, passer-by, sit in this plane-tree's shade
      under leaves shaken by Zephyr's delicate breath,
  where Nicagoras seated Maias' famous son,
      Hermes, to guard his orchard and his goods.

ALISTAIR ELLIOT 16.11

THYMOKLES

Thymokles was probably writing in the third century B.C. This poem was included in Meleager's *Garland*.

215

Remember, do you remember those solemn words –
Springtime is loveliest, time most elusive,
quicker than the quickest bird in the sky –
Look, your blossoms
all scattered on the earth.

PETER JAY 12.32

ARISTODIKOS

Probably a third-century B.C. poet, he was from Rhodes. This is one of his two poems; it is in the manner of Anyte.

216

Cricket, you'll sing no more
in Alkis' elegant house,
shrill-voiced in the sunlight.
For now you've flown away
to the grassy fields of the dead
and golden Persephone's
flower-meadows, wet with dew.

BARRISS MILLS 7.189

RHIANOS

Rhianos came from a small town in Crete. The *Suda* says he was originally a slave. He was active perhaps in the second half of the third century; he wrote lengthy epic poems – five titles are known – and edited Homer. This suggests that he worked at Alexandria. Ten epigrams survive, mainly dedicatory and pederastic. The most interesting is the ironic thank-you poem given here.

217

Archinos, this retsina bottle contains
Precisely half pine-resin and half wine.
Cuts from a leaner goat, I've never seen
(Though Hippokrates who sent them, the dear man
Deserves *every* thanks).

PETER JAY HE9

DIOSKORIDES

Dioskorides was writing towards the end of the third century. His forty-odd poems, influenced by Asklepiades and Kalli-machos, show his capacity for lively, realistic love-poems, and an interest in earlier literature. He lived in Nikopolis – probably the suburb of Alexandria.

218

My downfall: those pink articulate lips
Divinely flavoured portals to a mouth
Where soul dissolves . . . eyes darting
Beneath black brows, snares for the heart,
And the milk-white breasts, well shaped,
The twin rosebuds, fair beyond other flowers.

To itemize thus – is this to cast dogs a bone?
The poet's pen – secret as reeds of Midas?

PETER WHIGHAM 5.56

219

Zephyr, kindliest of winds,
Fetch back my loved one, Euphragoras;
Extend not that sojourn you began:
Brief months stretch to years for us in love.

PETER WHIGHAM 12.171

220

The first fruits from her fruitful bed
  This fan that cooled once her cheeks
Accept, Venus of Zephyrs, from Parmenis
  Whose heats your breezes gratefully allay.

PETER WHIGHAM 6.290

221

A Thracian page-boy
    mastered
you, Anacreon,
    Master of all-night
ceremonies,
    Enchanter of the Nine,
who wept
    often in your cups
for Smerdies,
    for Bathyllus.
Let wine spout
    in fountains
where you lie,
    ambrosia
nectar,
    from the gods.
Let your garden-grave
    bear
the evening violet,
    the stock, sweet-breathing,
myrtles
    for garlands
dew-fresh,
    that, in the House of Dis,
happy with wine,
    to a fine measure

dancing
   you may clasp forever
your golden love,
   Eurypyle,
in your arms.

PETER WHIGHAM 7.31

222

Hiero's former Nurse
Silenis, who liked wine
Straight & plentiful
Rests in these vine-fields,
May her old body
Buried amid vines
Feed in death the vats
She loved in life.

PETER WHIGHAM 7.456

DAMAGETOS

The author of twelve epigrams, Damagetos was a Peloponnesian, most probably from Sparta, active in the last quarter of the third century B.C. Among his commemorative epigrams are pieces about men killed on both sides of the Social War of 220–217 B.C. between the Achaian League (backed by Philip V) and the Aitolian League (backed by Sparta).

223   *On the Tomb of Orpheus*

A tomb on the Thracian approaches of Olympus holds
Orpheus, the one whom the Muse Calliope bore.
The oaks could not but obey him, and the mindless
Rocks kept pace to his beat, and the woodland beast-packs.

He found out the occult initiation rites of Bacchus, and
  likewise
Structured the linked line in epic metre.
Spellbound, with his lyre, he held the heavy mind
Of Him Whom we speak well of, the unmollifiable,
And that wrath likewise which no enchantment can bind.

JOHN HEATH-STUBBS and CAROL A. WHITESIDE 7.9

224

In the name of the God of strangers, we beg you
Carry tidings, man, to our father
Charinus in Aeolian Thebes,
Menis and Polynicus have ceased to be.
Say this also: we do not repine
At the treacherous lot assigned us,
Although we fell by the hand of the Thracians, but
For old age lying heavily on himself,
In harsh bereavement.

JOHN HEATH-STUBBS and CAROL A. WHITESIDE 7.540

225   *Epitaph of a Sailor*

And Thymodês also, lamenting a death unforeseen,
Raised up this empty tomb for Lykos his son:

For him there is no grave, not even in a far land:
Some Thynian beach or Pontine island holds him,

And there, cheated of all the rites of burial,
His bones gleam naked on an unfriendly shore.

DUDLEY FITTS 7.497

ALKAIOS

The epigrammatist from Messene – not to be confused with
the Lesbian lyric poet, Sappho's contemporary – is respon-
sible for twenty-two poems. He lived in the time of Philip V
of Macedon (238–179 B.C.) – the third poem here was written
about 197 B.C. Wilamowitz regards him as the last Hellenistic
poet to show any real originality. Certainly his political
epigrams are unique; the cause of his hatred for Philip is not
known, though it may date from Philip's attacks on Messene
in 215–214. The terrorist, empire-building king was defeated
by the Romans at Kynoskephalai in 197 B.C., and his influence
was limited to Macedon for the next dozen years. He was
notorious as a poisoner (Alkaios' second poem is on two of his
victims). The first poem is most naturally taken as ironic.
Alkaios is said also to have written 'iambic invectives' and
parody.

226   *Philip of Macedon*

Enlarge your fortifications, Zeus –
Philip climbs everything –
and shut heaven's bronze gates.
Land and sea are enslaved
to Philip as it is; only
the road to Olympus is left.

ALISTAIR ELLIOT 9.518

227   *Philip V of Macedon*

Wine destroyed the Centaur, not just you,
    Epikrates, and young and handsome Kallias.
Or rather, that one-eyed bastard did, wine-bearing
    you to hell – so send him up a similar health.

ALISTAIR ELLIOT 11.12

228   *Philip at Kynoskephalai*

Not wept for and not buried *in this tomb*
we lie, traveller: thirty thousand men,
destroyed by the fighting Aetolians and Latins
brought by Titus from broad Italy,
a calamity to Emathia; while His Boldness,
Philip, went off faster than any deer.

ALISTAIR ELLIOT 7.247

229

I hate Eros. He is loathsome and will not
hunt animals, but takes my heart for a target.
What good is it, a god igniting a man?
What boast-worthy prize will he get for my head?

PETER JAY 5.10

230

Fair Protarchus doesn't want to,
later he will when youth runs on
taking his torch with him.

THOMAS MEYER 12.29

231

Nicander, ooh, your leg's got hairs!
Watch they don't creep up into your arse.
Because, darling, if they do, you'll soon know
How the lovers flee you, and years go.

TONY HARRISON 12.30

232   *Hipponax*

Even dead the old man grows
on his tomb in prickly rows
never grapes, nothing sweet:
things that tear at hands and feet,
choke you and twist your lips awry.
If you should be passing by,
pray Hipponax' sleep is good,
and his corpse in a genial mood.

ALISTAIR ELLIOT 7.536

PHILIP V OF MACEDON

Philip (238–179 B.C.) is credited with this neat riposte to
Alkaios' poem (no. 228 above).

233

Traveller, on this ridge a leafless, barkless tree,
one gaunt cross, is planted: Alcaeus's.

EDWIN MORGAN 16.26b

ARTEMIDOROS

A scholar and lexicographer, Artemidoros from Tarsos was a pupil of the famous scholar Aristophanes of Byzantium. He lived in the second century B.C., and compiled lexicons of the Doric dialect and of the terminology of cookery. This poem was prefixed to his edition of the Greek pastoral poets.

234

The pastoral Muses once were scattered; now
they are together in one fold, one flock.

ANTHONY HOLDEN 9.205

ZENODOTOS

This author of three epigrams may possibly be Zenodotos the Stoic, the second-century B.C. pupil of Diogenes. An earlier candidate is Zenodotos of Ephesos (born *c.* 325 B.C.), who in about 285 became the first Head Librarian at Alexandria, and edited Homer, Hesiod and some of the lyric poets.

235   *A Statue of Eros*

Who carved Love
                    and placed him by
this fountain,
                    thinking
he could control
                    such fire
with water?

PETER JAY 16.14

ANTIPATER OF SIDON

Author of eighty-odd poems, Antipater (as his name, Anti-patros, is commonly anglicized) lived through the latter part of the second century B.C. Cicero speaks of him as '*ingeniosus et memor*' (talented and with a good memory), and tells the story of how he always caught a fever on his birthday each winter. He knew and influenced Q. Lutatius Catulus and other Roman poets of the time. How long he spent in Rome is not known.

His style is highly rhetorical and ornate. He had a reputation as a great improviser of verses, and this may account for some of his repeated variations on stock themes like Myron's Cow. Gow and Page comment that though he had few ideas of his own, he was 'sufficiently skilful to vary others' agreeably'. Leonidas is the source of several of his poems.

236

> Reporter of the courage of heroes,
> Gods' interpreter, a second
> Sun in the lives of Greeks,
> Radiance of the Muses, Homer, ageless
> Mouthpiece of the whole world –
> Buried, stranger, in this sea-beaten earth.

PETER JAY 7.6

237

> Never again, Orpheus
> Will you lead the enchanted oaks,
> Nor the rocks, nor the beasts
> That are their own masters.
> Never again will you sing to sleep

The roaring wind, nor the hail,
Nor the drifting snow, nor the boom
Of the sea wave.
You are dead now.
Led by your mother, Calliope,
The Muses shed many tears
Over you for a long time.
What good does it do us to mourn
For our sons when the immortal
Gods are powerless to save
Their own children from death?

KENNETH REXROTH 7.8

238

This is Anacreon's grave. Here lie
the shreds of his exuberant lust,
but hints of perfume linger by
his gravestone still, as if he must
have chosen for his last retreat
a place perpetually on heat.

ROBIN SKELTON 7.30

239

This is the grave of grey-haired Maronis
on which you'll observe a carved stone goblet.
Tippler and gossip, she's not at all sorry
either for children or destitute husband.
Though dead and buried, one thing still irks her –
that the emblem of Bacchus the wine god's
not full to the brim with good wine.

TONY HARRISON 7.353

240

– Lysidice, I'm anxious to find out the meaning
of the carvings Agis has made on your gravestone,
for the reins, the muzzle and the bird of Tanagra
famous for owls that rouse men to battle,
are not what we normally expect to be pleasing
to stay-at-home housewives, but spindles and looms.

– *The nightbird proclaims me an early riser,*
the reins show how I managed a household,
the horse's muzzle that I wasn't a gossip
but a woman of beautiful silence.

TONY HARRISON 7.424

241 *Priapos of the Harbor*

Now Spring returning beckons the little boats
Once more to dance on the waters: the grey storms
Are gone that scourged the sea. Now swallows build
Their round nests in the rafters, and all the fields
Are bright with laughing green.
                              Come then, my sailors:
Loose your dripping hawsers, from their deep-sunk graves
Haul up your anchors, raise your brave new sails.

It is Priapos warns you, god of this harbor.

DUDLEY FITTS 10.2

242

Bitto gives to Athena
Her thrumming loom comb,
The tool of a poor living,
And says, 'Hail, goddess, take it back.

A widow of forty, I
Abandon your gifts, and turn
Instead to the business of
Love. Desire is stronger than age.'

KENNETH REXROTH 6.47

243

This mangled tentacle of the huge scolopendra,
the deep-sea calamary as long as eight fathoms,
smeared over with foam and torn by the coral,
was found spreadeagled here on the seashore
by Hermonax, when about his usual business
of fisherman, hauling his usual catches.
And now he has left it here hanging
for Ino and her offspring Palaemon,
for the gods of the sea, a sea-monster.

TONY HARRISON 6.223

244

Already prepared in the golden chamber
the nuptial couch strewn over with saffron
for Clinareta the bride of Pitana.
Nicippus and Demo her doting parents
were eager to lift up the pine-torch
when sickness descended and took her
over the waters of Lethe and sadly
her girl friends beat at their bosoms
instead of the door of the bridal chamber
the appropriate rite for bereavement.

TONY HARRISON 7.711

245   *Erinna's* Distaff

Short in measure, narrow in theme, Erinna
Took this little epic from the Muses

And she is still remembered, is not shuttered
In the shadows, under night's murky wing.
And we, friend, we hordes of later poets?
– Here we are, lying in heaps, rotting,
Forgotten.

           Better a swan's low song
Than the cackling of crows
Echoing through spring clouds.

PETER JAY 7.713

246

This piece of Lydian earth holds Amyntor,
Philip's son, hardened by battles to iron war.

No lingering disease dragged him off to his end,
killed, with his shield held high above his friend.

TONY HARRISON 7.232

247   *The Ruins of Corinth*

Where are your fabulous Doric beauty, the fringe
of your towers, Corinth, your ancient properties –
the temples of gods, the homes, the Sisyphean
women, and your once countless inhabitants?

There is no trace of you left. Doomed city,
war crushed and gorged everything.

We alone, the Ocean's Nereids, remain
unravished – halcyons, sole tenants of your affliction.

PETER JAY 9.151

248

Who hung these shields here still all shiny,
these spears with no blood on, these helmets undented,
dedicating to Ares arms as ornaments only?

Will no one clear this rubbish from my house?

The banqueting halls of unbellicose softies
are fitter for those than the walls of the War God.

I want hacked trophies, the blood of the dying,
or else I'm not Ares, the plague of mankind.

TONY HARRISON 9.323

249

Antiodemis, Aphrodite's pet cherub, from a baby
cosseted on the costliest fleeces of purple,
a sleepy hypnosis in her languishing pupils,
halcyon of Lysis, star turn of stag-parties,
whose arms flow like water and seem almost boneless,
a woman of *Petit Suisse* softness and whiteness,
has been sent by the Government over the water
to make use of these graces and cause Rome to soften,
and set weapons aside and lay off from warfare.

TONY HARRISON 9.567

MELEAGER

Meleager (the Greek form is Meleagros) was born in Gadara –
the Old Testament's Ramoth-Gilead – in about 140 B.C. The
son of a Syrian, Eukrates, he was brought up in Tyre but
spent his later life on Kos, of which he became a citizen. He
died at an advanced age, perhaps about 70 B.C.; a marginal
note on the Palatine manuscript says that he flourished in the
reign of the last Seleukos (96–95 B.C.). The little that is known
about his life comes from his three autobiographical poems;
these also mention his Menippean satires, which he called
Charites (Graces) – essays in a mixture of prose and verse,
presenting Cynic philosophy in popular form.

Meleager's importance as the compiler of a critical an-
thology of Greek epigrams has already been noted. His
Garland was certainly not the first such collection, but its
survival at least until the time of Kephalas, who used it for
his anthology in the tenth century A.D., suggests that it was
one of the best. It was probably compiled on Kos in the early
years of the first century – too early to include poems by
Meleager's fellow Gadarene, Philodemos. It included epi-
grams from the time of Archilochos to Meleager's own day
and was evidently a large collection – 4,000 or more lines,
perhaps. Best of all, it preserved his own poems in quantity –
just over 130 of them.

Meleager transcends the limitations of the genre by sheer
versatility and inventiveness. His work as an editor was
important for his writing, because his intimate knowledge of
earlier epigram prompted him freely to adapt and combine
the themes of old poems into new entities. In a lesser talent
this habit would soon have resulted in tedious imitations; but
Meleager absorbs and transforms the whole tradition. He
could write equally well with elegant restraint and simplicity,
or with highly complex, flamboyant elaboration. He was
master of every mode and style of epigram, employing the
whole gamut of traditional erotic imagery and ringing all the
changes on it. His poems have an air of playful experiment.
Meleager has been accused of being too literary a poet, or too
ingenious to be 'sincere'; but the authenticity is in the com-
plete control of his medium, the subtle modulations of style
and sureness of touch.

Meleager's poetry had a considerable influence on the early
Roman erotic poets such as Q. Lutatius Catulus, and motifs
from Meleager appear in Catullus and the Augustan elegists.
Robert Herrick imitated and adapted a few of his poems, and
is perhaps the most Meleagrian of English poets.

By Cypris, Cupid!
I'll burn the Bow!
burn the Arrows!
burn that fancy
Scythian Quiver!
burn, Cupid, burn
Love's bitter
armoury.
   You titter?
Why? You wrinkle up
your silly nose?
You'll titter when
I've clipped those wings
turned lust to lead
& bound brass bands
about your feet.
But chained too near
where my Heart lies,
that were indeed
to set the lynx
to watch the fold –
best did I not
seek to best you:
take instead these
feathered shoes, on them
& those incal-
culable wings
go! – plague elsewhere
some other (yet
ingenuous
devotee of
Fairest Cypris.

PETER WHIGHAM 5.179

251

Love in silence shall
its levy of tears
draw from the eyes, ears
fill with clamour,

familiar impress
takes (already)
the heart,

darkness & light
powerless both
this charm to unwind:

Those wings, my Cupids
so strong in urging love
so weak now
at the time of separation.

PETER WHIGHAM 5.212

252

Cicala stoned with dew,
making your loud meadow-music
                                        alone
hidden somewhere
                        among high leaves
the sunburnt skeleton,
                        its thin serrated
legs, scratching
            a lyre's melody!
– Sing something fresh
for the tree-nymphs
                maelid & heliad
a *responsus* for Pan in the meadows

& something for me
                    fugitive from Love
that Meleager may take his siesta at noon here
blissfully, in the plane-tree's shade.

PETER WHIGHAM 7.196

253

Burn not too oft who flutters at thy flame
Cupid:
        Psyche, like thee, has wings.

PETER WHIGHAM 5.57

254

Cupid at Venus' breast
with Venus' dice
    gambols at dawn:

Gambols? Gambles!
    The stakes each morning –
    Meleager's heart.

PETER WHIGHAM 12.47

255

By Timo's locks
    that keep Love captive,
by Demo's skin
    whence all sweet scents steal
(deluding sleep),
    by Ilias' skilled foreplay
& my ever-watchful lamp
    (each separate Venus-act
attentively recording),
    all but the last breath of my lips
has been spent in your service –

You require that also?
Venus, it is yours:
  the poet's last gasp,
his latest (you may say)
  ejaculation!

PETER WHIGHAM 5.197

256

Asclepias who loves to love
invites with summer-seeming eyes
to sail upon her inland seas.

PETER WHIGHAM 5.156

257

Inconstant Dawn, thou tak'st thy time
when others with Demo lie.
Why, when my turn comes,
so mockingly punctual?

PETER WHIGHAM 5.173

258

White violets flower
lilies on hill-slopes
narcissus nodding to rain-showers

and the queen of lovers' hopes
the sweet persuasive rose,
Zenophile, more fair than those:

o hills o fields your laughter rings
falsely through the flowered spring
for she outshines your garlanding.

PETER WHIGHAM 5.144

259

Volatile mosquito,
at her ear a-
buzz with love-bites
hum these words:
   '*One wakeful waits.*
   '*Thou heedless sleep'st.*
   '*Love slips away.*'

Hence, impish Muse!
Mosquito, hence!
Ma pian' piano
with your buzzing
lest thou sting an
husband me-ward,
rancorously bent.

Bring me my girl.
This Herculean
chore perform &
thou shalt have from
grateful Meleager
fitting accoutrements
withal:
   One hero's club to swing!
   One lion pelt to wear!

PETER WHIGHAM 5.152

260

Counts itself lucky
  the wine-cup!
Lip slipt
  'twixt thy lips
pouring

sweet gossip
Zenophile.

Lucky the cup,
more fortunate
still, Meleager
my lip to thy lip
inclining/you
with a swig at my love
downed,
like a flask of retsina!

PETER WHIGHAM 5.171

261

Lost! Cupid!
One lost Cupid!
Since daybreak.
Meleager's delectable
bed empty.
One lost boy!
Viz & to wit:
winged,
cheeky,
a chatterbox,
laughs & cries at the same time,
smirks,
distrusted by all his acquaintance,
origin unknown,
Zeus, Gea, Poseidon,
disclaim liability,
armed & certainly dangerous,
beware!
But a moment –
You say you have found him?
Where?

Lo! with fierce bow
who lurks below
her lashes, shoots
where eyen flash:
ZENOPHILE!

PETER WHIGHAM 5.177

262

Soul counsels flight
from Heliodore's affections,
'Those pangs, those tears'.

Soul warns
            but warns
sans will to flight:

incontinent &
warning still soul
turns & loves her.

PETER WHIGHAM 5.24

263

Pour this wine
& say this
name:
            'Heliodora!'

Pour again
repeat the same
till the wine &
name are one.

Crown my forehead
with these petals
dewy with the
scent she sheds.

See! The rose droops
(friend of lovers)
grieved that on
another's breast

my Heliodore
now rests her head.

PETER WHIGHAM 5.136

264

More than Apollo's golden lyre
Cupid (with Meleager) would prefer
Heliodora's voice in Meleager's ear.

PETER WHIGHAM 5.141

265

The petals fall from Heliodora's image
that, flower of flowers, outfaces all.

PETER WHIGHAM 5.143

266

Wreathe violets white
myrtle & slight
narcissus wreathe
wreathe laughing lilies
crocus & hyacinth
yellow, blue
Love's friend the rose:

Heliodore's
myrrhed brows,

wreathed curls
swim in petals.

PETER WHIGHAM 5.147

267

In heart's space hath Eros
set shaping my spirit
to her spirit, the sweet
gossip – *Heliodora*!

PETER WHIGHAM 5.155

268

Love cast!
Love filed!
Heliodora's
finger
                nail
whose deli-
cate scratches
prick the heart.

PETER WHIGHAM 5.157

269

Busy with love, the bumble bee
philanders through the petal'd spring
& lights on Heliodora's skin.

And have you left the stamen-cup
to tell me Cupid's arrow stings?
til rueful Heart heaves up:
                'Enough'?

Thou loved of lovers, Bee, buzz off –
what zestful petals wait your tupping!
Such news to me was never new
whose honey's long been mixt with rue.

PETER WHIGHAM 5.163

Mother of gods
  Night
loved of lovers,
  by pact in love
& love's toys
  grant
whoso smugly shares this night
  Heliodora's sheets
fired
  next flesh that offers
(nightly) insomnia –
  douse his desire
let him sleep
  cold on her breast
useless
  as Endymion.

PETER WHIGHAM 5.165

271

Night & Night's longing
cruel tears at crueller dawn,

does Heliodora show
still my love?

Can thought (that's cold)
warm to old kisses?

Does she (as I)
take tears to bed,

kiss in dream & strain
phantom to breast?

Or lies she now new love beside?

Lamp, light never that.
Votive, light her alone.

PETER WHIGHAM 5.166

272

She's gone! Call Rape! Call Robbers! Violence!
Yet Mars against Cupid makes no sense.
Torches ho! Wait: her footsteps – All is well!
Back into my chest, heart, where safe hearts dwell.

PETER WHIGHAM 12.147

273

Sweetly hath Dorcas of Lycaenis learnt:
'Kisses like coins prove true or false with time.

PETER WHIGHAM 5.187

274

'Tis Timarion,
my Desire,
whose kisses sting
whose looks burn
– lips of honey
eyes of fire!

PETER WHIGHAM 5.96

275

Love's night & a lamp
judged our vows:
that she would love me ever
& I should never leave her.
Love's night & you, lamp,
witnessed the pact.

Today the vow runs:
'Oaths such as these, waterwords'.
Tonight, lamp,
witness her lying
        – in other arms.

        PETER WHIGHAM 5.8

276

Foresworn now the love-vows!
  And your proclivities
Zenophile
  clamour from your appearance:
those ringlets, dripping
  with fresh application of seductive scents,
those eyes,
  heavy with sleepless nights,
and *what* is that flower doing
  dangling behind your ear?
and your hair, matted
  tousled in who knows what love-tussles –
besides which, you're *smashed*!

Go! The guitar thrums.
The castanets clatter.
Go! Woman common to all.

        PETER WHIGHAM 5.175

277

Dorcas, be off! & tell her this,
tell her not once or twice but thrice –
don't loiter here! be off! – but wait,
you don't know what the message is!

Say what you said the other day
& add – at least – not *that,* but say
– say *every thing*: keep nothing back!
Tell her it all – but, no! not *you*:

Meleager has gone on before
& knocks already at her door.

PETER WHIGHAM 5.182

278

At 12 o'clock in the afternoon
   in the middle of the street –
      Alexis.

Summer had all but brought the fruit
   to its perilous end:
      & the summer sun & that boy's look

did their work on me.
   Night hid the sun.
      Your face consumes my dreams.

Others feel sleep as feathered rest;
   mine but in flame refigures
      your image lit in me.

PETER WHIGHAM 12.127

279

As honey in wine / wine, honey
   Alexis in Cleobulus
Cleobulus in Alexis
   sweet-haired & lovely each
as he with whom the other
   mingles ... product

142

of such two entwined
  potent
as vineyards of deathless Cypris.

PETER WHIGHAM 12.164

280

I was thirsty.
It was hot.
I kissed the boy
with girl-soft skin.
My thirst was quenched.
I said: Is that what
upstairs you're up
to Papa Zeus,
is that what strip-
ling Ganymede
at table serves,
under Hera's
watchful eye?

Lip-spilt wine
from soul to soul
as honeyed-sweet
as these vast draughts
Antiochus
pours now for me!

PETER WHIGHAM 12.133

281

It is true that I held Thero fair,
  Apollodatus a torch of love –
not so no longer:
  that light is out.

143

Mine now woman's love.
The delights of hirsute sex
let us leave to Welsh shepherds.

PETER WHIGHAM 12.41

282

And now I, Meleager, am among them,
those whom I mocked,
the young men crying through the evening
to their señoritas.
For Cupid has nailed me to your gates,
Myiscus,
on my brow cut mocking words:
'Lo! The Fruit of Favours long Preserved.

PETER WHIGHAM 12.23

283

The regions of Tyre are noted
for the delicate beauty of their people.
And do not the bright regions of the sky
pale when Myiscus steps forth?

PETER WHIGHAM 12.59

284

Eyes,
flatterers of Soul
looking on naught
save that which soul desires,
as mine,
blind to all else
save that alone which Myiscus can yield.

PETER WHIGHAM 12.106

285

All that he is ... does ... is attractive
   even his name: Myiscus
      & love goes

where he goes in him
   as in Cypris beauty
      itself fulfils itself

& Cypris gives birth to Eros.
   Not affect but effect of love.
      Rue spills from the comb.

PETER WHIGHAM 12.154

286

The breath of my life – no less,
   this rope that constrains
me, Myiscus, to you
   – you have me fast.

Sweet boy,
   even a deaf-mute
could *hear* what you *look*!
   Look blackly at me,
winter breaks out in clouds.
   Smile with clear eyes,
& spring giggles
   coating me with petals.

PETER WHIGHAM 12.159

287

Whose the hand unloosed Clearista's zone
   at bride-night, in her bride-room?
Death, in guise of the bridegroom.

Evening, & flutes & clapping hands
   clamour at bridal door.
At dawn the funeral wail. No more

the Hymen song. The very lights
   that lit the bridal bed
light now Clearista's journey to the dead.

PETER WHIGHAM 7.182

288

Goat-foot Pan has quit his flocks.
What to him the hillslopes?
What to him the herds of mountain goats?
Their upland pastures pleasure him no more.

For Daphnis is dead. Daphnis, the fire
in sly-foot Pan, is stilled.
And Pan must now through cities go.
Others shall serve the wild flocks.
Not for Pan where Daphnis haunts no more.

PETER WHIGHAM 7.535

289

Tread lightly, Stranger!
  Here, among the Faithful Dead
An old man lies,
  Sleeping the sleep
That all must sleep –
  Meleager, son of Eucrates,
Whose verses truly blend
  Love's sweet & sad tears,
The Muses,
  & the ribald Graces.
Tyre of Heavenly origin,

146

MELEAGER

Gadara's Holy earth,
Made him man;
　Meropian Cos
Harboured his old age.
　Be you Syrian: 'Salam!'
Phoenician: 'Audoni!'
　Greek: 'Chairè!'
And see, before you leave this place,
　You say the same to him.

PETER WHIGHAM 7.419

3

OTHER HELLENISTIC POETS

ARISTON

Author of three epigrams, strongly influenced by Leonidas of Tarentum. The poem included here is based on Leonidas' poem which immediately precedes it in the Anthology.

290

> If you mice are looking for *food*, you'd better look
> elsewhere, for mine is a frugal shack.
> Do you fret for the Good Life, friends – dried figs,
>   and protein-laden cheese? . . .
> But if you attempt my books with your teeth
> once more, you will rue it, mice.

W. G. SHEPHERD 6.303

CHAIREMON

There are no clues to Chairemon's date: he may have written at any time between 300 and 100 B.C.

291   *Epitaph*

> Athenagoras begot Eubulus –
> more unfortunate than all in his luck,
> excelling all in glory.

RICHARD EVANS 7.469

292

We of Sparta fought the Argives – equal in number and
    arms;
  Thyreae was the prize of the spear.
We both without thinking gave up our homeward journey
    and leave the telling of our death to birds.

RICHARD EVANS 7.721

DIONYSIOS

Dionysios was a common name, and the headings of these
two poems in the manuscripts – 'Dionysios the Sophist' and
'Dionysios of Andros' respectively – do nothing to help
identify or date either.

293

      You hold a bunch of roses, Rose.
      Are they for sale? Or, Rose, are you?

EDWARD LUCIE-SMITH 5.81

294

      No wonder I slipped, being soaked
      with Zeus's rain and Bakchos' wine.
      Two against one – and gods
      against a mortal.

BARRISS MILLS 7.533

DIOTIMOS

There seem to be at least two poets of this name; probably
nine of the eleven 'Diotimos' epigrams are pre-Meleager.
The excellent poem included here pre-dates Erucius who
imitated it. I give two versions of it.

295 *Cold Pastoral*

Homeward at evening through the drifted snow
The cows plod back to shelter from the hill
But ah, the long strange sleep
Of the cow-herd Therimachos lying beneath the oak,
Struck still, still, by the fire that falls from heaven!

DUDLEY FITTS 7.173

296

Homing at dusk – the snow falls on them – cattle
   Drift by themselves into the shed.
Look, still beside the oak Therimachos sleeps
   The long sleep: laid to rest by fire from heaven.

ALISTAIR ELLIOT 7.173

GLAUKOS

Six epigrams are ascribed to Glaukos; three of them to a
Glaukos of Athens, which I omit. Glaukos of Nikopolis
(perhaps the suburb of Alexandria) is the author of the three
poems included here; he is not datable, but must be pre-
Meleager. Propertius may have had the second poem in mind
in his elegy on Paetus (3.7, lines 11–12):

Seabirds now hover over your bones: you have
the whole Carpathian Sea for a tomb.

297

Time was when once upon a time, such toys
As balls or pet birds won a boy, or dice.
Now it's best china, or cash. Lovers of boys,
Try something else next time. Toys cut no ice.

PETER JAY 12.44

153

298

No, not earth, nor a stone slab,
But the whole vast surface of the ocean that you see
Is Erasippus' tomb.
He and his ship drowned together. – Where
And in what unknown depths his bones wander
Seabirds alone can tell.

CLIVE SANSOM 7.285

299   *Pan and the Nymphs*

'O Nymphs, did Daphnis, passing by,
Stop here to rest with his shaggy white goats?
Tell me truly.'
              'Yes, yes, piper Pan,
And there on the poplar's bark he carved for you
A letter saying *O Pan, Pan, come!*
Come to Maleia, to the mount of Psôphis:
I shall wait for you there.'
              'Goodbye, dear Nymphs; I go.'

DUDLEY FITTS 9.341

KARPHYLLIDES

Karphyllides (or Karpyllides) is author of two epigrams, the
better of which is included here. Gow and Page believe that
this epitaph belonged to Meleager's *Garland*; in which case
he pre-dates 90 B.C., though Mackail places him much later,
in the second century A.D.

300

Passer-by, don't blame this memorial
for giving no cause of mourning, even death.
I left children of my children, enjoyed one wife
to my old age, gave weddings for three brides
whose sleepy babies often filled my lap
with never an illness or a death to weep for;
and now they have made their offerings for sweet sleep
without sorrow and sent me to the place of honour.

ALISTAIR ELLIOT 7.260

NIKARCHOS

Not to be confused with the contemporary of Lucilius, poems
by this Nikarchos appeared in Meleager's *Garland*.

301

Take note who stoop,
I am the goat-foot, Pan the Great,
Guardian of this spring,
Reticulator of all falling waters,
Heed my warning!

You may drink as much
As you please and fill your pitcher here
But never dare defile
The crystal issue of the Nymphs by washing
Your filthy feet in it!

If you do so,
Fear my ithyphallic armour,
You shall not speak a word
But submit upon the instant to be buggered –
That's my rigid law!

And if by chance
You're pathic and like such punishment,
I have another weapon:
My club is harder than my prick and with it
I'll break your head wide open!

PETER PORTER 9.330

302

Sweet Nicarete, who served Athene's shuttle
And by the loom which decent girls attend on
Made warp and woof to overlay and straddle,
One day in new allegiance took these symbols
Of female bondage (work basket and bobbins
And all the other stuff) and made a bonfire
Of the lot outside her house, exclaiming:
'Get knotted, home-based tyrants, woman's shackles,
Marking my dull days even as you waste them,
Winding my once-bright youth into a grave sheet.'
Instead, our little Nicarete set up
The lyre, the garlands and such proper emblems
As Violettas use to grace their calling,
Her humble prayer to her new Goddess running:
'Be my protector, Cypris, and I offer
You ten per cent of all I make: I'm changing
My trade from the upright to the horizontal.'

PETER PORTER 6.285

PAMPHILOS

Nothing is known about this poet, who was included in
Meleager's *Garland*. He might be any one of a number of
men named Pamphilos. Two poems are extant, and are
reminiscent of Mnasalkes and Nikias.

156

303 *To the Swallow*

why sing sadly sad daughter of Pandion
all day long these little notes –
do you long for the maidenhead Tereus
of Thrace took with unbelievable power?

DENNIS SCHMITZ 9.57

PHANIAS

There is some slight linguistic evidence that Phanias was one
of the latest poets of Meleager's *Garland*, and that he perhaps
lived in Italy and knew Latin well. Seven epigrams, in the
manner of Leonidas, are extant.

304

By Themis & the wine that made me tipsy,
your love won't last much longer, Pamphilus.

Already there's hair on your thigh,
down on your cheeks & another lust ahead.

But a little of the old spark's left in you,
so don't be stingy – opportunity is love's friend.

THOMAS MEYER 12.31

305

The stick he used to tap out feet
    (both kinds), the belt and cane which
lay side by side to maintain order,
    the well-oiled tawse, the stinging slipper
with its one thin sole, the skull cap
    which kept his hairless head from laughter –
these tokens of his long schoolmastering

Callon dedicates to the Lord Hermes:
his limbs are bound by age and he
   must soon depart the ageless world of boys.

PETER PORTER 6.294

306

It's a sign of the times when even barbers
   take the long-haired way to meditation.
Eugathes of Lapithe has ditched his tools
   of trade – his upright mirror, his sheet
to catch the clippings, the velvet bed his
   razors sat on, his cheaper combs for poorer
customers, his shining scissors for display,
   his manicuring kit (pointed nail-cleaners,
little clippers, cuticle removers), even the chair
   his customers chatted in, and he's gone
to *Epicurus' Garden* to hear mantras
   on the bells and finger-cymbals. Poor Eugathes,
like Bottom, he 'has a reasonable good ear
   in music; let's have the tongs and the bones.'
He'd have starved to death in ecstasy
   if he hadn't remembered where he put
his barbering gear and gone back to work.

PETER PORTER *after* 6.307

307

Here Lysis set an empty tomb
In honour of his dear son Mantitheus.
The unrecovered body rots elsewhere but
Here the loved name is mourned forever.

PETER PORTER 7.537

ANONYMOUS EPIGRAMS

308

Her saffron gown,
      her crown of dark-green ivy
still redolent of myrrh,
      her hood
Alexo dedicates these
      to delectable Priapos
of the effeminate leer,
      his holy
night-festival's souvenirs.

PETER JAY 5.200

309

Till the good morning star, Leontis
lay sleepless, enjoying herself
with Sthenios, the golden boy.
Since that all-night affair, her lyre
which with the Muses' help she played then
lies in the shrine of Kypris.

PETER JAY 5.201

310
           Lais' Mirror

I – who giggled so scornfully at Greece,
Kept young admirers swarming at my door –
Give Aphrodite this glass, since I'd ignore
My face now – and can't see it as I was.

PETER JAY 6.1

311

You too, Clenorides, homesickness drove
    deathwards, braving an icy, southerly squall.
Treacherous weather held you, the wringing swell
    rinses right out of you the youth I love.

TONY HARRISON 7.263

312

This is a sailor's grave, while opposite
There is a farmer's. Land or sea
Death is the same, does not discriminate.

PETER JAY 7.265

313

Sailors, I wish you safety on sea and land.
The tomb you're passing is a shipwrecked man's.

PETER JAY 7.269

314

Before your hair was ever cut
Or your third birthday come,
Kleodikos, your parents stood
Weeping beside your tomb.
And by the unknown Acheron
You pass your unreturning youth,
Your single bloom.

ALISTAIR ELLIOT 7.482

315   *The Tomb of Ibykos*

I celebrate Rhegion, Italy's tip, licked by
    shoals of Sicilian water, because
Ibykos, who loved both boys and his lyre, is buried
    there, his many pleasures spent, under

an elm-tree whose leaves cast shade on his tomb, piled high with
thick ivy and a bed of white reed.

PETER JAY 7.714

316   *The Achaian Invasion of Sparta*

The smoke rises. Never before
Conquered or occupied,
Lakedaimon, you see the smoke
Of the Achaian camp
By the banks of Eurotas.
There is no shade. Birds nest
Miserably on the ground. Wolves wait,
Hear no sheep bleating.

PETER JAY 7.723

317   *Inscription for a Statue of Pan*

Be still O green cliffs of the Dryads
Still O springs bubbling from the rock
                                   and be still
Manyvoiced cry of the ewes:
                         It is Pan
Pan with his tender pipe:
                         the clever lips run
Over the withied reeds
                     while all about him
Rise up from the ground to dance with joyous tread
The Nymphs of the Water
                     Nymphs of the Oaken Forest.
DUDLEY FITTS 9.823

318

It's the Enobarbus Complex:
'I will praise any man that will praise me.'
The corollary goes 'If someone doesn't like me
I can't like him.' Being so experienced
At liking and loathing, I have no difficulty
Recognizing them in others.

PETER PORTER *after* 12.103

319

Graces, if the beautiful Dionysios
Chooses me, lead him into
Beauty that increases season by season.
But if he turns me down for someone
Else, and loves him,
Let him be thrown out like a stale
Berry with the dry sweepings.

PETER JAY 12.107

320   *The Serenader*

Boy, hold my wreath for me.
The night is black,
                    the path is long,
And I am completely and beautifully drunk.
Nevertheless I will go
To Themison's house and sing beneath his window.
You need not come with me:
                    though I may stumble,
He is a steady lamp for the feet of love.

DUDLEY FITTS 12.116

Why all the racket, you chattering birds?
Don't bother me here, warmed by the boy's
delicate flesh. You nightingales in leaves,
sleep, I beg you, you babbling women,
shut up!

THOMAS MEYER 12.136

4

THE ROMAN PERIOD

c. 90 B.C.–A.D. 50

DIODOROS ZONAS

Writing of notable men from Sardis, Strabo mentions Zonas and Diodoros of Sardis (see p. 230), who were relatives: 'the two Diodoroses, the orators: the elder was called Zonas, a man who regularly pleaded the cause of Asia; at the time of the invasion of King Mithridates he was accused of attempting to incite cities to secede from him, but he defended himself and was cleared of this slander. The younger Diodoros (who was a friend of mine) is the author of historical works as well as lyric and other poems, in which he displays the ancient style of writing very well.' Zonas was perhaps born about 125 B.C.; he is a skilful writer.

322

A pomegranate just splitting, a peach just furry,
a fig with wrinkled flesh and juicy bottom,
a purple cluster (thick-berried well of wine),
nuts just skinned from their green peelings – these
the guardian of the fruit lays here for Priapus:
for this single shaft in the wilds, the seed of trees.

ALISTAIR ELLIOT 6.22

323

For Demeter winnowing, for the Hours who haunt the
    furrows,
    out of his needy ploughland Heronax took
a share of threshed corn and all-seed vegetables
    and put them on this flat-topped tripod here,
a little out of his little: for the piece of land he got
    here on the bitter hill-crest is not big.

ALISTAIR ELLIOT 6.98

167

324

from the field's plane tree
Telemon wolf-killer hangs
this hide this wild olive
staff he threw so often

bless him woodland god
by taking these poor gifts
by giving him hunting rights
where you rule, this mountain

DENNIS SCHMITZ 6.106

325

Who in the waters of this reedy lake –
Black Charon! – pole the boat of corpses down
to Hades, reach your hand out from the gang-plank
for Kinyras' son coming aboard and hold him.
His sandals trip the child there and he fears
to put his bare feet on the sandy shore.

ALISTAIR ELLIOT 7.365

326

Come tawny bees
out of the hive
feed yourselves on these tips:
shrivelled thyme to nibble round,
poppy petals,
raisins, violets, down of quinces.

Nibble them all,
make wax boxes
so the bee-saviour Pan
keeper of skeps can taste for himself,

and smoking you out
with honeying hand leave you a little.

ALISTAIR ELLIOT 9.226

327

Spare the mother of acorns, man. Cut down some paliurus,
old mountain pine or sea-pine, or ilex or dry arbutus.
But keep your axe out of the oak: remember our forefathers
said that once upon a time the oaks were our first mothers.

ALISTAIR ELLIOT 9.312

328   *Pan Asks about Daphnis*

Girls of the riverside, Nereids, did you see
Daphnis yesterday washing his dusty head?
Into your waters he jumped, with his apple-cheeks
burnt by the dog-star just a little red.
Is he beautiful? Tell me. Or am I
a deformed goat in the heart as in the thigh?

ALISTAIR ELLIOT 9.556

PHILODEMOS

Philodemos of Gadara (*c.* 110–30 B.C.) studied philosophy in
Athens where his tutor was the Epicurean, Zeno. Cicero and
Atticus were among his fellow-students. He moved to Italy
probably in the early seventies, and lived near Naples –
according to Cicero, so as to be near his friend and patron L.
Calpurnius Piso Caesoninus. He taught with Siron at the
Epicurean school in Naples. It was the centre of Epicurean
activity in Italy, and its importance in the history of Roman
poetry lies in the fact that Vergil and Horace, to mention only

the best-known names, were among those taught by Philodemos.

Piso was not, perhaps, Philodemos' only patron, but seems to have been the most important. Several half-legible papyrus rolls of Philodemos' prose works were discovered in the ruins of Piso's villa at Herculaneum; they are Epicurean philosophical treatises, and are still in the course of publication. He also wrote on other subjects, and fragments of his treatise on poetry are among the papyri. In this he propounded a theory of art which is opposed to the 'classical' position his protégé Horace later adopted in the *Ars Poetica*. Philodemos, in criticizing Neoptolemos of Parion's theories, rejects the idea of a utilitarian purpose for poetry, and its corollary, the separation of form from content. He believed that a poem should be an organic whole, and that form was a property of content. Neoptolemos wished to limit the content of poetry to 'reality'; Philodemos allows poets the licence to choose unreal or fantastic themes. 'Even if [a poem] edifies,' runs one of the tantalizing fragments of his treatise, 'it does not edify *as a poem*.' L. P. Wilkinson's article 'Philodemos and Poetry' in *Greece and Rome* (May 1933) gives a good account of his poetic theory; see also C. L. Neudling's *A Prosopography to Catullus* (1953), pp. 137ff. Neudling points out that Philodemos and Catullus had a number of friends and acquaintants in common, including, for example, L. Manlius Torquatus, for whom Catullus wrote the beautiful wedding hymn (Catullus poem 61). Philodemos' views on poetry accord well enough with Catullus' practice to suggest more than casual acquaintance between them, a notion which is lent weight by the evident imitation of one by the other in a poem: compare Catullus poem 13 (the invitation to Fabullus) with poem 347 here. The Socration ('Little Socrates') of Catullus poem 47 is surely Philodemos – Catullus did not hesitate to abuse close friends in his epigrams.

PHILODEMOS

Vergil and Horace were both influenced by Philodemos, Horace as much perhaps by his poetry, which he alludes to several times, as by his Epicureanism. If Horace rejected his teacher's poetics, that is influence. Propertius and Ovid echo him; Cicero describes him, without mentioning him by name, in his attack on Piso (*In Pisonem*, 68ff.). Philodemos' twenty-nine epigrams are among the most original of the period. Seven other poems are more dubiously ascribed to him.

329

That silent publicizer of unheard-of news,
the lamp, Philainis, stupefy with olive drink;
then out you go, since Love alone does not appreciate
live audience. And as the door is shut, Philainis,
turn the key.
            Then Xantho dear, turn in with me . . .
But you, my mattress so enamoured of erotica,
get your impressions of our untried love techniques.

WILLIAM MOEBIUS 5.4

330

Sixty sun-decked years Charito has gotten to,
but still dark is the shock of her hair,
still firm, without the aid of corsetry,
those pale marble cones of her breasts,
and ambrosia condenses on her tight skin,
every inducement does, blandishments galore.
You lover-boys, who don't turn tail at wild intensity,
come forward and forget her sunny decades.

WILLIAM MOEBIUS 5.13

331

    – Hello there. – *Hello there yourself.*
    – What's your name? – *What's yours?*
    – Let's not get too involved right away.
    – *Let's not.* – Are you busy?
    – *I have my full-time admirers.*
    – Like to have dinner with me?
    – *If you like.* – Splendid. How much
    does it come to? – *Nothing fixed in advance.*
    – How exotic! – *After you've had me in bed,*
    it's up to you what you give.
    – Fair enough! What's your address?
    I'll call for you. – *You look it up.*
    – When can you make it? – *Whenever you want.*
    – I want to right now. – *Lead the way.*

                  WILLIAM MOEBIUS 5.46

332

    'I know, fair lady, how to love the lover well,
    and I know as well how to bite the biter back:
    don't hurt too much the man who leans on you,
    or try to bring the irate in the poet out.'
    I strained my voice to get my warning in,
    but you were as receptive to my terms
    as the surf along Ionia. Now you, high
    in your emotion, moan . . . but I
    between the swells of Naias sink me down.

                 WILLIAM MOEBIUS 5.107

333

    With Demo I fell in love, of Paphian origins.
    Nothing very amazing. Next with Demo of Samos.
    Not much in that. And again with Demo of Naxos.

No laughing matter! Fourth, with the Argolian Demo.
The Fates themselves must have hit on my name,
since with every Demo Philodemo's heart is warm.

WILLIAM MOEBIUS 5.115

334

With the night half over, I slip
out on my husband, and get here
soaked through by a downpour.
Why do we sit and make faces
and don't, as we talk, take a respite,
as it is normal for lovers to do . . .

WILLIAM MOEBIUS 5.120

335

A small thing and moreover black is she,
but kinkier than parsley is Philainion's,
and sleeker than down is her complexion;
and her talk unfolds more magically
than sheer underthings; and she's unselfish
about everything, and presses few demands.
May I settle for Philainion as is, until,
oh golden Cypris, I find a more developed one.

WILLIAM MOEBIUS 5.121

336

Double-horned, nocturnal Moon,
fancier of all-night activities,
shine, penetrate the windows' slits,
train your beam on golden Kallistion.
Heavenly peeping on what lovers do
is no impudence. You do cast bliss
on her and me, I know that, Moon –
did not Endymion give your soul its fire?

WILLIAM MOEBIUS 5.123

337

The naked warmth of you is still
encased in bud, the unspoiled freshness
of the early grape is not yet dark . . .
but already the erotic Urges
born yesterday make swift arrows sharp,
Lysidike, and fire breaks out
behind the scene. Let us be off,
urged frantically, before the shaft
is on the string. The prophet in me
feels a fire of vast dimension soon.

WILLIAM MOEBIUS 5.124

338

The strumming and patter,
the meaningful glances,
the vocalizations,
and the fire just set off
by Xanthippe, my soul,
will 'combust' you; the wherefore,
the when or the how I don't know,
but as you're inflamed,
poor victim, you'll get the idea.

WILLIAM MOEBIUS 5.131

339

Oh feet, oh legs, oh thighs
that formed the deathrow
I deserved, oh rump,
oh groove, oh smooth tummy,
oh shoulders, oh slim neck,
oh breasts, oh arms, oh eyes
that I am driven crazy by,
oh masterful rhythm,

oh first-rate tongue,
oh high-pitched delivery
that turns me on.
She may be Flora
of Italian race
and not sing Sappho's verse,
but Andromeda
of Indian race
was the love of Perseus.

WILLIAM MOEBIUS 5.132

340

You cry, carry on in tones of pity,
you dwell on trivia, are prone to jealousy,
you often crush me in your arms
and are thoroughly affectionate.
As a lover, then, you qualify:
but when I comment, 'Here I lie with you,'
and you hesitate, you're totally disqualified.

WILLIAM MOEBIUS 5.306

341

Wax-contoured, in your face a Muse,
magic skin, fine talker, pretty precious object
of the Penchants of two wings, Xantho,
play for me your magic with your misty hands;
'For a long while on a single slab
of cut stone I must make my bed
and sleep, not subject to mortality . . .'
Sing me again, Xantharia, yes, yes, that sweet refrain.

WILLIAM MOEBIUS 9.570

342

Cypris who puts the sea to rest,
and holds the bridegroom in her care,
Cypris who stands by the just, Cypris,
mother of the gust-footed Passions,
Cypris, I am the half-ousted
from the saffron bliss of Bridal Halls,
freezing my heart out in the snows of Gaul,
Cypris, the man of peace am I
who wastes no words with anyone,
splashed over by your dusky sea,
Cypris, who cares about landing,
who cares about wedlock, help me,
Cypris, my queen, into Naias' harbor.

WILLIAM MOEBIUS 10.21

343

Seven plus thirty years are gone,
    discarded pages of my life;
white hairs already streak my head,
    Xanthippe, couriers of the age
of common sense. But party games
    and the lyre's sweeping phrases
still absorb me; in my restless heart
    a fire burns on. Now let your poet,
Muses, with this girl, your Worships,
    write the last of his insanity.

WILLIAM MOEBIUS 11.41

344

Once I was in love. Who's been exempted?
I was a reveler. Who is still innocent
of those rites? But I was made crazy.
By whom? It was a god, wasn't it?

I pitch it out, as a greyness rushes
through my black bushiness, announcing
the age of common sense. Play I did,
in the time for play; with that run out,
I'll take as my preferred companion, thought.

WILLIAM MOEBIUS 5.112

345

Here it's rose-time again, chick-peas in season,
cabbages, Sosylus, first heads of the year,
fillets of smelt, fresh-salted cheese,
tender and furled up lettuce leaves ...
but we don't go way out to the point, Sosylus,
or picnic, as we used to, on the overlook.
Antigenes and Bacchios had the old party spirit,
but today we dump them in their graves.

WILLIAM MOEBIUS 9.412

346

White violets again and lyre orchestras,
Chian wine again, and myrrh from Syria,
and party fun again, and thirsty whores again,
I part with willingly. Whatever tends toward madness
I abhor. But tie narcissus in my hair, and tongue
the angled-flutes, rub my limbs with saffron balm,
moisten my palate with wine from Mytilene,
and bed me down with a virgin in her wild retreat.

WILLIAM MOEBIUS 11.34

347   *To Piso, on Epicurus' Birthday*

Tomorrow, the twentieth, we celebrate
the birthday of the founder of our cult;
a friend of whom the Muse is fond

177

would press you, dearest Piso, to stop by
at his simply furnished hovel about five.
In case you feel deprived of hearty sips
and swallowings of the potent Chian stuff,
the friends you'll meet are full of truth,
and the talk is, as you'll hear, more fancy-sweet
than any natural Phaiacian fare.
And Piso, if you bestow your glance on me,
we'll give this twentieth an extra flair.

WILLIAM MOEBIUS 11.44

348

This *quidam* gives that *quidam* for *one* round
five *talents*; he's a frigid screw, and she's
not pretty even. Five *drachmas* for *twelve* rounds
I pay Lysianassa, and I clearly get a better screw.
Either I have lost my faculties, or his pair
deserve imminent removal with an axe.

WILLIAM MOEBIUS 5.126

349

I, who used to score five, even nine times,
Venus, can now scarcely get it up once
between sundown and sunrise. Oh man!
Here's a case of slow death . . . lately,
a series of fatal strokes . . . I have it coming.
Old age, old age, how will you treat me,
later on if we meet, when now I'm so burnt out?

WILLIAM MOEBIUS 11.30

350

This stone incorporates three gods:
the head is unmistakably goat-horned Pan's
the chest and belly Heracles', the rest,

from thighs on down, belongs to wing-
footed Hermes. Never, stranger, refuse
an offering: in your single sacrifice
three immortal spirits will participate.

WILLIAM MOEBIUS 16.234

KRINAGORAS

Krinagoras of Mytilene is author of fifty-one poems. He was
born about 70 B.C. and was a public figure of some importance
in Lesbos, serving on three ambassadorial commissions: in
48 or 47 and in 45 to Julius Caesar in Rome, and again in 26/5
to Augustus Caesar in Spain. The poems display his familiarity
with Roman high society: it seems that he spent some time
in Italy after returning from Spain and lived until he was at
least eighty years old, perhaps even ninety. Krinagoras'
poems reflect historical events and personal experiences to a
degree unusual in Greek epigrammatists.

351

Turn on your left side, back to your right again,
  Krinagoras, on the empty bed:
You'll get no sleep, only exhaustion, till
  Lovely Gemella lies by you instead.

ALISTAIR ELLIOT 5.119

352

This silver thing I send you for your birthday,
Proklos, a brand-new polished pen
with such a nib, it parts so easily
and evenly flows across the rapid page –
a little gift, but with the greater feeling:
I hope it matches your new-gathered learning.

ALISTAIR ELLIOT 6.227

353

This wingtip feather from a hook-beaked eagle,
   lacquered with purple dye, cut sharp with steel –
good for picking gently at any morsel
   that might lurk in your teeth after a meal –
dear Lucius, from your friend, Krinagoras:
   a little token of how much I feel.

ALISTAIR ELLIOT 6.229

354

Roses used to bloom in spring,
   but now in full midwinter
we open out our scarlet cups
   smiling on your birthday –
nearly your wedding-day as well.
   Better to crown the brow
of the loveliest of women than
   to wait for the spring sun.

ALISTAIR ELLIOT 6.345

355   *Dedication of a Torch*

Antiphanes, son of the same, to Hermes
ran with this torch, prize in the young men's games,
still burning in his hand, like a memento
of what Prometheus ran from the gods with: flames.

ALISTAIR ELLIOT 6.100

356

This longed-for morning here is our sacrifice
   to Zeus the finisher, and Artemis goddess of childbirth:
to them my brother, still not even downy,
   vowed the first spring blossom of his cheeks.
Accept it, gods, and from these delicate whiskers
lead our Eukleides on till his grey hairs.

ALISTAIR ELLIOT 6.242

357

Back from the west, back from the war, Marcellus,
carrying his loot, at the rocky frontier post
first shaved his tawny beard – as the fatherland
had wished: it sent a boy, got back a man.

ALISTAIR ELLIOT 6.161

358

Eartha my mother's name, now earth
covers me as before my birth.
And this is just as good as the other.

I shall be long in this: the sun
soon snatched me from my earthly mother
in the great heat where I was grown.

Now in the strange under a stone
I lie, much wept for: Inachos,
apt servant of Krinagoras.

ALISTAIR ELLIOT 7.371

359

Unhappy men, why do we travel so,
emptily optimistic before death?
Here was Seleukos, perfect of his kind
in talk and manners, briefly at his prime:
on the far edge of Spain, a world from Lesbos,
he lies a stranger on the unmeasured coast.

ALISTAIR ELLIOT 7.376

360 *On the Death of Cleopatra-Selene*

She too went dark as dusk began, though rising,
　　the Moon, covering up her grief with night;
because she saw her lovely namesake breathless
　　Selene setting into gloomy Hades.
With her she had shared the beauty of her light
　　and with her death she mixed her proper darkness.

ALISTAIR ELLIOT 7.633

361

The linguist parrot flicked his flowery wings
and changed his wicker cage for greener things,
but constantly saluting Caesar's fame
kept on the hills the memory of his name.
All these quick-learning fowls began to strive
which should greet first the god that is alive.
Orpheus commanded animals with a word:
these birds sing 'Caesar' of their own accord.

ALISTAIR ELLIOT 9.562

362

Sailing to Italy – fitting out –
commissioning – to see the friends
I've been away from for so long.
I need a guide to take me round
the Cyclades, and old Corcyra.
Come too, my dear Menippos; bring
your circular tour (in three vols.),
professor of all geography.

ALISTAIR ELLIOT 9.559

363

Though you are sedentary always, though
   you never sail, or walk the inland roads,
you must set foot in Attica, go and see
   those long nights of Demeter's festival
unworried among the living, and when you come
   to the greater company, with a lighter heart.

ALISTAIR ELLIOT II.42

364

Though of white marble and dressed straight
   by the mason's upright rule,
this is not a good man's tomb.
   Sir, you must not estimate
the dead by stones. The stone is dumb
   and covers a black heart just as well.
Here lies the feeble rag that was
   Eunikidas, rotting in the dust.

ALISTAIR ELLIOT 7.380*

365

Foul sod covers a bad one here: this tomb
   crushes the hated skull, the pigeon chest,
the stinking saw-teeth,
   the chain-scarred shins of a slave;
the hairless and half-burnt leavings of Eunikidas,
   still full of green rot.
Ill-married earth, lie long and heavy
   upon the ashes of your filthy groom.

ALISTAIR ELLIOT 7.401

366

Here are grapes ready to turn to wine,
pieces of pomegranate ready split,
yellow marrow of seashore escargots,
almonds terrible to bite on, bees'
ambrosia, short-cake with sesame,
sweet cloves of garlic, pears with glassy pips,
ample interludes for the drinker's stomach:
for Pan with his crook, Priapus with his horn,
this simple feast, from Philoxenides.

ALISTAIR ELLIOT 6.232

367

Lucky shepherd, if only on the hill
I'd led sheep too,
up this grassy knoll
with bleating noises to the rams in front –
instead of dipping the steering oar
in the bitter brine.
So I went down, into the deep
and the whistling East wind brought me
in to this beach.

ALISTAIR ELLIOT 7.636

368

Forehead without scalp, dry shell without yolk of eye,
    composition of a tongueless mouth,
the weak stockade of mind abandoned to no grave,
    tears in the way of passers-by,
there you lie by a stump beside the path, to show
    the thrifty to what end they save.

ALISTAIR ELLIOT 9.439

369

How long in these empty thermals near the cold
  clouds gliding unhappy soul
will you sketch out your heaping dreams of wealth?
  Possessions never walk tame to our hands.
Go after the gifts of the Muses: and leave these
  faint forms to the rambling minds of others.

ALISTAIR ELLIOT 9.234

ERUCIUS

Fourteen epigrams are by an Erucius: it seems there were two
poets of the name, one from Kyzikos, one from Thessaly. I
omit the poem (*AP* 7.397) which the manuscripts give as by
the Thessalian. I give his name in the Latin form, supposing
(with Gow and Page) the Greek form, which I would trans-
cribe 'Erykios', to be a transliteration of what is only known
as a Roman name. He seems to have been active about
50–25 B.C. The first poem is the only extant epigram to use
the pastoral name Korydon, familiar from Vergil; the coincid-
ence in phraseology, too, of Erucius' first two lines and Vergil's
Seventh Eclogue, line 2 ff., suggests either a common model
or that Vergil knew Erucius' poem. (The *Eclogues* were
published in 37 B.C.)

370

Glaukon and Korydon, mountain herdsmen
and both Arkadian, pulled back the head
of this horned bull-calf to sacrifice
to the mountain-lover, Kyllenian Pan:
then they fastened the yard span of his horns
with a long nail to the broad trunk of a plane-tree:
a good offering to the god of grazing.

PETER LEVI 6.96

371

Tell me herdsman for the sake of Pan
who is the oaken idol where you pour the milk?
The wrestler from Tiryns who fought lions:
You fool, can you not see his bow?
Can you not see his wild-olive truncheon?
Greetings Alkides, calf-eater,
guard my hut, give me ten thousand cattle.

PETER LEVI 9.237

372

Kleson's goat snorted all night through the dark,
he kept the nanny-goats awake,
he sniffed a murderous tang of wolf
wafting up into the stony fold:
he woke the dogs, they scared the great beast,
and sleep hypnotized the goat-eyes.

PETER LEVI 9.558

373

I am Athenian, that was my city,
raving Italian war
took me from Athens long ago
to the city called Rome. Now I am dead,
island Kyzikos has covered my bones.
Farewell,
Earth who reared me, earth who took me,
earth in whose lap I lay at last.

PETER LEVI 7.368

374

I, the priest of Rhea, long-haired
castrato, Tmolian dancer, whose
high shriek is famed for carrying power,
now, at last, rest from my throes

186

and give the Great Dark Mother on
the banks of the Sangarius all:
my tambourines, my bone-linked scourge,
my brazen cymbals, and a curl

of my long heavy perfumed hair
in dedication, Holy Rhea.

ROBIN SKELTON 6.234

375

May supple-footed theatre-growing ivy
always dance on your glittering
monument, godlike Sophokles:
and your grave be sprinkled by bull-begotten
bees and run with Hymettos honey,
like Athenian wax tablets for ever,
and your hair crowned with ivy for ever.

PETER LEVI 7.36

376

Even though he lies underground
pour pitch on dirty-tongued Parthenios
who vomited such spit at the Muses,
such foul linen of filthy elegies:
he was so mad he said the *Odyssey*
was mud and the *Iliad* was shit.
Therefore the dark Furies have him
in middle Kokytos with his neck
in a collar like a dog's.

PETER LEVI 7.377

377

How massively, with what a fine stiff rise
that weapon shoots up, Priapos, from your thighs,
prepared it would seem for the wedding-night, athirst
for women, its whole being taut with lust!
But please do something – comfort that swollen cock,
put it away under your flowery cloak;
this is no deserted mountain-side
but a sacred city, Lampsakos, which you guard.

PETER JAY 16.242

ANTIPATER OF THESSALONIKA

Antipatros (usually anglicized as Antipater) is known only
from his epigrams in the Anthology. There is a problem in
distinguishing his poems from those of his earlier namesake,
the Sidonian: Gow and Page 'disclaim any capacity to
distinguish the two poets by style'. At any rate, there are about
ninety pieces probably by this poet, who lived from the last
half of the first century B.C. into the first decade or two of the
first century A.D. He was probably born in Thessalonika; L.
Calpurnius Piso Frugi (48 B.C.–A.D. 32), consul in 15 B.C. and
at some time proconsul of Asia, was his friend and patron.
Piso was interested in literature and himself wrote poetry;
Horace dedicated his *Ars Poetica* to his sons. Antipater seems
to have travelled to Asia, and to have worked in Rome as a
teacher of rhetoric. The last two poems given here are only
doubtfully his.

378

In my stars there's three times ten
of breath they say, plus three times two.
For me, though, three decades will do.
That's the limit set for men;
the rest is Nestor's – and even he
went to Hades finally.

ALISTAIR ELLIOT 9.112

379

Homer said everything beautifully, but to call
    Aphrodite golden was the best of all.
Because if you bring cash, there's no concierge
    underfoot and no dog chained at the door.
If not, there's Cerberus himself. Hell's greedy children,
    the only ones to do well doing the poor!

ALISTAIR ELLIOT 5.30

380

It is morning, Chrysilla. Some time ago the clarion cock
summoned away the jealous, queenly Dawn.
Curse you, most jealous of birds, who drives me out
from home to the innumerable chattering of striplings.
You grow old, Tithonos. Why else would you thus chase
your bedfellow Dawn from your pillow at first light?

W. G. SHEPHERD 5.3

381

That dried-up arse, Lykainis,
disgrace to Aphrodite,
with thinner buttocks than deers',
so that the drunkest goatherd
wouldn't live with her – eugh!
the wives of the Sidonians!

ALISTAIR ELLIOT II.327

382

Don't judge men by their gravestones. This slight tomb,
nothing to see, contains a great man's bones:
Alcman, you know, who played the Spartan lyre,
whom the nine Muses found extraordinary,
whom two continents claim, whether he were
Lydian or Spartan. Many mothers bear
any who make and sing with such an air.

ALISTAIR ELLIOT 7.18

383

The man who first built up with good strong words
    the high-browed songs of towering tragedy,
Aeschylus, son of Euphorion, far from Eleusis
    lies here and glorifies Sicily with his body.

ALISTAIR ELLIOT 7.39

384

Unlucky Nicanor, quenched by the grey and deep
naked you lie on some strange shore, some rock,
that rich home lost, the hopes of all Tyre lost.
And none of your possessions saved you: life,
and work, gone to the fishes and the sea.

ALISTAIR ELLIOT 7.286

385

Italian dust covers a Libyan: me,
    a virgin, by these sands not far from Rome.
Pompeia who had kept me like a daughter
    with tears buried me: a free person's tomb,
after other hopes. But at the ceremony
not Hymen lit the torch: Persephone.

ALISTAIR ELLIOT 7.185

386

The waves, the rough surf, swept me on the shore,
    a dolphin-emblem of our common fate.
But on land there's room for pity: those who saw
    wreathed me with flowers piously for the grave.
The sea bore and destroyed me. Who would trust it?
It wouldn't spare even the child it fed.

ALISTAIR ELLIOT 7.216

387

Gorgo, a Cretan bitch, on a deer's track
    ran, pregnant, saying prayers to both Dianas.
She gave birth at the mort and Eleutho granted
    both prayers: good hunting and good motherhood.
Now she gives milk to nine pups. Cretan hinds,
    run from the hunting class of the new born.

ALISTAIR ELLIOT 9.268

388

Deserted islands, broken sherds of land
held in by the Aegean's belts of noise,
you have copied Siphnos and the dry Cyclades –
their wretched loss of an archaic glory.
Or Delos, brilliant once, taught you her way,
the first to meet the god of desolation.

ALISTAIR ELLIOT 9.421

389

Yesterday when I'd drunk myself to bed
with water (neat), Bacchus came by and said:
'By the way you sleep, you're not Aphrodite's friend!
Well, sobersides, how did Hippolytus end?
Avoid imitations.' So he went away,
and water doesn't seem so nice today.

ALISTAIR ELLIOT 9.305

390

I'm not at all scared of the Pleiades setting,
nor of loud waves crashing on to rough headlands,
nor of thunder and lightning, but I'm frightened
of water-drinkers who hear all we say, and remember.

TONY HARRISON 11.31

391

Neither war, nor cyclones, nor earthquakes
Are as terrifying as this oaf,
Who stares, sips water, and remembers
Everything we say.

KENNETH REXROTH *after* 11.31

392

The gipsies tell me my life-line's a short one.
So it is, Seleucus, but I'm not very bothered.
There's one place for us all, and if I'm there the sooner
I'll get my business with Minos over and done with.
Drink! Wine's a conveyance. Let all the teetotal
go slogging on foot down to judgement.

TONY HARRISON 11.23

393

Theogenes sent us for Piso's pleasure –
two well-made bowls, with heaven in double measure.
– We're cut both from one sphere – joint demonstrations
of the southern stars, the northern constellations.
Why look in your Aratus? Just drink up
and see all *The Phaenomena* in your cup.

ALISTAIR ELLIOT 9.541

394

Watered by the Strymon and great Hellespont,
   tomb of Edonian Phyllis, Amphipolis –
nothing remains of you but Artemis' temple
   in ruins and this river so much fought round.
The great prize of the Aegeidae now we see
   like an emperor's rags spread on two banks to dry.

ALISTAIR ELLIOT 7.705

395   *To Telembrotos*

You can't win Love over
by crying. Does a fire
you can't blow out give in
to a little water?

Gold was always the cure
for Love, who born at sea
in Aphrodite's foam
was not at all put out.

ALISTAIR ELLIOT 9.420

396

Phoebus was a herdsman,
   Poseidon was a horse,
Ammon was the famous snake,
   and Zeus a swan of course,
all of them after girls, or boys,
   and trying to keep it quiet,
not bedding by persuasion but
   rape without a riot.
But Euagoras is made of brass;
   he doesn't need disguises:
he does them with no change of shape,
   both sexes and all sizes.

ALISTAIR ELLIOT 9.241

397

Europa (in Athens) does business
   at truly reasonable rates.
You needn't fear interruption
   or the gainsaying of whims;
also, she offers irreproachable
   sheets, and – in winter –
a coal-fire. This time, Zeus,
   come as you are. No bull.

ANDREW MILLER 5.109

398

All sea is sea. How mad it is to blame
the Cyclades, the narrow Hellespont,
the Sharpies, for their meaningless bad name.

Because, after I got away from them,
why did Scarphea harbour cover me?
Pray if you like for a good voyage home,

194

but Aristagoras, buried here, has found
the ocean has the manners of an ocean.

ALISTAIR ELLIOT 7.639

399

In winter on her hearth lighting some coal
old Gorgo died: thunder, shock, fear.
Chilled to the lungs she shut her eyes for ever.
So between age and death occasion waited.

ALISTAIR ELLIOT 9.309

400

Am I to blame the drink or the downpour? Together
Dionysus and Zeus make for treacherous walking.

This stone's for Polyxenus. Staggering home after a fuddle
out in the country, he went slithering off the soaked
   hillside
and now lies far, far away from Aeolian Smyrna.

Drinkers, watch out at night for rain-sodden cliff paths.

TONY HARRISON 7.398

401

When the deep-piled winter snow
melted on her roof, it caved
the timbers in and killed her, but
her neighbours did not make a grave;
they left her in her friendly room,
her tomb her home, her home a tomb.

ROBIN SKELTON 7.402

402

I was Hermocrateia: twenty-nine
  children I bore, and never saw one die.
Apollo never shot my sons; his sister
  Artemis never made me mourn my girls.
Instead she came to ease my labour pains
  and Phoebus led the boys as well to manhood,
unharmed by illness. See how well I beat
  Niobe in children and in sober words.

ALISTAIR ELLIOT 7.743

403   *A Water-mill*

Hold back the hand that works the mill; sleep long
  you grinding-women, though cocks announce the day:
Demeter has put your work out to the Nymphs
  who jump on to the very top of the wheel
and spin the axle which with twisting cogs
  revolves the Nisyrus millstones' hollow weights.
We taste the archaic life again, by learning
  to feast on Demeter's produce without work.

ALISTAIR ELLIOT 9.418

404   *The Temple of Artemis at Ephesos*

I've seen Babylon's walls wide enough to take traffic.
I've seen the statue of Zeus on the banks of the Alpheus.
I've seen the Hanging Gardens and the Sun's Colossus,
the enormous labour of the Pyramids towering upwards,
the immense tomb of Mausolus, but once I'd set eyes on
the temple of Artemis with the clouds almost touching
it put all other marvels into the shade. Except for Olympus
I'd say the Sun shed its light on nothing sublimer.

TONY HARRISON 9.58

405

To Epicles

Already Autumn, and from the belt of Boötes
already there flares the bright flame of Arcturus.

The vineyards already are waiting for pruning
and countrymen patch up their thatches for winter.

You've neither a cloak nor a warm indoor tunic;
you'll shiver, blaming the star that you're frozen.

TONY HARRISON II.37

406

Priapus seeing Kimon with a stand
said, 'I'm divine, but he makes me feel unmanned.'

ALISTAIR ELLIOT II.224

407

'They pray for children? Let them!' cried Polyxo,
her belly torn apart by her new three,
and fell dead in the midwife's hands, and they,
three boys, slipped from her open loins to the ground,
a living birth from a dead mother, one god
taking from her, offering life to them.

ALISTAIR ELLIOT 7.168

408

These are Aristophanes' marvellous plays,
so often crowned with ivy from his deme.
What Dionysian pages, and how clear
that ringing voice of comedy edged with charm –
heroic dramatist fit to take on Greece,
hating the bad and making fun from it.

ALISTAIR ELLIOT 9.186

409

Mentorides, please tell us who
caused this too-obvious change in you
    and by what crafts or arts.
Your arsehole's moved out of its place
diagonally to your face,
    which doesn't breathe: it farts.
And there from your anterior cheeks
a voice out of the basement speaks:
    a hole of many parts!

ALISTAIR ELLIOT *after* 11.415

410

Glykon, glory of Asia
born in Pergamum,
thunderbolt to athletes,
firm-footed, a new Atlas
with unconquered hands,
is down: one never thrown
among the Italians,
never in Greece, never
in Asia, was tripped by Hades,
who throws everyone.

ALISTAIR ELLIOT 7.692*

MARCUS ARGENTARIUS

Author of thirty-seven epigrams, Argentarius is (with Philo-
demos) one of the most elegant and varied epigrammatists of
the period. His poems are influenced by the Alexandrians and
by Meleager, with whom he has some kinship in spirit and
style. 'Good-humoured irony is the hallmark of his style,'

say Gow and Page. Argentarius has been identified with the
witty, malicious Greek rhetorician known to Seneca the
Elder; if so, he lived over the turn of the first centuries B.C.
and A.D.

411

> Look at this, golden-horned moon
> And you stars who light the sky
> Until Ocean enfolds you:
> Ariste, that cunning bitch
> With the sweet breath, has left me!
> Six days I've hunted in vain.
> But we'll catch her, never fear,
> If I send Aphrodite's
> Greyhounds after her: she won't
> Resist the sight of silver.

FLEUR ADCOCK 5.16

412

> Melissa means honeybee; yes, you're true
> To your name, my love: you bring me
> Mouthfuls of honeyed kisses; and when
> You claim your fee, how you sting me!

FLEUR ADCOCK 5.32

413

> Love is not just a function of the eyes.
> Beautiful objects will, of course, inspire
> Possessive urges – you need not despise
> Your taste. But when insatiable desire
> Inflames you for a girl who's out of fashion,
> Lacking in glamour – plain, in fact – that fire
> Is genuine; that's the authentic passion.
> Beauty, though, any critic can admire.

FLEUR ADCOCK 5.89

414

A rather skinny beauty, you'll find,
is Diocleia – thin as a wand;
but a charming girl: you'll be impressed.
– Then I'll fling myself on her narrow chest
and with nothing much to keep us apart
I shall lie close up against her heart.

FLEUR ADCOCK 5.102

415

Take off those flimsy nets, Lysidice;
Don't twitch your bottom teasingly at me,
Walking about in your transparent dress –
Although it suits you well, I must confess:
The muslin clings so tightly to your sides
It shows more of your body than it hides.
But if you find that an amusing trick
I'll drape a see-through veil over my prick.

FLEUR ADCOCK 5.104

416

About Menophila's morals there are strange rumours:
They say her mouth, to astronomers, can provide
An image of heaven: under one small roof
The sword of Orion, with room for the Twins beside.

FLEUR ADCOCK 5.105

417

Here's to Lysidice: pour in ten ladles, boy;
And now one for my sweet Euphrante. Only one,
You ask me? Do I rate Lysidice so high
Above her? No, by Bacchus, whose wine I so enjoy;
But one Euphrante equals ten of anyone –
Just as the moon outshines all else in the night sky.

FLEUR ADCOCK 5.110

418

You loved Menophila when you were rich,
But poverty has cured you of that itch,
Sosicrates: now that you've lost your money
Your love's gone too. The girl who called you Honey,
Darling, and Sweetheart, now asks 'Who are you?
What city are you from? What do you do?'
You've learnt the hard way what that song's about:
Nobody knows you when you're down and out.

FLEUR ADCOCK 5.113

419

Hetero-sex is best for the man of a serious turn of mind,
But here's a hint, if you should fancy the other:
Turn Menophila round in bed, address her peachy behind,
And it's easy to pretend you're screwing her brother.

FLEUR ADCOCK 5.116

420

Isias my love, with your scented breath
Sweeter than any perfume: wake up.
Here is a symbol for you: this garland
Is in full, fresh bloom now; but towards
Morning you will see it wither. Take it
In your hands; and think of your beauty.

FLEUR ADCOCK 5.118

421

That's your third sneeze now, my good lamp.
A happy omen. Can it mean,
Perhaps, that my sweet Antigone
Will come to my bedroom? Let it be true!
Then, lord lamp, you'd rank with Apollo
As a prophet, and deserve a tripod.

FLEUR ADCOCK 6.333

422

Once I was reading Hesiod
When Pyrrha came along.
I dropped him on the ground and sang:
What's the *Works and Days* to me, old man?

ALISTAIR ELLIOT 9.161

423

Damned bird, why have you ruined my sleep
And disturbed my delicious dream
About Pyrrha? Is this how you pay for your keep
And your whole egg-laying harem?
By the sceptre of holy Serapis
His altar, on which I swore,
Shall have your corpse as a sacrifice:
You'll not crow at night any more.

FLEUR ADCOCK 9.286

424

My name was Pnytagoras; I died by drowning.
Waves washed over me, I shared the depths
With diving seabirds, a sad corpse;
While on the shore my mother mourned
By an empty tomb, shorn of comfort.
On the Aegean I fell to my fate,
Reefing ropes in a northerly gale;
And still my seafaring was not finished:
I sailed again in the ship of the dead.

FLEUR ADCOCK 7.374

425

This is Callaeschrus' empty tomb:
He lost his life in the deep current
Passing through the Libyan straits

At the season when Orion, setting
With fearful power, drags the swollen
Ocean upside down from its bed.
There he was drowned; and the salt sea
Hustled his corpse; monsters feasted
Upon him; and his gravestone shows
Nothing but this mute inscription.

FLEUR ADCOCK 7.395

426

Here lie a grasshopper and a
Cicada. Myro made their tomb.
She scattered a handful of dust
Over their grave and wept sadly.
Hades took the music-maker
And Persephone the other.

FLEUR ADCOCK 7.364

427

Blackbird, singing on the highest branch
Of the oak, you are in danger.
That tree is bad for you: on it grows
Mistletoe, a hazard for birds.
Fly off to the vine, with its curly
Tendrils hidden by shady leaves.
It bears grapes for the wine-harvest. Perch
There (you will be safe) and pour out
Your liquid notes: Bacchus loves a song.

FLEUR ADCOCK 9.87

428

Welcome, old friend, long-necked bottle,
Dearest companion of my table
And of the winejar, with your soft gurgle
And your sweetly chuckling mouth: welcome;

You secret witness of my poverty
(Which you've done little enough to aid)
At last I hold you in my hand again.
But I wish you had come to me undiluted,
Pure as a virgin to her bridegroom's bed.

FLEUR ADCOCK 9.229

429

Drunk I observe the golden dance of stars
Each evening; I like other dances too,
With petals dropping from my crown, and touchy
Fingers at foreplay on a booming harp:
A life as orderly as heaven's own
(With Orpheus' Lyre and Ariadne's Crown).

ALISTAIR ELLIOT 9.270

430

Trader, untie the long stern-cables;
Cast off your safely-moored ships; unfurl
Their canvas and put out to sea.
The season of winter storms is past.
Friendly west winds gently ruffle
The blue-green waves now, and the swallow,
Eager for offspring, twitters as he
Builds with his beak a wattle-and-daub
Bridal chamber. Flowers are springing
Up from the soil. So be persuaded
By the god Priapus: embark now
On all kinds of adventuring.

FLEUR ADCOCK 10.4

431

Come, Gobrys, there are other gods besides the Muses.
Literature is fine: enjoy your share of it,
But give Aphrodite and Bacchus a chance.
One offers the delights of sex: try them;
And a glass of good wine is a pleasure too.

FLEUR ADCOCK 10.18

432

Dead, you will lie under a yard of earth,
Far from daylight and all delighting.
So drain the cup; take your pleasures whole;
Embrace that beautiful girl, your wife;
And pin no hopes on 'immortal wisdom':
Cleanthes and Zeno lie as deep as any.

FLEUR ADCOCK 11.28

433

Aristomache loved a drink:
The old chatterbox was fonder
Of Bacchus than his nurse had been.
But when the days of wine were over,
When she had breathed her last on earth
And gone below, she said to Minos:
'Bring me a jug: I'll fetch and carry
Muddy water from Acheron.
That's a suitable punishment
For a husband-murderer like me.'
This she was not; but she lied, hoping
Even in death to see a jar.

FLEUR ADCOCK 7.384

434

Psyllus lies here. Procuring was his trade.
He kept a bunch of girls and hired them out

For parties. Not a nice business: he made
A fat profit out of the weak, no doubt.
But spare his grave, now that he's dead and gone,
You who pass by; don't throw a scornful stone.
Remember this: the service he laid on
Induced the lads to leave our wives alone.

FLEUR ADCOCK 7.403

435

Your kink, Heraclea, is sucking off
Young men: it's an open secret in the town.
How could you bring yourself to do it, though?
Did someone grab your plaits and force you down
To the act? Or is it just that, being named
After great Heracles, you feel that this
Entitles you, whenever it may arise,
To pay his club the tribute of a kiss?

FLEUR ADCOCK 9.554

STATILIUS FLACCUS

Fourteen poems are by this otherwise unknown author, who
was active about the turn of the first centuries B.C. and A.D.
His poems seem not to have been included in Philip's *Garland*. One of his poems (*AP* 7.542) was translated into Latin
by Germanicus, another (no. 438 here) by Ausonius, the
fourth-century scholar-poet.

436

Flaccus gave me, the silver lamp,
 faithful to love, to faithless Napé.

By her perjured bed I dwindle, watching:
  she suffers her shameless passions.
In our separate insomnias
  Flaccus and I are burning.

W. G. SHEPHERD 5.5

437

Bowlegged, pinchered sand-digger –
backward-running, neckless, eight-footed,
shell-backed, hard-skinned swimmer –
Kopasos the fisherman dedicates
this crab to Pan – the first fruits
from the harvest of his line.

BARRISS MILLS 6.196*

438

X finds gold and leaves his noose for Y who's
  left the gold and therefore needs the noose.

EDWIN MORGAN 9.44

439

Just as he gets a beard,
Lado, the lovely, a bitch to lovers,
loves a boy. Justice is quick.

THOMAS MEYER 12.12

APOLLONIDES

Apollonides probably lived in Asia; he has been identified
with a rhetorician who lived in Nikaia in the reign of Tiberius.
Some of his poems refer to events of the period 6 B.C.–A.D. 15.
Thirty-one of his epigrams are extant.

440

Lacking rich acres, thick grape-crops
Old Euphron, his plough as old as he,
Scrapes share-cropper's soil –
Grape-harvest thin, hard found:
First-fruit gifts ever meagre.
But let the year's crop swell,
Shall not the god's tithes too increase?

PETER WHIGHAM 6.238

441

Beeman Cliton hews
From the flower-fed hive
Sweet honey-crop, Spring's
Gift, ambrosial, pressed
From combs of his far-
Roving flock . . . Let but his
Multitude of singing bees
Fill full with honeyed wine
Their wax-built cells.

PETER WHIGHAM 6.239

442

Snow, clothing sky & mountain,
Drives the shy, pointed deer
To valley river, whose moisture
Still is warm. Improvident frost
Chains them there in painful ice.
Villagers, without fishing gear,
Catch what escaped the hunter's snare.

PETER WHIGHAM 9.244

443

The cup clinks out, my friend,
Diodorus, 'Sleep apes but Death'.
Wine! Here is wine. No water add,
But drink till your knees sag.
Soon, too soon, will come the day
When we no more shall drink
Together. Rouse up, Diodorus!
Age, sobriety, have touched our brows.

PETER WHIGHAM 11.25

BIANOR

Twenty-two poems are ascribed to this name: twice he is called 'Bianor of Bithynia' and once 'Bianor the Grammarian'. The poem on Sardis (no. 446) was written sometime after its destruction by an earthquake in A.D. 17.

444

In the clear water by the beach
an octopus was swimming, and
a fisherman, who saw it, grabbed
and threw it high upon the land,

afraid his prey might trap him if
he wasn't careful. There it flailed
its tentacles and writhed until
it happened on a timorous wild

half-sleeping hare among the reeds,
and strangled it. Thus, all unplanned,
the fisherman's sea-plunder brought
him further plunder from the land.

ROBIN SKELTON 9.227

445

The house fell head-first, quietly crushing all but a child –
    on him it fell gentler far than a Zephyr.
Even the ruin showed mercy to childhood. O mothers,
    great boasters, the stone sensed your birth-pangs.

RICHARD EVANS 9.259

446

Sardis, the old city of Gyges and Alyattes,
    Sardis the Great King's Asiatic Persia,
which in the old days built Croesus a palace,
    taking the richness from Pactolus' stream –
now, now to one doom you are swept altogether away,
    swept to the depths through an open chasm.
Boura and Helike were broken like you, but you,
    Sardis, were drowned on land as those in the sea.

RICHARD EVANS 9.423

447   *Paradox*

    This man: this no-thing: vile: this brutish slave:
    This man is beloved, and rules another's soul.

DUDLEY FITTS 11.364

BASSUS

Thirteen epigrams appear under the name of Bassus in the
Anthology: half of them are 'by Lollius Bassus', and he is
doubtless the author of them all. A poem on the death of
Germanicus (A.D. 19) places Bassus in the first half of the first
century A.D.

448

I refuse to turn into gold.
               As for a bull
or a melody-making swan at the shore –
you can keep it. As far as I'm concerned
Zeus can handle the stunts. I'll give
Corinna her two quid, and stay down to earth.

PETER JAY 5.125

POMPEIUS

Two poems, probably of the early first century A.D. He is
probably the Pompeius Macer Junior who committed suicide
in A.D. 33 (Tacitus, *Annals* 6.18); his father, the Procurator of
Asia, was a friend of Ovid and also wrote poetry.

449   *Mycenae*

even if I am only more dust
piled on this desert & even

if I am plainer than a common
stone you just happen to look at –

look again at that other famous
city Ilium whose walls I broke

underfoot to empty Priam's house
& you will know how mighty young

Mycenae was – if my old age wronged
me I still have Homer's testimony

DENNIS SCHMITZ 9.28

450

Lais, who was a lovely flower
in everyone's eye & alone

collected the Graces' lilies
with her eyes no longer

follows the gold traces
of the Sun's horses, sleeps

a destined sleep
goodbye to celebrations

lover's sorrows, those who wish
to be loved & the lamp her confidant

DENNIS SCHMITZ 7.219

THALLOS

A Greek from Miletos, but it is evident from a poem (*AP* 6.235) in celebration of Caesar's birthday that he lived in Rome. Which Caesar is meant is not certain – either Germanicus or Gaius is possible – but at any rate Thallos belongs to the first half of the first century A.D. Five poems are ascribed to him.

451
Now the green plane-tree hides the lovers, hides the lovers'
    rites, its holy leaves are roof and curtain,
its branches are hung with clusters of vine
    heavy and sweet with pleasures of the season.
Undying plane-tree! long may your rich thick green
    conceal the happy friends of Aphrodite!

EDWIN MORGAN 9.220

HONESTUS

A series of brief, partially preserved epigrams 'by Honestus'
were found inscribed on the bases of statues in the sacred
grove of the Muses under Mount Helikon. One of them, on
Livia Augusta, dates him fairly certainly to the reign of
Tiberius, and must have been written about A.D. 30. Honestus
is a rare name, and doubtless the poet of those inscriptions is
also responsible for ten epigrams of variable quality in the
Anthology. Perhaps his best poem is that on Thebes.

452

> The very day one son was drowned
> she lit the other's funeral pyre;
> two griefs, two gifts, destroyed her heart,
> one given water, and one fire.

ROBIN SKELTON 9.292

453

> I would never marry a young girl or an old woman.
> I'd pity, or respect, too much to love.
> Neither unripe grape nor raisin for me, but
> a beauty ripened for the bridal room.

EDWIN MORGAN 5.20

454   *Thebes*

> By the lyre I rose, fell with the flute –
> Thebes. Alas for the discordant Muse;
> the lyre-charmed remnants of my towers lie mute,
> the stones self-risen for my song-built walls:
> your effortless gift, Amphion, who walled in
> the seven-gate city with your lyre's seven strings.

PETER JAY 9.250

ANTIPHANES

'Antiphanes' is the author of ten poems; there is however no way of distinguishing poems by Antiphanes of Macedon, to whom no. 455 is expressly ascribed, from those of a Megalopolitan namesake responsible for at least one poem (not included here), and probably others. Gow and Page note points of verbal similarity between the work of Antiphanes and Philip – cf. nos. 456 and 458 with Philip's 467 and 474. They regard Antiphanes as the better poet and Philip as his imitator.

455

> When Cytherea slipped her wily sash off
>   she gave it to Ino as a lover's fetish
> to draw all men and break their hearts; but Ino
>   bends its holy power on me alone.

EDWIN MORGAN 6.88

456   *The Lost Bride*

> At the bridal bed of star-crossed Petalê
> Hadês, not Hymen, stood:
>   for as she fled
> Alone through the night, dreading Love's first
>   stroke
> (As virgins will), the brutal watch-dogs seized her.
>
> And we, whose morning hope had been a wife,
> Found scarce enough of her body for burial.

DUDLEY FITTS 9.245

457

Man's makeshift days would flash past at the best,
    even if we all reached white hair and stick.
We've scarcely touched our peak when – Oh while it lasts
    pour from the great jug: pour song, love, wine!
Senile tagtail years are waiting. A hundred pounds
    you'd give in vain when the genitals are asleep.

EDWIN MORGAN 10.100

458

Piddle-paddling race of critics, rhizome-fanciers
    digging up others' poetry, pusillanimous bookworms
coughing through brambles, aristophobes and Erinnaphils,
    dusty bitter barkers from Callimachus' kennels,
poet's-bane, nightshade of the neophytes,
    bacilli on singing lips: get off, get down, get lost!

EDWIN MORGAN 11.322

PHILIP

Philip (Philippos) of Thessalonika has eighty-nine poems in
the Anthology. Nothing is known of him from other sources;
from the poems we gather that he either enjoyed or aspired
to patronage at the Imperial Court. He is largely a conven-
tional poet: many of his poems are derivative of earlier poems
by Leonidas and other writers. He lived in Rome and pub-
lished his *Garland*, containing new poetry written since
Meleager's *Garland*, in about 40 A.D. A prose translation of
his prefatory poem to the *Garland* is given in Appendix 1.
The last poem here is only doubtfully by Philip.

215

459

Bronze warship-beaks, old voyage-avid weapons,
   kept here as relics of the battle of Actium,
hide like a hive the rich sweet wax of bees
   which hum and swarm so heavily about them.
Caesar rules generous and just: trophies of war
   in his hands deliver fruits of peace.

EDWIN MORGAN 6.236

460

Sosicles the farmer dedicated these sheaves
   from the furrows of his few acres to you
Demeter, friend of the wheat; his harvest was good.
   May later reapings also blunt his sickle.

EDWIN MORGAN 6.36

461

His anchor, seaweed-probing, boat-securing,
his pair of oars that thrust through the swell,
the lead-weights his net soars up from,
his wicker creels marked out by floats,
his showerproof hat with its wide brim,
his evening flint for light at sea –
to you, King Poseidon, he dedicates these,
Archides, ending his beach-wanderings.

EDWIN MORGAN 6.80*

462

The whistling bellows of his furnace,
the sharp-toothed file that burrs the gold,
the fire-tongs with their twin crab claws,
the hare's feet that mop up the scrapings –
dedicated to Hermes by Demophon
the goldsmith, as age silts up his eyes.

EDWIN MORGAN 6.92*

463

A yellow-coated pomegranate, figs like lizards' necks,
   a handful of half-rosy part-ripe grapes,
a quince all delicate-downed and fragrant-fleeced,
   a walnut winking out from its green shell,
a cucumber with the bloom on it pouting from its leaf-bed,
   and a ripe gold-coated olive – dedicated
to Priapus friend of travellers, by Lamon the gardener,
   begging strength for his limbs and his trees.

                        EDWIN MORGAN 6.102

464

     To Pan the forest-ranger, Gelo the hunter
     dedicates me, his spear, long-used,
     worn-edged, also the tatters of his
     ravelled hunting-nets, his throttling nooses,
     his trip-snares made of sinews, eager
     to snap beasts' legs, his dogs' hard collars –
     since time has undermined his stride
     and his hill-walking days are dead and gone.

                EDWIN MORGAN 6.107*

465

    Queen of black-earth Egypt, divine Isis
      in linen robes, accept my well-set offering:
    flaky sacrificial cake on the wood-embers;
      two dazzling water-loving geese; nard
    crumbled around seed-seething figs; raisins
      like lizard-skins; fragrant frankincense.
    But most, great queen: save Damis from poverty
      as you did from the sea, and a gold-horned kid is yours.

                EDWIN MORGAN 6.231

466

    – *Young Hermes, who placed you at the starter's mark?*
     – Hermogenes. – *Son of?* – Daimenes. – *Where from?*
    – Antioch. – *And why you, I wonder?* – I helped him
     in the race. – *What race?* – Isthmus and Nemea.
    – *So he ran there?* – And won. – *And beat?*
     – Nine boys. He was winged with my feet.

EDWIN MORGAN 6.259

467

A moment ago the shrill flute whistled in the bridal
    chamber,
    the house clapped hands and sang at Nikippis' wedding.
But shrieking split the marriage hymn, we watched
    the poor girl die before she became a wife.
Weeping Hades, why did you tear bride from groom
    when ravishing is your own great delight?

EDWIN MORGAN 7.186

468

Look at these most wretched remains of a man,
    scattered on the sand, drawn with waves through rocks,
a head here, scalped, and teeth knocked out, a hand
    five lonely fingers, some ribs lacking all flesh,
a foot left flat and slack, the tendons gone,
    limbs torn from their sockets. This man
in a score of pieces was once whole. It is better
    for those that are never born to see the sun.

EDWIN MORGAN 7.383

469

Stranger, beware! This terrible tomb
rains verses! The very ashes of Hipponax
have screaming iambics to hurl at Bupalus.
Let sleeping wasps lie. Even in Hades
nothing has soothed his spite. From there
he shoots straight metres in lame bursts for ever.

EDWIN MORGAN 7.405*

470

I am a plane-tree. I was sound and strong when the blasts
  of a stormy sou'-wester uprooted me and threw me flat.
Yet a bath of the grape makes me stand again, I breathe
  both summer and winter a rain sweeter than the sky's.
I died to live, and I soak the relaxing liquor
  that makes others bend but only makes me stand
    straighter.

EDWIN MORGAN 9.247

471

I, a ship, built on the profits
from my master's amorous trade
slide into the sea the Goddess
took as birthplace. He that made
my beauty calls me Courtesan,
for I am kind to one and all;
board me boldly; I don't ask
a lot for passage, and install
most gladly those who wish to come –
natives, aliens, every fellow –
and I ride as well on land
as on the sweet tempestuous billow.

ROBIN SKELTON 9.416*

472

The sky will extinguish its stars, and the sun
   will appear shining in the folds of night,
and the sea will be a well of fresh water for men,
   and the dead will come back to the land of the living,
before forgetfulness of those ancient lines
   can steal from us the far-famed name of Homer.

EDWIN MORGAN 9.575

473

You were a pretty boy once, Archestratus, and
   young men burned for your wine-rosy cheeks;
you had no time for me then, on the game with those
   who took your bloom away. Now bristly and black
you push your friendship in my face, holding out
   straw after others have got your harvest.

EDWIN MORGAN 11.36

474

A long farewell to all you universe-swivelling optics,
   and to all you Aristarchoid acanthologizing bookworms!
What do I care about aphelion or perihelion,
   or the generations of Proteus or Pygmalion?
Clarity, clarity always! and may some tenebrous saga
   wither the bones of the Hypercallimachoids!

EDWIN MORGAN 11.347

475

Old Nico brought wreaths to the tomb of Melite
   the virgin. Hades, was your judgement just?

EDWIN MORGAN 7.187

5

OTHER POETS OF THE
ROMAN PERIOD

ADAIOS

Ten poems are ascribed to Adaios of Macedon; they include
historical epitaphs on Philip II of Macedon and Alexander the
Great, as well as poems of country life.

476

> John spared his patient labouring ox,
> worn out by years and the plough,
> the answer of the bloody axe,
> and thanked it for its service; now,
> somewhere, half-lost in meadow grass,
> it lows in soft requited ease,
> glad of the respite from the plough,
> rejoicing in release.

ROBIN SKELTON 6.228

477

> They say dogs killed you. No, Euripides,
> not lust for women either, as no friend
> to love in darkness, but Hades and old age.
> And you lie in Macedon, honoured, the king's friend.
> I say your tomb's not here though, but the stage
> at Bacchus' festival, the scenes, the costumes.

ALISTAIR ELLIOT 7.51

478

> If you see someone beautiful
>   hammer it out right then.
> Say what you think; put your hands full
>   on his bollocks: be a man.

But if 'I admire you' is what you say
and 'I'll be a brother to you' –
shame will bar the only way
to all you want to do.

ALISTAIR ELLIOT 10.20

ALPHEIOS

Nothing is known of Alpheios of Mytilene, twelve of whose
epigrams remain.

479

Andromache's lament is still in our ears; we still
watch Troy struck flat; and Ajax goes on struggling
in his fight for ever; and Hector is tied to the chariot
for ever and dragged round the city walls – all
through the lines of Homer, man of no fatherland
though honoured east and west like no other man.

EDWIN MORGAN 9.97

480

Where are the birth-places of the heroes?
The few you see hardly break the plain.
I passed you by, Mycenae, and knew you,
dead, more desolate than a goat-field,
talked of by goat-herds. 'It stood here' (said
the old man) 'covered in gold, the giants built it . . .'

EDWIN MORGAN 9.101

ANTIMEDON

Antimedon 'of Kyzikos' – the rare name is generally 'corrected' to Automedon, for no reason at all – is unknown, and no other poems by him survive. The poem is quite original in theme. It was probably included in Philip's *Garland*, so could have been written at any time from about 90 B.C. to A.D. 40.

481

Drinking together in the evening we are human.
When dawn comes, animals
we rise up against each other.

PETER JAY II.46

ANTISTIUS

Antistius has four pleasant poems in the Anthology. He may be identifiable with C. Antistius Vetus, an eminent Macedonian whom Tacitus mentions as exiled for treason in A.D. 21; but this is no more than a possibility.

482   *Priapus the Scarecrow*

Here erect I guard the land
    and Phrikon's crops and hut.
You're open-mouthed at how I stand –
    but keep your legs tight shut.
Laugh, but never trespass or
    I'll show you shaggy bums
your hair is no protection for
    I drill whatever comes.

ALISTAIR ELLIOT 16.243

ARCHIAS

At least three poets share this name, which is attached to thirty-seven epigrams. Of the four printed here, the first two are probably by the same unspecified author; the third is ascribed to 'Archias of Macedon', and the last to 'Archias of Byzantium'. Since these four poems probably fall into the period between Meleager and Philip, I place them together.

483

Desire, get your bow ready
　　　　　and go quietly after
　　　　　　　　　　another mark.

I have not even
　　　　　one dot
　　　　　　　　left for wounding.

ALAN MARSHFIELD 5.98

484

'Get away from Eros!'
　　　　　　　　– the labour's lost; I cannot
get away on foot
　　　　　from a close-tracking flying thing.

PETER JAY 5.59

485   *Hektor of Troy*

Stone, who was his father that lies beneath you?
What was his name? His country? What was his death?

His father was Priam. Ilion his country. His name
Was Hektor. He met death fighting for his land.

DUDLEY FITTS 7.140

Not even in death can I,
Theris, my shipwrecked body
Delivered on the travelling wave,
Escape these unresting, unwelcoming
Shores; for here, under
The tide-lashed reefs which break
Into spray the calamitous ocean,
Have strangers fashioned my grave;
And therefore sadly, eternally,
I listen, even in death,
To the sea's perilous thunder.

CLIVE SANSOM 7.278

AUTOMEDON

Author of a dozen lively epigrams, all humorous and satirical. There is no information about him, and nothing in the poems to date him.

487

That Asiatic striptease girl
    who goes in for those
poses – obscene
    to her delicate nails:
I like her.
            Not because she can flick you
    all the erotic positions
or softly soft hands
    this way and that way.
But because she knows how to flutter
    my ragged old man

and does not flinch
    from the withered skin.
She tongues it, teases it,
    knots herself round it.
Only let those thighs
but once, ah!, go down,
    and she raises a horn
    from the bleaks of Hell.

ALAN MARSHFIELD 5.129

488   *The Impotent Lover*

You send for her, you tell her to come, you get everything
    ready,
    but if anyone really comes, what will you
get up to? Think how things stand with you, Automedon:
    this cock that was spirited and stiff is dead now
and shrivelled between your legs. How they'll laugh if you
    put to sea empty-handed, an oarsman who's lost his oar.

W. S. MERWIN 11.29

489
    Nicetes begins with gentle declamation,
        Forestays in sail, a light breeze going;
    But when the squall comes on, with full sail out
    And canvas fastened he runs the central sea,
    A weighty merchantman, until, the term of his words
        Reached, he arrives well-sailed at
    Waveless harbours.

FREDERICK GARBER 10.23

490

– Phoebus, accept this dinner that I bring you.
– If I'm allowed, I will. – But you're the son
Of Leto, what could you fear? – Only Arrius.
No robber-kite can match his talon's grasp,
This tender of fatless altars: once the pomp's
Over, the gift goes off with him. Ambrosia
 Holds potent stuff, or else
I'd hunger as you do.

                                It's good I'm a god.

FREDERICK GARBER II.324

491

Having dined yesterday on a goat's leg
And a ten-day-old, yellowish cabbage-stalk
The texture of hemp, I refrain
From naming my host.

                                He's a shit –

And I am bound to suspect
He might invite me back.

PETER JAY II.325

492   *The Gymnastics Teacher*

Yesterday I dined with Demetrius, the boys'
  gymnastics teacher, luckiest of men. One was lying
in his lap, one was draped on his shoulder, one served him
  food, one drink – what a quartette! So I said to him (in
jest) 'Good friend, do you
  have exercises for them at night too?'

W. S. MERWIN 12.34

DIODOROS

It is uncertain which of a number of authors this Diodoros is; the name may have been extrapolated from this poem on the assumption that the poet is describing an accident in his own house. This may be the Diodoros of Sardis who was Strabo's friend (see preface to Diodoros Zonas, p.167).

493

A young child of Diodoros's house
fell from some steps and broke its neck.
Yet, when the master came running,
it stretched out its arms for his sad aid.
Earth, do not crush the bones
of a slave's child: be kind to Korax,
who died at two years old.

W. G. SHEPHERD 7.632

EUENOS

There appear to be several poets of this name, responsible altogether for eleven epigrams. The first poem here is 'by Euenos the Grammarian'; the second 'by Euenos of Askalon'; the last two by plain Euenos. The lacunae in 'B kw rm' are, of course, supplied by the translator, although the version is otherwise a translation not an adaptation.

494

B kw rm

Hated by the Muses!
serial eater!
mutilat r!
living in a h le,
feeding n st len qu tati ns –
why d y u lie in ambush (blackskin)
graving y ur spiteful image
in my h ly *Numbers*?
B kw rm!
fly fr m the Muses –
far away –
keeping y ur evil l ks
  ff the g d acc unt
  f my arithmetic b ks!

ALISTAIR ELLIOT 9.251

495

Vine v. Goat

Eat me to the root,
I shall still bear fruit –
an offering to spice
(goat!) your sacrifice.

ALISTAIR ELLIOT 9.75

496

If hate is painful and if love's a pain,
I'll choose the wound that is not quite in vain.

ALISTAIR ELLIOT 12.172

497 *To a Swallow*

Relish honey. If you please
Regale yourself on Attic bees.
But spare, O airy chatterer,
Spare the chattering grasshopper!

Winging, spare his gilded wings,
Chatterer, his chatterings.
Summer's child, do not molest
Him the summer's humblest guest.

Snatch not for your hungry young
One who like yourself has sung –
For it is neither just nor fit
That poets should each other eat.

JOHN PEALE BISHOP 9.122

GAETULICUS

Gaetulicus is probably to be identified with Gn. Lentulus
Gaetulicus, consul in A.D. 26 and legate of Upper Germany
from 30–39. He wrote epigrams in Latin as well as Greek;
Martial acknowledges him as an influence along with Catullus,
Pedo and Marsus. Nine Greek epigrams remain, and a
meagre three lines of his Latin verse. A popular army-com-
mander, Gaetulicus was executed in 39 after the discovery of a
plot against the emperor Gaius, in which he was implicated.

Against this identification is Philip's exclusion of the poems
from his anthology, though he should have known them; but
this is quite inconclusive.

498

Here, by the seashore, there lies
Archilochus, whose Muse was
Dipped in viper's gall, who stained
Mild Helicon with blood. The
Father knows it, mourning for
His three daughters hanged, shamed by
Those bitter verses. Stranger,
Tread softly, lest you rouse the
Wasps that settle on this tomb.

EDWARD LUCIE-SMITH 7.71

ISIDOROS

An unknown poet of the pre-Philip period. He is said to be
'from Aigai'.

499

My name is Eteocles. The sea seduced me from my farm
    to be a merchant against my nature.
I was on a voyage across the Tyrrhenian Sea
    when a quick sharp squall tore the ship
from air and sent me down with it. Different winds
    ruffle the threshing-floor and belly the sail.

EDWIN MORGAN 7.532

JULIUS POLYAENUS

Nothing is known about this author of three good epigrams.
It is unclear from no. 500 whether Corcyra (Corfu) was his
homeland or not.

500

Although your ears must be plentifully occupied
With the many-voiced anxieties of your worshippers
And the thanks of those whose prayers you have answered,
O Zeus, who watch over the sacred earth of Corfu,
Listen to me also
And grant me this that there may be a term
To this exile of mine and that I may go and live
In my own country, released from my long labours.

JOHN HEATH-STUBBS and CAROL A. WHITESIDE 9.7

501

    Always it's hope that skims time from our lives.
    The last dawn bypasses all our schemes.

PETER JAY 9.8

MACCIUS

If one poet is responsible, as Gow and Page think, for the
twelve poems ascribed to 'Maccius' or 'Maecius', the form
of his name is uncertain. I follow Gow and Page in preferring
Maccius. The praenomen Quintus precedes Maccius in the
manuscripts at one point. The poems yield no information
about him; he is one of the best contributors to Philip's
Garland – skilful, polished and inventive in language.

502

        Philistion's a hard bitch:
        in her book 'penniless lover'
        is a mere contradiction in terms.
        She seems more bearable now? She

mellows? One may die from the bite
of a less than totally hostile snake.

W. G. SHEPHERD 5.114

503

I swore, love, by your
   dominion, to rest
two nights away from Hedylion.
   You must have laughed,
knowing my searing malady.
   For I will not keep
the second oath –
   the winds can have it.
I'd rather for her sake sin
   than by keeping
my word, lady, perish
   of piety.

ALAN MARSHFIELD 5.133

504

Your pleasures, Priapus, are the island's coast
with its rough seaworn rocks, its rugged peak.
For you, Paris the fisherman has hung up
this hard-shelled lobster won with the lucky dip
of his rod. He happily stacked away the roast
meat with his rotten teeth, leaving the shell
for you, with a small request, kind spirit: luck
enough with the nets to silence his barking stomach.

PETER JAY 6.89

MYRINOS

Four poems by Myrinos, who is otherwise quite unknown, show him to be a talented, inventive poet with a mastery of elaborate effects. The first poem is a devastating parody of the dedicatory mode of epigram.

505

Time topples Statyllios like a doddery oak.

Death hauls the old queen off, but before he goes,
he solemnly dedicates to the God of Cock:

his summer frocks dyed Dayglo puce
one shoulder-length, blonde, greasy, lacquered wig
two glittering, sequined, high-heeled shoes
an overnight grip stuffed full of drag
and flutes still smelling of cachous and booze.

TONY HARRISON 6.254

506

'L' may stand for fifty, Lais,
but yours is from 'millennium',
you lay as old as minstrelsy
and mistress to Methuselah.
Never mind, dye your white hair
and call the men 'Daddy-O'.

ADRIAN WRIGHT 11.67

PARMENION

Eighteen poems are ascribed to Parmenion, a Macedonian of
the period between Meleager and Philip.

507

You poured down like gold,
Olympian Zeus,
on Danaé,
so that the girl
might yield
as girls do when given a present
not shrink
as from His presence.

PETER JAY 5.33

508

Zeus paid Danaé in gold:
thus I pay you.
I can't use
more than Zeus.

PETER JAY 5.34

509

The protection of a cheap coat suffices. I
Who graze on the Muses' flowers, will not be slave
To any table. I hate wealth's inanity,
The hot-bed of hangers-on. I wait
On no one's frown, I know
A meagre diet's freedom.

PETER JAY 9.43

237

510

The gutsy bugs grabbed grub from me till disgusted.
Grudging the bugs as they grubbed disgusting me I grabbed
    them.

PETER JAY 9.113

511   *Thermopylai*

The man who altered the paths of earth and sea,
Sailed on the land and marched across the water –
Him Spartan courage and three hundred spears
Resisted. Be ashamed, mountains and sea!

PETER JAY 9.304

512   *The Statue of Nemesis at Rhamnus*

I am the stone the Persians put to bear
their trophy, neatly changed to Nemesis,
just goddess seated on the bank at Rhamnus,
witness to Athens' victory and art.

ALISTAIR ELLIOT 16.222

PINYTOS

One poem by Pinytos exists. He is probably the Bithynian
Pinytos who became a teacher of literature at Rome, and was
a freedman of Nero's secretary Epaphrodites. This would place
him in the middle of the first century A.D.

513 *Epitaph: Sappho*

The grave has the bones and dumb name of Sappho,
but her softest wise words are deathless.

LEE T. PEARCY 7.16

SERAPION

Serapion was from Alexandria. There is no indication of his
date, but his poetry appeared in Philip's *Garland*. This is the
only extant poem.

514

This is the skull of a hard-working man – either
A merchant, or a fisher in the sea's confusion.
Tell mortals that, while we hunt after other
Prospects, this prospect is our final solution.

PETER JAY 7.400

ANONYMOUS EPIGRAMS

515 *A Field*

Once I belonged to Achaimenides –
Now to Menippos. Some day
I shall pass on from this man to the next.
Achaimenides once thought I was his,
It is the turn of Menippos to share the illusion
Since I belong to no man at all, but fortune.

PETER JAY 9.74

516

The curtain rung down on his wise old age,
Diogenes in Hades encountered Croesus
who panned so much gold from the river.
The Cynic sat down by the Millionaire
and laughed – 'It seems I am now
a man of more substance than you.
Your fortune is lost. But mine –
whatever I had, I have it still.'

W. G. SHEPHERD 9.145

517   *Epitaph on a Tomb near Rome*

Squander for me no scent of myrrh
Spread no myrtle on my tomb
Kindle me no burning pyre
What's the use of such waste

My dust will turn to clay & mire
For all your purple, flowing wine
Give the living their desire
Dead men conspicuously have no taste

FRANK KUENSTLER 11.8

518

Woman-love can't touch my heart
but men's brands heap up hot
coals on me that won't go out.

This heat is as hot as man is
stronger than woman; this lust
that much more.

THOMAS MEYER 12.17

519

I would but I can't
make you my friend;

you never ask or give
when I ask or take
what I'd give.

THOMAS MEYER 12.19

520

Now we flourish
as others have
before,
still others will
in the future,
whose progeny
we'll never see.

PETER JAY *M*12.25

521

Epitaph in the Borghese Gardens

Powder-light let dust lie
On Musa, who had blue eyes,
Who made bird-sweet music,
That all heard, all praised,
Who, silent now, stone-still,
Here lies.

PETER WHIGHAM *M*3.45

522

Epitaph of a Dog

Stranger by the roadside, do not smile
When you see this grave, though it is only a dog's.
My master wept when I died, and his own hand
Laid me in earth and wrote these lines on my tomb.

DUDLEY FITTS *K*627

6

THE ROMAN EMPIRE

c. A.D. 50–450

ANTIPHILOS

Some fifty poems are ascribed to Antiphilos. He came from Byzantium, and was a younger contemporary of Philip; one poem (not included here) probably refers to the emperor Nero in A.D. 54. He is conventional in themes, but ingenious in vocabulary and phrasing.

523   *Gifts to a Lady*

I've not much of my own, lady, mistress, but I
  believe that the man who's yours heart and soul stands
a full head above most men's riches.
  Accept this tunic, the soft pile of flowered purple,
this rose-red wool, this nard in a green glass
  for your dark hair. I want the first to enfold your body,
the wool to draw out the skill of your fingers,
  the scent to find its way through your hair.

W. S. MERWIN 6.250

524   *A Quince Preserved through the Winter,*
                      Given to a Lady

I'm a quince, saved over from last year, still fresh,
  my skin young, not spotted or wrinkled, downy as the
    new-born,
as though I were still among my leaves. Seldom
  does winter yield such gifts, but for you, my queen,
even the snows and frosts bear harvests like this.

W. S. MERWIN 6.252

525 *Epitaph of a Sailor*

Tomorrow the wind will have fallen
Tomorrow I shall be safe in harbour
Tomorrow
        I said:
                and Death
Spoke in that little word:
The sea was Death.

           O Stranger
This is the Nemesis of the spoken word:
Bite back the daring tongue that would say
    Tomorrow!

                DUDLEY FITTS 7.630

526 *A Torrent Cuts Off the Poet's Path*

Wild water-head, what's your reason
  for exalting yourself, cutting off the path,
the way? Must be drunk with rain-water. That's no crystal
  from the nymphs you're flowing with.
Even the clouds that filled you were muddy.
    You'll dry up. I'll be here to see it. The sun
can tell the true stream, born of the source, from the
    bastard.

                W. S. MERWIN 9.277

527

    Give me a mattress on the ship's poop some day –
    The awnings above resounding with the spray's thud,
    A fire forced upward from the hearth-stones, a pot
    Standing on it, and the empty ferment of bubbles.
    Let me see the steward preparing the meat,

My table a plank laid on the deck, the give
And take of the dice, and the sea's whispering.
This was the luck I had recently,
Who love all things commonplace.

PETER JAY 9.546

528

Even then I said
                when her magic
                was infantile
'She will snare us all
                when she's older.'
They laughed at my prognostication.
                But the time I spoke of
                            has come
and what can I do?
                To watch her is absolute fire.
                            If I turn away:
more worry.
            If I ask for it:
                'I'm a virgin.'
                        And I am done for.

ALAN MARSHFIELD 5.III

529   *On the Death of the Ferryman, Glaucus*

Glaucus, pilot of the Nessus strait, born
  on the coast of Thasos, skilled sea-ploughman,
who moved the tiller unerringly even in his sleep,
  old beyond reckoning, a rag of a sailor's life,
even when death came would not leave his weathered deck.
  They set fire to the husk with him under it
so the old man might sail his own boat to Hades.

W. S. MERWIN 9.242

530

Earthquaked, my house collapsed
in a heap around my bedroom,
whose walls withstood the blast.
Then it shook again. Not the earth,
this time, but another dread
in a smaller cave – the pang of birth.
Nature was my only midwife.
Later, we emerged to our sun
which shone on earth and child and life.

LEE T. PEARCY 7.375

531   *Imaginary Dialogue*

This cloak of purple, Leonidas, Xerxês gives you
Praising your courage in battle.
                              Let Xerxês keep
His gift for traitors. Cover me with my shield:
I want no richer burial.
                         But you are dead.
Must you hate the Persians even when you are dead?
Soldier, the love of freedom can not die.

DUDLEY FITTS 9.294

532   *On Diogenes the Cynic*

Shoulder-bag, cloak, unleavened barley-cake, stick
   for walking, clay cup – these the wise Cynic thought
enough for living. And of these there was one too many:
   when the wise man saw a ploughman pick up water
in the palms of his hands, he shouted, 'Clay cup, I don't
   need you!
What have I been lugging you around for?'

W. S. MERWIN 16.333

LUCILIUS

Lucilius (not to be confused with the much earlier Roman satirist of the same name) was patronized by Nero, and thus was a contemporary of the poet Lucan, and the novelist-poet Petronius. He is the author of 120-odd extant poems, and was a grammarian by profession.

Lucilius was the first poet to exploit the humorous potential of the epigram, often by means of rather extravagant hyperbole, and to concentrate on giving it a climactic 'point'. He influenced Martial, though he is a much more limited and uneven writer.

533

Here I am launching my Second Book of Epigrams –
   Inspire me, you gods, that I may produce
A superb exordium to smooth the progress
   Of my poems. Perhaps the Hesiod touch will suit:
'Let us begin our song inspired by Helicon
   And its Muses', that's not a bad beginning
When you've got a flock of sheep to tend –
   Or another style: 'Sing, O Goddess, the wrath
And tell me of the man, O Muse' – thus Homer,
   Mouthpiece to trumpet-toting Calliope,
Protector of Three Epics. Perhaps it's all too high
   As preface to my work (second books
Are notorious for getting bad reviews) – so this:
   'Olympian Muses, Daughters of Time
And Memory, nothing could save me if the Emperor Nero,
   Himself a poet, had not paid me hard cash.'

PETER PORTER *after* 9.572

534 *Nikylla*

Some say you dye your hair, Nikylla. That
blackest of black – you bought it in the market.

PETER JAY 11.68

535

Olympicus, the welter-weight,
took such a beating in the ring
his nose, his chin, his forehead,
his ears and eyelids all disappeared
in one thick cabbage spheroid
sitting on his neck. His bad luck
didn't end there. When his father died,
his brother imitated him
and claimed his share of the
inheritance, while Olympicus
was shown the door as an impostor.
What a fate, to be robbed
not just of your money but your face!

PETER PORTER 11.75

536

Cleombrotus the bruiser
    retired from the ring
to an even fiercer arena –
what happens to him at home
makes the Isthmian and Nemean Games
    like pillow fights.
    His Old Woman's in Olympic Class,
she'd hammer the daylights out of
        Herakles himself.
    No wonder Cleombrotus

dreads going home more than he ever
    did the ring.
  When he gets his wind back
and faces her again, she hits him with
    every blow in the book
    until he concedes the fight,
then he has to pay for losing by
    screwing her good and hard,
    which no sooner done
earns him a second and severer beating
      for failing to
    satisfy her.

PETER PORTER II.79

537

HIS GRATEFUL OPPONENTS SET UP THIS
STATUE OF APIS THE BOXER WHO STOOD
THUS IN THE RING HARMING NOBODY

PETER PORTER II.80

538

A recent earthquake
set everything in motion
except Erasistratus
the sprinter, who's
still on his mark.

PETER PORTER II.83

539

Marcus in the armed hoplites' race
kept on running after midnight
when the stadium gates were closed,
the race officials taking him
for one of the decorative stone statues

fringing the circuit of the course.
When they opened the stadium gates
for the new season, in came Marcus,
puffing across the line, one year late
and still a whole lap behind.

PETER PORTER 11.85

540

Tiny Erotion, borne away
By a gnat had this to say:
'O Father Zeus, do you need
A companion for Ganymede?'

PETER PORTER 11.88

541

Hermogenes is rather short,
He looks up microbes' mini-skirts,
And high above him, snowy-topped,
Loom peaks of objects that he's dropped.

PETER PORTER *after* 11.89

542

Lean Gaius, who was thinner than a straw
And who could slip through even a locked door,
Is dead, and we his friends are twice bereft,
In losing him and finding nothing left
To put into the coffin: what they'll do
In Hades with a creature who is too
Shadowy to be a Shade, God knows,
But when we bear him to his last repose,
We'll make it stylish – mourners, black crêpe, bier,
The lot, and though he won't himself appear,
His empty coffin's progress will be pious –
THE DEATH OF NOTHING, FUNERAL OF GAIUS!

PETER PORTER *after* 11.92

543

> Further adventure of Skinny Marcus –
> Deciding to blow a trumpet, he put his lips
> To the mouthpiece and before he could make
> A sound fell headfirst down the shaft.

PETER PORTER 11.94

544

> Final adventure of Skinny Marcus –
> Finding himself next to one of Epicurus' atoms
> He knocked a hole in it with his head
> Only to disappear for good down the middle.

PETER PORTER 11.93

545

> As thin little Proclus was fanning the fire,
>   The smoke swept him up and out, higher and higher,
> Till floating forlornly past cloud after cloud,
>   He made his way down through the fall-out and vowed
> He'd never go gliding with atoms again
>   Nor trip over hailstones, nor drown in the rain.

PETER PORTER *after* 11.99

546

> Gently, so as not to rouse
> His skinny girl Demetrius fanned
> Her with a very cautious hand –
> And blew her right out of the house.

ALISTAIR ELLIOT 11.101

547

As a poet put it once, an ant
may seem 'a monstrous elephant' –
especially when Menestratus
is riding it. O what a toss,
when thrown from high and trodden on,
he'd time for just one last quotation:
'By Heavens, 'twas bravely done,
First to attempt the Chariot of the Sun,
And then to fall like Phaëton.'

PETER PORTER *after* 11.104

548

Lifted by a little breeze
Chaeremon floated up like chaff
And would have spun right up to heaven
If he hadn't hit instead
A spider web and, caught there, hung
With his feet above his head
Five days and five nights, and then
On the sixth climbed down a thread.

ALISTAIR ELLIOT 11.106

549

Doubly unfortunate are those who dwell in Hell –
    Eutychides the Lyric Poet,
out of breath at last, has had burned with him
    twelve lyres and twenty-five
albums of songs, which poor Charon will have to
    ferry over the charcoal waters.
Alas, where will music-lovers take refuge now
    Eutychides will be singing for eternity?

PETER PORTER 11.133

550

I'm round at Heliodorus' place –
 first he gives me a slice of raw beef,
then pours me three glasses of wine
 rawer than the beef – finally
 to flush the lot out of me
he drenches me with a veritable cyclone of epigrams.
 All this puts me in mind
 of the sins of Odysseus's companions
 who ate the Oxen of the Sun –
if Heliodorus' tasteless meat passes for
 Trinacrian spare ribs,
then the only appropriate punishment
 is not drowning at sea
but being tipped headfirst down the backyard well.

PETER PORTER II.137

551

 There's one Grammarian I know
 Who cuts my talking to *Dead Slow* –
 I'm making all my usual slips,
 Then think of him – it glues my lips!

PETER PORTER II.138

552

Zenonis has a splendid tutor for her son –
 all day long the bearded fellow
teaches grammar, and at night he's still at work
 demonstrating to the mother
declensions, figures, moods, conjunctions
 and other usages. If only the son
had half the taste for learning that the mother has.

PETER PORTER *after* II.139

553

Orator Flaccus can commit solecisms
Without saying anything at all –
Even his yawns are ungrammatical
And he snores with a barbarous accent,
His hand signals when driving
And his facial expressions are
Entirely neologistic, he's a walking
Lexicon of Bad Taste – so that when
I see him I'm struck dumb in turn –
A single word would be a pleonasm.

PETER PORTER *after* 11.148

554

My Dad was worried about his brother,
    frightened he wouldn't live long,
  so he went to every astrologer in town
and got the same report – nothing to worry about
    he'll live to a ripe old age.
Only Hermoclides foretold his early death
    but that was at the funeral.

PETER PORTER 11.159

555   *On Kriton the Miser*

To ease his rumbling stomach our Kriton sniffs
Not mint,
But the product of the Mint.

DUDLEY FITTS 11.165

556

When Hermocrates the Miser lay in bed,
Desperately sick, he called for pen
And paper to make calculations – what
Would it cost in doctors' fees and medicines
To get well and how did this compare
With the cost of dying, assuming a minimum
Expenditure per day until he went?
He found recovery cost a penny more –
It pays to die, he said, and stiffened out
In readiness on the sheets. There he lies,
A halfpenny stuck between his grinning teeth
And all his wealth as pickings for his heirs.

PETER PORTER II.171

557

Aulus
is childless:
when he saw his new-born baby,
all he could think of
was how much it
would cost him
if it grew up,
so he drowned it in the sea –
the only family a miser needs
is money.

PETER PORTER II.172

558

Eutychides the thief was in a rare
Dilemma when burgling a church.
He decided if he stole the Bible it
Wouldn't count as sacrilege since
They couldn't ask him to swear on it.

PETER PORTER *after* II.175

559

Light-fingered Dio takes after the God of Thieves,
His hands, if not his feet, certainly have wings.

PETER PORTER II.179

560

Bad actors love to play great villains
And the badness gets into their performances.
Consider Hegelochus, who once emptied
A whole Greek city playing Nauplius.
Nauplius is an evil name to Greeks,
Once he destroyed the victorious fleet from Troy,
Now he's creating havoc on our stage
Impersonated by vain and strutting freaks.

PETER PORTER II.185

561

Diophon, seeing
another man
crucified on
a higher cross
than him, died
of envy.

PETER PORTER II.192

562

Poor Calpurnius, the most Schweikian soldier
in the land,
was frightened out of his wits by one of those
big murals
in the Imperial War Museum, *The Battle of the Ships*.
He passed out
under the picture after having surrendered to the
Trojan troops –

'Take me prisoner, you heroic warriors, beloved
    of Ares,'
he cried in terror. When we brought him round
    he wanted
to know where he'd been wounded and only believed he
    was alive
after agreeing his ransom with his captors on the wall.

PETER PORTER *after* 11.211

563

    Well, Menestratus, you ask me what I think
       of your pictures of Deucalion and Phaëton:
    I'd flood the first one down the lavatory
       and throw the second into the fire.

PETER PORTER 11.214

564

        Eutychus the painter
        Fathered twenty sons.
        And did he get a likeness?
          Not once!

ALISTAIR ELLIOT 11.215

565

Apollophanes married for an alibi
and paraded as bridegroom through the town –
'It won't be long before I'm the father
of a bouncing babe,' he boasted,
but the only thing he ever fathered
was suspicion of his manhood.

PETER PORTER 11.217

566

It's said you take a long time over a bath,
        Heliodora –
understandable, I suppose, for a woman
        nearly a hundred
and still on the game. But I'm sure it's really hope
        springing eternal
that, like Pelias, you'll get your powers back
        by being parboiled –
the trouble is you ought to read the legend, you're
        just bones already.

PETER PORTER 11.256

567

With a lucky charm around his throat,
A copper bracelet on his wrist
And a protective ring, Diophantus
Should have been safe at all times,
But he saw Dr Hermogenes in a dream
And never woke up again.

PETER PORTER 11.257

568

Mean old Hermon
dreamt he'd spent
all his money
and hanged himself
for fear of
dreaming it again.

PETER PORTER 11.264

569

Lazy Marcus once dreamed
he was running all night –
he's never gone to sleep since.

PETER PORTER 11.277

570

Crown your Bacchus with lettuce leaves, not ivy.
This wine might do for a French Dressing!

PETER PORTER 11.295★

571

Wig, rouge, honey, wax, teeth:
with a make-up bill like yours
you'd save money buying a face.

PETER PORTER 11.310

572

Lysimachus' cushion caught Antiochus' eye,
And never again did it catch Lysimachus' eye.

ALISTAIR ELLIOT 11.315

573

Asclepiades the Miser was horrified
to discover a mouse living under his roof.
                        'My dearest Mouse,
I am a very humble man, my home is no
place for a Magnifico like you.'
                        The Mouse smiled
sweetly: 'My good friend, Asclepiades,
I shall cost you nothing, I want only
                        bed, not breakfast.'

PETER PORTER 11.391

NIKARCHOS

Doubtless contemporary with Lucilius, and similar to him in manner, Nikarchos has forty-two humorous epigrams in the Anthology. He lived at Alexandria.

574

> I like a woman built on ample lines,
> A Daimler of a girl or a Dowager –
> One gives a well-sprung ride, the other
> Makes *you* the plat-du-jour when she dines!

PETER PORTER *after* 5.38

575

> *The path of glory leads but to the grave:*
> Then must I miss this evening's programmed rave?
> Whether I go to shades of Underground
> With gouty legs or leaping like a hound
> Is all the same to me, since I'll be carried
> By able-bodied men when I am buried,
> So let me drink my liver dry, go lame
> With ten thromboses in my swollen frame –
> It's quite absurd to give up all your vices:
> They come by courtesy of Dionysus!

PETER PORTER *after* 5.39

576

> Niconoë has just inched past her prime
> (Which was, God knows, in old Deucalion's time
> When human sin was washed clean by the Flood –
> *Then* the sun's heat was running in her blood),

But of such times we have no knowledge, so
We think she might pursue her heat below:
This is the way with many ancient ladies,
Their best chance of a husband is with Hades.

PETER PORTER II.71

577

Another doctor story. Our G.P., Marcus,
Whose very touch turns healthy flesh to carcase,
Just put his hand on stone-faced Zeus – *O Weh!*
They're burying the King of Gods today!

PETER PORTER II.113

578

Diodorus the hunchback
Went to Socles the quack;
Socles took three stones
Weighing about three tons
And piled them on his spine
Right along the line.
The treatment did the trick
(The joke is rather sick)
And now you can't deny
He's straighter than a die!

PETER PORTER II.120

579

Agelaus was kind to Acestorides,
    who, if he'd lived, would have been lame.
Agelaus decided to operate.

PETER PORTER II.121

580

Have you heard the latest miser story,
 how old Dinarchus, about to hang himself,
stayed alive because of the cost of dying?
 A strong enough rope was five new pence
and since he couldn't beat the salesman down
 Dinarchus insulted him hoping he'd
murder him in anger. Alas, Dinarchus
 will never die till death gets cheaper,
but he's touched the top of avarice – he'll
 be known for all time as the man who
bought immortality for five new pence.

PETER PORTER II.169

581

Phido the miser's crying
Not because he's dying
But for paying thirty quid
For his pearl-lined coffin lid!
Just let him off this bill,
He'll make a codicil,
And since there's so much room
Beside his skin and bone,
Bury two for the price of one –
Put in his little son.

PETER PORTER II.170

582

Listen! The night-raven's song
Bodes death before long.
Demophilus sings instead –
The night-raven's dead!

PETER PORTER II.186

583

The Law should have ear-plugs, not bandaged eyes.
 A recent case: one stone-deaf man was suing
Another just as deaf and the judge was deafer than either.
 The plaintiff contended he was owed five months'
Rent, the defendant said his accuser ground corn
 At night to elude the excise men. The judge
Impartially summed up: 'What are you two quarrelling
    about?
 She's your Mother and you must both maintain her.'

PETER PORTER II.251

584

All great events have harbingers.
When Nicon's coming, look out for
His nose: you'll see it like a billhook
Down the road. Now hurry up the hill
And scout the countryside around;
Somewhere or other, round a bend,
A man is following that nose.

PETER PORTER II.406

585

If blocked, a fart can kill a man;
if let escape, a fart can sing
health-giving songs; farts kill and save:
a fart is powerful as a king.

ROBIN SKELTON II.395

LEONIDAS OF ALEXANDRIA

Forty poems by this astrologer-poet patronized by Nero, Vespasian and Domitian appear in the Anthology. They are notable mainly for their ingenuity: thirty poems (including the two printed here) are *isopsepha* – verses in which the letters of each couplet, if added up as though they were numerals, come to the same figure.

586

We oxen are not only good
at cutting furrows with the plough,
but excellent at hauling ships
up from the sea to land; we know
the oarsman's trade as well as that
of ploughman; therefore, sea, command
your dolphins to be just as deft
and yoke them up to work the land.

ROBIN SKELTON 9.347

587

You send me reams of snowy paper,
and elegant Egyptian pens;
Dionysus, do not offer
poets imperfect gifts again,
but use your head! Consider! Think!
What use are these without some ink?

ROBIN SKELTON 9.350

TRAJAN

Born in A.D. 53, the Spanish-born Trajan was Roman Emperor from 98 to his death in A.D. 117. His single epigram is notable for a technical hitch: as Paton puts it, 'in *rhĭnă* the emperor has been guilty of a false quantity.'

588

Point your nose to the sun
mouth open wide
– hold it! You're a time-signal
for everyone.

PETER JAY 11.418

AMMIANUS

Author of twenty-nine mostly humorous epigrams. Active in the reign of Hadrian (A.D. 117–38), he was influenced by Martial.

589

Dawn after dawn after dawn
then suddenly the Dark One –

Consumption, Dropsy, Fever –
a pit and earth flung over.

TONY HARRISON 11.13

590

John's efforts to extract a thorn
failed miserably. He was so thin
that when the pin approached his foot
it was the foot that pierced the pin.

ROBIN SKELTON 11.102

591

You think that beard has made you wise,
but 'Cut it off' is my advice;
that goatish fly-swat is the cause,
not of your learning, but your lice.

ROBIN SKELTON 11.156

592

Distaste

Not because you suck
off a sugar-cane
do I detest you, but
because you also
do it, without the cane.

PETER JAY 11.221

593

May the soil cover
your interred corpse
lightly, pathetic Nearchos,
so that the dogs
have less trouble dragging you out.

PETER JAY 11.226

594

Supper at Apelles'
            was a garden-butcher's work –
feeding-time not for friends
            but a herd of cattle.
Radishes, chicory, fenugreek,
            lettuce and onions, leeks,
mint, basil, rue
            and asparagus –
I was afraid he would then
            bring out the hay,
so I left
            after the soggy lupins.

PETER JAY II.413

ASKLEPIODOTOS

Known only for this poem, composed in Hadrian's time,
which was inscribed with the author's name on the base of
one of the so-called 'Memnon statues' opposite Thebes in the
Nile valley. The statue was said to speak when touched by the
first rays of the sun.

595

Hear in the sea, Thetis, Memnon's alive
    and shouting, warmed by the torch of dawn, his mother,
under the Libyan hills in Egypt where
    the driving Nile cuts through the gates of Thebes.
But your son speaking, war-hungry Achilles?
    Not a word in the Trojan plain or Thessaly.

ALISTAIR ELLIOT M9.19

STRATO

Strato of Sardis lived early in the second century A.D.; his *floruit* is generally given as A.D. 125. Nearly a hundred poems of his are extant, largely because of the absorption into the Palatine Anthology of a collection edited by Strato entitled *Mousa Paidiké* (Pederastic Poems). The *Mousa Paidiké* presumably incorporated all Strato's own homosexual verse, but it appears (as Book 12 of the Palatine Anthology) in an imperfect form – heterosexual poems having found their way into the book. Strato is an adept and witty writer of light, mildly pornographic verse, using the Alexandrian erotic conventions.

596

'Let's start from Zeus,'
as Aratus said, & I won't

trouble you today Muses.
If I love boys & keep

their company, what's that
to Helicon's Muses?

THOMAS MEYER 12.1

597

Boy's cocks, Diodore,
have three phases,
or so those in the know say.

Leave 'em alone & they babble,
let 'em swell & they wail,
but when a hand yanks 'em,
those pricks talk;

that's all you need to know.

THOMAS MEYER 12.3

598

I delight in the prime of a boy of twelve,
but a thirteen-year-old's better yet.

At fourteen he's Love's even sweeter flower,
& one going on fifteen's even more delightful.

Sixteen belongs to the gods, & seventeen . . .
it's not for me, but Zeus to seek.

If you want the older ones, you don't play
any more, but seek *& answer back.*

THOMAS MEYER 12.4

599

The numbers in *ass*
add up the same as
gold. I figured this
out doing easy
arithmetic once.

THOMAS MEYER 12.6

600 *Heterosexual Poem*

A virgin has no subtle cunt-control
No basic kissing technique
No natural smell on her flesh
No cool conversation that is seductive
No ingenuous look in the eye.
Beginners are even worse, they're all
Frigid behind. Which is not, after all,
Where your hand is supposed to wander.

TEDDY HOGGE 12.7

601

Once I came across
some beardless doctors
love had left alone
grinding up
nature's antidote for it.

Surprised,
they begged me,
'Keep it quiet.'

'Mum's the word,'
I said,
'if you can cure me.'

THOMAS MEYER 12.13

602

The bath-house bench pinched Graphicus' bottom.
So even a plank has feelings, and I am a man . . .

W. G. SHEPHERD 12.15

603

I swore to you, son of Kronos, never, not even to myself,
to mention the felicity Theudis has promised to grant me.
But O, my rebel soul –
    I can't dam back the Word – I must
speak (forgive me, Lord): HE SAID YES – YES, HE
    WOULD...
How thwarted the pleasure, Zeus, of Good News
    unpronounced!

W. G. SHEPHERD 12.179

604

Those snooty boys in all their purple drag!
We'll never get our hands on one of those!

There like ripe fig trees stuck up on a crag –
food only for vultures and high-flying crows.

TONY HARRISON 12.185

605

If my kisses wrong you, then tit for tat,
punish my lips with yours.

W. G. SHEPHERD 12.188

606

Long hair, endless curls trained by the devoted
'Artistry' of a stylist beyond the call of
Nature, do nothing for me. What I like's a
Boy's body hot from the park, all grimy
And the sight of his flesh rubbed down with oil.
Nice, and artless; none of the pretty 'enchantment'
Laid on by your merchants of the romantic.

TEDDY HOGGE 12.192

607

I am provoked
by the delicious boy next door.
His laugh of complicity is not
that of a novice.
He is twelve years old.
Green grapes may be touched, but his ripe
chastity will be guarded.

W. G. SHEPHERD 12.205

608   *To Kyris*

You recline that magnificent pair of buttocks
Against the wall . . . why tempt
The stone, which is incapable?

TEDDY HOGGE 12.213

609

Give, and take the cash.
– 'I don't need your money!
Then give, like a prince.

W. G. SHEPHERD 12.214

610   *Private Poem*

Now, damn you, you're stiff, uptight –
nothing doing.
Yesterday when there was, you got up –
to fuck all.

TEDDY HOGGE 12.216

611

There was this gym-teacher
Who took his chance while giving
A lesson to a smooth lad –
He whisked him over his knee, and started
Doing his press-ups there right up him, hand
Working his balls. At which moment the father
Comes looking for his son; the gym-teacher
Throws the boy flat on his back,
Leaps on top and grips him tight round the neck.
Father knows a thing or two about wrestling
And says, 'Easy, please! You'll have it right off.'

TEDDY HOGGE 12.222

612

Meeting a lovely boy face to face
I may strive to avert my eyes – I may
succeed, but must at once glance back.

W. G. SHEPHERD 12.227

613

Off with you, boy! Pretended prude!
Low-minded liar! Recently,
You swore to me such sport was done.
'Never again!' you said. Not ever?
I know the where, the how, the who,
And how much you got paid for it.

EDWARD LUCIE-SMITH 12.237

614

Grey already the hair at my temples
Cock hanging limply from my shanks
Balls out of service, age hard upon me
Dammit, I want to screw a boy, but can't.

TEDDY HOGGE 12.240

615

Vive La Différence

Brainless creatures simply fuck. But we
Thinking beings invented buggery.
One up to us! Man under woman's thrall
Has nothing over a brainless animal.

TEDDY HOGGE 12.245

616

A pair of brothers love me. Which
To be slave to? I adore them both.
One goes, the other approaches –
One now best when he's with me
The other, when I think about him in absence.

TEDDY HOGGE 12.246

617

Who knows when love has had its day
who never leaves can never say
for can who cannot please today
    say yesterday he did?
And pleasing still are those who may
be sure what now does not gainsay
    tomorrow shall forbid.

CHRISTOPHER LOGUE 12.248

618

>He's a dragon, see,
>DRAG   ON
>but other reptiles
>poke into his hole.

TONY HARRISON 11.22

619   *Two Plus Two*

Two passive and two active – you'd imagine
That makes four in bed. But no – they're three.
How come (indeed)? Count twice the middleman –
Letting them both have it, communally.

TEDDY HOGGE 11.225

620   *His Apology*

Someone later may hear these playthings, thinking
Their love-aches were all mine. Not so:
These are the scribblings which for one or another
Boy-lover I tossed off – being blessed with the knack.

TEDDY HOGGE 12.258

CLAUDIUS PTOLEMAEUS

Active about A.D. 120–50, Claudius Ptolemaeus of Alexandria
was a great mathematician, geographer and astronomer. The
Ptolemaic System is named after him. His two most important
works were the astronomical *Great Collection* (known to the
Arabs as the *Almagest*) and the *Geography*, which remained a
standard work until modern times. Minor works are also

extant, often in Latin versions of Arabic translations. Of the two poems bearing his name, *AP* 7.314 is likely to be a namesake's. I give two versions of *AP* 9.577, Bridges's for its interest as a successful experiment in English quantitative elegiacs.

621   *Star-Gazing*

That I am mortal I know and do confess
My span of day:
                                    but when I gaze upon
The thousandfold circling gyre of the stars,
No longer do I walk on earth
                                    but rise
The peer of God himself to take my fill
At the ambrosial banquet of the Undying.

DUDLEY FITTS 9.577

622

Mortal though I be, yea ephemeral, if but a moment
I gaze up to the night's starry domain of heaven,
Then no longer on earth I stand; I touch the Creator,
And my lively spirit drinketh immortality.

ROBERT BRIDGES 9.577

LUCIAN

Ludian (Loukianos) of Samosata in Syria lived about A.D. 115–80. He is famous for his satirical and fantastic prose dialogues, essays and stories, many of which are extant; for a selection see *Satirical Sketches*, translated by Paul Turner. Educated in rhetoric, he travelled widely as a successful lecturer before taking up philosophical studies in Athens. Later he became an administrator in Egypt. Some forty of his epigrams are in the Anthology.

623

To Glaukos, and to Nereus
To Ino's son Melikertes
To the Deep-Sea-Lord, son of Kronos
And the gods of Samothrace
I, Lucilius, saved from the sea
Give this hair cut from my head:
I've nothing else left to offer.

PETER JAY 6.164

624

I was Kallimachos, age five,
had no grief; then pitiless death
cut me off.
Don't mourn me. I had a little life,
a little part of its evil.

PETER JAY 7.308

625

A worthless man is a leaking wine-jar: pour in
every grace and favour, you pour in vain.

EDWIN MORGAN 9.120

626

Enjoy your fortune as if you were about to die,
eke out your goods as if you were about to live.
Only the sage can yoke these ideas together,
and find the measured marriage of thrift and excess.

EDWIN MORGAN 10.26

627

For mortals, mortal things. And all things leave us.
Or if they do not, then we leave them.

EDWIN MORGAN 10.31

628

Do tell me, Hermes, what was it like when the soul
of Lollianus went down to Persephone's house?
I can't believe he'd be silent. 'Now listen to me –'
Good God, to meet that man even when he's dead!

EDWIN MORGAN 11.274

629

A beard-wagging stick-waving beggarman Cynic
unlocked his wisdom to us one supper-time.
At first he refused the lentils and radishes:
'Righteousness is not the slave of the belly.'
But then his eyes popped at some sharp-sauced quivering
white pork slices that unhooked his prudence,
he quickly asked for a portion, and ate in earnest:
'Pork slices are no drag on righteousness.'

EDWIN MORGAN 11.410

630

We were all drunk, and Acindynus was determined to keep
sober.
The fool! To us he was the fuddled man out.

EDWIN MORGAN 11.429

631

If you really imagine wisdom grows with a beard –
ask my hairy goat to do a Plato.

EDWIN MORGAN 11.430

632

> I am Priapus. I was put here according to custom
>   by Eutychides to guard his scraggy vines,
> the idiot. A great cliff round me too. Well,
>   all a thief gets here is me.

EDWIN MORGAN 16.238

SKYTHINOS

This poet cannot be identified with the namesake from Teos, Plato's contemporary, who wrote in iambic verse an account of the philosophic doctrines of Herakleitos. He is perhaps a contemporary of Strato, to judge from the content of his two poems.

633

> Great woe, fire & war come on me:
> Elissus, filled with love's ripe years
> (sixteen, that deadly age) has all charms
> & a voice & lips that read & kiss like honey.
>
> What am I to do? He tells me: just look.
>
> So I lie awake & let my hands fight unfilled love.

THOMAS MEYER 12.22

634

> And now you're ready who while she was here
> Hung like a flag in a calm. Friend, though you stand
> Erect and eager, in your eye a tear,
> I will not pity you, or lend a hand.

J. V. CUNNINGHAM *after* 12.232

DIOGENES LAERTIOS

Diogenes is best known as the author of a work on the lives
of the philosophers which is still partially extant and is im-
portant as the main source for our biographical knowledge
of the Greek philosophers. He lived in the first half of the
third century A.D.

635   *Tauromancy at Memphis*

At Memphis the horn'd bull told our friend
Eudoxos of his approaching end.
That is the story I have heard.
But lest you think me so absurd
As to believe that bulls can chatter,
Or bull-calves either, for that matter,
Hear what happened: the prophetic brute
With its long wet tongue lapped the fine new suit
Eudoxos was wearing, as much as to say
Your demise is arranged for this very day.
Whereat our friend obligingly
Went home & died. Age? 53.

DUDLEY FITTS 7.744

636

Nor, by God, shall we neglect
to tell how this one died of gout,
however curious it may seem
that he, who used to get about
by using other people's feet,
could suddenly become so well
that in the space of one short night
he scampered all the way to Hell.

ROBIN SKELTON 7.112

PALLADAS

The Anthology contains over 150 poems by Palladas of Alexandria, a teacher of literature by profession. Most critics agree that he is not – from the purely literary point of view – a very skilful writer; 'but his deadly earnestness tells', as C. M. Bowra put it. A pagan in the age of the rise of Christianity, his verse is imbued with a deep-rooted, bitter pessimism and melancholy, and it is this Swiftian satirical quality which makes him an impressive figure. Both detached and passionate, his gnomic blasts carry great conviction.

His dates are usually given as A.D. 360–430, but C. M. Bowra in an important essay, 'Palladas and Christianity' (reprinted in *On Greek Margins*, 1970), makes out a strong case for putting his birth about A.D. 319 and his death around the end of the century. In 391 Bishop Theophilos of Alexandria, encouraged by the new anti-pagan laws of Theodosius, led the local Christians in a campaign of riots, destruction of temples and plunder against the pagans (see poem 647). By now an old man, Palladas evidently lost his job teaching ancient (pagan) literature. He came to terms with the violent advent of Christianity, even though he had been (to judge from poem 673) a member of some organization connected with pagan affairs. *AP* 9.171, not included here, tells how he sold his books and took up an unspecified new job; poem 674 probably hints at this change in his circumstances. There is no evidence in the poems that he came to any belief – indeed the inference is that he remained a pagan at heart. However, he regarded resistance to the Christian persecution as useless and stupid – more, I think, because of his general attitude of resignation to the buffetings of fortune than from any sympathy with their cause.

637

It's no great step for a poor man to the grave.
He's lived his life out only half-alive.

But when the man of plenty nears the end of his,
Death yawns beneath him like a precipice.

TONY HARRISON 10.63

638

Ignorant of all logic and all law,
Fortune follows her own blind course,
kind to the criminal, trampling on the just,
flaunting her irrational, brute force.

TONY HARRISON 10.62

639

So, Mister Moneybags, you're loaded? So?
You'll never take it with you when you go.

You've made your pile, but squandered time. Grown old,
you can't gloat over age like hoarded gold.

TONY HARRISON 10.60

640

Totting up the takings, quick Death can
reckon much faster than the businessman,
who, balancing, blacks out for ever, still
with the total ringing on the till.

TONY HARRISON 11.289*

641

Racing, reckoning fingers flick
at the abacus. Death's double quick
comptometer works out the sums.
The stiffening digits, the rigid thumbs
still the clicking. Each bead slides,
like a soul passing over, to the debit side.

TONY HARRISON 11.290

642

God is philosophical and so can wait
for the blasphemer and the reprobate.

He calmly chalks their crimes up on His slate.

TONY HARRISON 10.94*

643

God rot the guts and the guts' indulgences.
It's their fault that sobriety lets go.

TONY HARRISON 10.57

644

Born naked. Buried naked. So why fuss?
All life leads to that first nakedness.

TONY HARRISON 10.58

645

Life's an ocean crossing where winds howl
and the wild sea comes at us wave after wave.

With Fortune our pilot, weather fair or foul,
all alike drop anchor in the grave.

TONY HARRISON 10.65

646

Fate didn't hustle Gessius to his death.
He ran there well before it, out of breath.

TONY HARRISON 7.682

647

Death feeds us up, keeps an eye on our weight,
and herds us like pigs through the abattoir gate.

TONY HARRISON 10.85

648

Think of your conception; you'll soon forget
what Plato puffs you up with, all that
'immortality' and 'divine life' stuff.

Man, why dost thou think of Heaven? Nay,
consider thine origins in common clay!
is one way of putting it, but not blunt enough.

Think of your father, sweating, drooling, drunk,
you, his spark of lust, his spurt of spunk.

TONY HARRISON 10.45

649

Born crying, and after crying, die.
It seems the life of man is one long cry.

Man, pitiful and weak and full of tears
shows his face on earth, and disappears.

TONY HARRISON 10.84

650

The ignorant man does well to shut his trap
and hide his opinions like a dose of clap.

TONY HARRISON 10.98

651

This is my mule, a poor, long-suffering hack
with iambic front legs and trochaic back.

Backwards or forwards, he'll take you home
both ways together like a palindrome.

TONY HARRISON 11.317

652

Poor little donkey! It's no joke
being a pedant's not a rich man's moke
preened in the palace of an alabarch.
Exist on all the *carets* that I mark
in pupil's proses, little donkey, stay
with me patiently until the day
I get my (patience's first morpheme) pay.

TONY HARRISON 11.383

653

Thanks for the haggis. Could you really spare
such a huge bladder so full of air?

TONY HARRISON 9.486

654

Life's a performance. Either join in
lightheartedly, or thole the pain.

TONY HARRISON 10.72

655

Why this desperation to move heaven and earth
and try to change what's doled out at your birth,
the lot you're made a slave to by the gods?

Learn to love tranquillity, and against all odds
coax your glum spirit to its share of mirth.

TONY HARRISON 10.77

656

I was promised a horse, but what I got instead
was a tail, with a horse hung from it almost dead.

TONY HARRISON 11.293

657

A drink, to drown my sorrows and restart
the circulation to my frozen heart!

TONY HARRISON 11.55

658

Cuckolded husbands have no certain sign
that trusted wives are treacherous, like mine.
The ugly woman's not *de facto* pure,
nor every beauty fast. You're never sure.
The beddable girl, though every bidder woos
with cash and comfort's likely to refuse;
there's many a plain nympho who bestows
expensive gifts on all her gigolos.

The serious woman seemingly man-shy
and never smiling. Does that mean chastity?
Such gravity's worn only out of doors.
At home in secret they're all utter whores.
The chatty woman with a word for all
may well be chaste, though that's improbable.
Even old age gets goaded into lust,
senility's no guarantee. What can we trust?

I've got twelve gods to swear my honour by,
she, convenient Christianity!

TONY HARRISON 10.56

659

When he comes up to the bedroom
and switches on the light,
the poor man with the ugly wife
stares out into the night.

TONY HARRISON II.287*

660

Mere ants and gnats and trivia with stings
vent their aggression like all living things,
but you, you think that *I* ought to be meek,
lay myself open, turn the other cheek;
not even verbal comebacks, but stay dumb
and choking on my gag till Kingdom Come!

TONY HARRISON 10.49

661

The women all shout after me and mock:
Look in the mirror, you decrepit wreck.
But I'm too near the end to give a toss
for trivia like grey temples and hair-loss.
A nice, fresh deodorant, some after-shave
for banishing the bad smell of the grave,
a few bright flowers in my falling hair,
a good night's drinking, and I just don't care.

TONY HARRISON II.54

662

The theft of fire. Man's worst bargain yet.
Zeus created Woman, He was that upset!

A woman desiccates a man with cares
and soon gives Golden Youth his first grey hairs.

But Zeus's married life in Heaven above
's no cloudy mattress of ambrosial love.

Zeus with Hera of the golden throne
longs to be divorced and on his own.

He often has to shove Her from the sky
to a dog-house cumulus to sulk and cry.

Homer knew this well and shows the two
squabbling on Olympus as mere mortals do.

Thus a woman nags and haggles though she lies
beside the Deity of Deities.

TONY HARRISON 9.165

663

Man stole fire, and Zeus created flame
much fiercer still; Woman was its name.

Fire's soon put out, but women blaze
like volcanic conflagrations all our days.

TONY HARRISON 9.167

664

Zeus isn't such a raving Casanova
if he's seen this girl and passed her over.

No galloping bull or strong-winged giant swan
to get his hands on this proud courtesan,

who's Leda, Europa, Danaé all rolled
into one, worth ten showers of his gold.

Is a courtesan too common to seduce
and only royal virgins fit for Zeus?

TONY HARRISON 5.257

665

women all
cause rue

but can be nice
on   occasional

moments   two
to be precise

in bed

& dead

TONY HARRISON 11.381

666

Don't fash yourself, man! Don't complain.
Compared with those dark vastnesses before
and after, life's too brief to be a bore
and you'll never pass this way again.

So until the day you're in your grave
and inevitably you become an incubator
for the new-born worms, don't you behave
as though damned here and now, as well as later.

TONY HARRISON 10.78

667

Each new daybreak we are born again.

All our life till now has flown away.

What we did yesterday's already gone.

All we have left of life begins today.

Old men, don't complain of all your years.
Those that have vanished are no longer yours.

TONY HARRISON 10.79

668

Maurus the rhetor's elephantine conk's
amazing, amazing too that voice that honks
through blubber lips (1 lb net each)
spouting his loud, ear-shattering speech.

TONY HARRISON 11.204

669

Where's the public good in what you write,
raking it in from that shameless shite,

hawking iambics like so much *Betterbrite*?

TONY HARRISON 11.291*

670   *The Murderer & Sarapis*

A murderer spread his palliasse
beneath a rotten wall
and in his dream came Sarapis
and warned him it would fall:

*Jump for your life, wretch, and be quick
or in a second you'll be dead.*
He jumped, and tons of crumbling brick
came crashing on his bed.

The murderer gasped with relief,
he thanked the gods above.

It was his innocent belief
they'd saved him out of love.

But once again came Sarapis
in the middle of the night,
and once more uttered prophecies
that set the matter right:

Don't think the gods have let you go
and connive at homicide.
We've spared you that quick crushing, so
we can get you crucified.

TONY HARRISON 9.378

671

Mein breast, mein corset und mein legs
ja dedicates to Juice like all gut Griegs.

TONY HARRISON 6.85

672

The blacksmith is a logical man
to melt an Eros down and turn
the God of Love into a frying pan –
something that can also burn!

TONY HARRISON 9.773

673

A lifetime's teaching Grammar come to this –
returned as member for Necropolis!

TONY HARRISON 10.97

674

Hope! Fortune! *Je m'en fous!*
Both cheats, but I've come through.

Penniless but free, I can ignore
Wealth that looks down on the poor.

TONY HARRISON 9.172

675

Poverty's better than any arrogant
Conservative Government grant!

TONY HARRISON *after* 10.93

676

'I know all,' you say; of incompleteness, you have
    enough.
You taste others' all; of your own, you have nothing.

SAM BRADLEY 11.355

677   *The Lyf So Short*

But the brief pleasures of life! but the
Headlong fugue of time passing!
                    Waking,
Sleeping, playing, contriving, with Time against us,
Marching always against us, swerving us
To our end –
            and that's nothing.

DUDLEY FITTS 10.81*

678

A sad and great evil is the expectation of death –
And there are also the inane expenses of the funeral;
Let us therefore cease from pitying the dead
For after death there comes no other calamity.

EZRA POUND *after* 10.59

679   *Meditation*

Praise, of course, is best: plain speech breeds hate.
But ah the Attic honey
Of telling a man exactly what you think of him!

DUDLEY FITTS 11.341

680   *Monks*

If solitaries, why so many?
So many, how are they then sole?
O crowd of solitaries
feigning solitude!

PETER JAY 11.384

681

Having slept with a man
the grammarian's daughter
gave birth to a child, in turn
masculine, feminine & neuter.

PETER JAY 9.489

682

Whose baggage from land to land is despair,
Life's voyagers sail a treacherous sea.
Many founder piteously

With fortune at the helm. We keep
A course this way & that, across the deep,
From here to nowhere. And back again.
Blow foul, blow fair
All come to anchor finally in the tomb.
Passengers, armed, we travel from room to room.

FRANK KUENSTLER *after* 10.65 (cf. 645 above)

GREGORY

St Gregory of Nazianzus (*c.* 330–90) is most famous as the friend and associate of Basil and Chrysostom, and as the author of forty-five *Orations* and many letters. His writing has survived in enormous quantity. Book 8 of the Palatine Anthology contains just over 250 of his very repetitive poems – there are more. Gregory was a reluctant bishop; forcibly ordained a priest by his father, he eventually succeeded him as bishop in Nazianzus, but resigned because of intrigues against him, and spent his retirement writing. As Paton says, 'Gregory evidently enjoyed making verses.'

683 *On Naucratius, Brother of St Basil*

This fisher, netted like a fish,
in being trapped escaped life's mesh.

ROBIN SKELTON 8.158

684

Leave my tomb. Employ your pick
upon your cabbage patch instead,
for I have nothing in my pit
but the watchful angry dead.

ROBIN SKELTON 8.227

685

> Why do you heave apart my stone?
> The feeble dead are all I own;
> my wealth is nothing more than bone.

ROBIN SKELTON 8.233

JULIANUS

Flavius Claudius Julianus (A.D. 332–63) was Roman Emperor for the last eight years of his life. He is famous as 'the Apostate' who attempted to subvert Christianity in favour of paganism by means of social sanctions rather than actual persecution. Soldier and economic reformer, he also found time for a great deal of varied prose-writing.

686   *Beer*

> What kind of Bacchus are you? By the real
> Wine-god, I don't know you. Zeus's son
> I know: he smells of nectar, you of goat.
> Were the Celts short of grapes, so turned to corn?
> If so, and they made you from wheat and oat,
> Your name's not Bacchic – it's Cereal.

PETER JAY 9.368

'THE DELPHIC ORACLE'

The authority of the Greek oracles (which were always given in verse) declined sharply with the rise of Christianity. The tradition was that this poem was delivered by the Oracle to Oribasius, the emperor Julian's emissary, in about A.D. 350

when Julian was trying to restore the temple of Apollo at Delphi. But it is certainly a forgery – either by a pagan attached to the old religion, or (much more probably) by a Christian attempting to expose the futility of Apollo and his oracle. In an essay on the poem in *On Greek Margins*, C. M. Bowra makes out a good case for the poem having been written shortly after the destruction of the temple of Apollo in A.D. 396/7 by someone who knew Gregory of Nazianzus' published denunciation of Julian's archaizing religious beliefs; especially a passage on the collapse of oracles, which the poem is closely modelled on.

687

> Go tell the king – the carven hall is felled,
> Apollo has no cell, prophetic bay
> Nor talking spring; his cadenced well is stilled.

PETER JAY *OBGV* 627*

RUFINUS

Thirty-six poems by Rufinus are among the first hundred-odd poems of Book 5 of the Anthology; it seems probable that he made an anthology of erotic verse in which he included his own poems. There is no means of dating him: any time between the second and fifth century A.D. is possible. One poem is written in the form of a letter from Ephesos, and suggests that he lived not very far away. He is a spirited performer.

688   *Leaving the Boys Behind*

boy-mad no longer
            as once before
                        I am called
woman-mad now
                        from scabbard to thimble
instead of boys' unalloyed skin
                                    I go in for
chalky complexions
                        and the added-on crusts
                                    of cochineal
dolphins shall pasture
                        in the Black Forest
and nervous deer
                        in the grey sea

                        ALAN MARSHFIELD 5.19

689

            a silvertoed virgin
                was washing her body
                drenching the golden
            apples of her breasts
                their flesh like yogurt
            the plump cheeks of her bum
                tossed against one another
            as she swung about
                flesh as lithe as water
            a hand spread down
                to cover
                        much swollen
                the fairflowing conduit
            not the whole thing
                but as much as she could

                ALAN MARSHFIELD 5.60

690

Europa's kiss
   even if
      brushing the lips
is sweet
   even if reaching
      the outer mouth
but she does not reach
   with outer lips
      her grappling
tongue
   drags the soul
      out of your fingers

ALAN MARSHFIELD 5.14

691

Pallas and
   golden-shoed Hera
took one glance
   at Maionis
and from the roots of their souls
   cried
no more
   will we take off our clothes
let one bum verdict
   suffice
it is not nice
      to be not nice
         twice

ALAN MARSHFIELD 5.69

692   *Amymone*

dear Love you'd better know
that the virgin Amymone
mulled my vitals
no end
she would flirt with me
till at the critical moment
I dared to

she blushed
what else
she felt that pain
I managing with some trouble
now I am told she is pregnant
what next
do I go or stay?

ALAN MARSHFIELD 5.75

693   *Letter from Ephesos*

my sweetest Elpis
I wish you much joy
if any without me
is possible
by your eyes
I can bear no longer
this asceticism
this lonely
dismemberment from you
always tear-wet I visit
Koressos Hill
or the temple
of Artemis the Great

but tomorrow I shall be
back home and I'll fly
to your eyes bestowing unnumbered
good wishes
Rufinus

ALAN MARSHFIELD 5.9

694 *Prodike*

when Prodike seemed
alone I begged for it
holding her
marvellous knees
I said save a man
almost utterly gone
allow me life's
vanishing breath
my words brought a tear
but she dried it
and with a fastidious linger
gradually withdrew
her hands

ALAN MARSHFIELD 5.66

695

Let us wash each other's body
Prodike
and crown ourselves
and swill neat wine
from bigger cans
life's joy is miniscule
then age mars
the residue
and at last death

ALAN MARSHFIELD 5.12

did I not say we grow old
    Prodike
did I not foretell
  solvents of love
should quickly come
  wrinkles grey hair
tattered body
  a mouth with none
of its gone charm

  does anyone
unctuous and pleading
  visit you now
high-minded lady
  no you're like
a burial mound
  that we pass by

ALAN MARSHFIELD 5.21

so it's hullo now
the bright face you
were frugal with
is devilled away

so you flirt now
that you've dismantled
the hair that once
stirred at your throat

high-minded lady
press no more
I do not take
spikes for flowers

ALAN MARSHFIELD 5.28

698 *Melissias*

Melissias denies she's in love
            but her body screams
she has absorbed
            a quiver of darts
her walk is fitful
            and her breath fitful
while her eyes have gone into
            smitten hollows
by your dam
            the chapleted Kypris
you tiny Lusts
            hot up this girl
till the strict thing cries
            I'm on heat

ALAN MARSHFIELD 5.87

699 *The Waterfront Girls*

Felucca and Pinnace
            those two whores
are always blockading
            the harbour of Samos
fly boys all such
            vikings of lust
the man who grapples
            and goes down on them
            gets sucked right in

ALAN MARSHFIELD 5.44

700

where is Praxiteles where
                    the hands of Polykleitos
that gave life
                    to the old masterpieces
who will fabricate Melite's
                    fragrant hair her burning
eyes and the marvel
                    that is her neck
where are the sculptors
                    where are the masons
                              such a shape
like the effigy of a god
                    deserves a temple

ALAN MARSHFIELD 5.15

701

you have Hera's eyes Melite
        the hands of Athene
the breasts of the Paphian
        the ankles of Thetis
wealthy the man who sees you
        thrice prosperous who hears you
a demigod who kisses
        and a god who makes you his wife

ALAN MARSHFIELD 5.94

702

Rhodope is so stuck up
                    because of her beauty
if I ever say hi
                    she acknowledges
with an arched eyebrow
                    if I let a bouquet

305

hang at her door
                          she tracks it to earth
with an angry foot
                          wrinkles and ruthless age
            pst
                  come quickly
do you at least
                  prevail upon
                              Rhodope

ALAN MARSHFIELD 5.92

703

            here Rhodoklea
                        is a garland
            a braid of delicate
                        flowers laced
            with my own hands
                        there are lilies
            roses
                        moist anemones
            soft narcissus
                        dark-gleaming violets
            wear it
                        cease to be haughty
            both flowers and you
                        will cease one day

ALAN MARSHFIELD 5.74

704

Rhodope, Melite and Rhodoklea
                              contested
to see who possessed
                  the best quim
I was the judge

RUFINUS

and like those three
          famous seraphs
they stood naked
        damp with wine
between Rhodope's thighs
         gleamed the one eye
like a rosepatch cut
        by a foaming stream
(and Melite's
       like watered silk
between frills folded
      an aching dark)
while Rhodoklea's
      was like clear glass
          its wet surface
like a newly minted
       temple carving
but I knew what Paris
        suffered for his choosing
so I at once did the honours
        to all three angels

ALAN MARSHFIELD 5.36

705

if girls were nice
after lovemaking
no man could fuck them enough
but after bed
all girls
are nauseating

ALAN MARSHFIELD 5.77*

706

lay neither the scrawny
              nor thick
choose the mean
              between
one lacks some measure
              of body
the other has gained
              too much
choose neither lack
              nor enormity

ALAN MARSHFIELD 5.37

707

I have armoured my feelings
    with syllogisms
        against desire
and it will not defeat me
        being one against one
a mortal will grapple
    with an immortal
but if it has liquor
    to aid it
what can I alone
    do against two

ALAN MARSHFIELD 5.93

708

I hate an easy woman
and I hate a prude
the one comes over too slowly
and the other's too sudden

ALAN MARSHFIELD 5.42

709

I do not enjoy
          an extortionate night
I prefer bedsit girls
          to your suave madams
the suave flesh reeks
          of arrogant scent
and a chauffeur escorts it
          to the gamy tussle
the other chicks
          have a look and smell
               that's at least their own
they're easy to make
          and do not cost
               a night on the town
I copy Pyrrhos
          who always preferred
to Hermione his wife
          the au pair girl

ALAN MARSHFIELD 5.18

710   *The Slave Girl*

who flogged you and threw you out
  and only naked
who had such a soul of starch
  and no eyes
did he catch you with someone else
  when he came back early
well it happens so many pussies
  are at it love
from now on when someone's with you

309

and he's away
wedge the front door in case
it happens again

ALAN MARSHFIELD 5.41

711

her eyes are gold
her cheeks are glass
her mouth more pleasing
than rose petals
her throat is marble
her breasts dazzle
her feet are whiter
than silver Thetis
if sometimes thistledown
flickers in her hair
I avoid the thought
of white stubble

ALAN MARSHFIELD 5.48

712 *In Spite*

Melissa where is the golden
esteemed sight
of your notorious beauty
where is your classy
capricious pride
your long throat
and the golden bangles
on your swaggering feet
now your hair is
impoverished gritty

round your feet are rags
such is the end
of a bachelor girl

ALAN MARSHFIELD 5.27

THEON

Theon was from Alexandria. He was probably active in the
fifth century A.D.

713   *For the Cenotaph of a Lost Soldier*

You are the charge of halcyons now, it may be:
But – oh Lenaios! – your mother
Bends in still anguish above your empty tomb.

DUDLEY FITTS 7.292

JULIANUS

Julianus of Egypt has seventy poems in the Anthology. He
was active in the first half of the fifth century A.D., and is
referred to as 'an ex-prefect of Egypt'.

714   *Lais' Mirror*

You gave me beauty, Cytherea,
but gradual time has withered me;
now, since your gift is gone, I give
the glass that kept it company.

ROBIN SKELTON 6.19

715

> I kept singing this, and I will call it out from the grave:
>> 'Drink, before you put on these clothes of dust.'

W. S. MERWIN 7.32

716

> 'Drink was the end of you, Anacreon.'
>> 'But I liked it.
> You never touch it, and you'll arrive here just the same.'

W. S. MERWIN 7.33

717

> Though you rule the dead, under the earth, who never
>> smile,
>> Persephone, welcome the shade of the gentle laugher,
> Democritus. It was laughter alone that led
>> your mother away from grief, when her heart was sore,
>> after she lost you.

W. S. MERWIN 7.58

718   *Epitaph in Dialogue on the Sceptic*
                Philosopher Pyrrho

> Are you dead, Pyrrho?
>> *I don't know.*
> If your share of life is measured out,
>> how can you still presume to doubt?
>> *I don't know.*
> Death doubts not, Pyrrho.

LEE T. PEARCY 7.576

719

Anastasia, the Graces blossom and you were their flower,
   and in your time the marriage bed
and before your time the grave held you. Father
   and husband weep for you bitterly. Even the boatman
of the dead weeps over you, not a whole year
   with your husband: sixteen and buried.

W. S. MERWIN 7.600

720   *On a Young Wife*

   O black winter of savage death
that froze the spring of your unnumbered charms.
   The tomb tore you from brilliant day
   in this, your bitter sixteenth year.
   Your husband and father – blind with grief –
think of you, Anastasia, who were our sun.

WILLIS BARNSTONE 7.601

721   *An Unguarded House*

   Thieves, find some other house, worthy of robbing.
   Sleepless poverty mounts guard over this one.

W. S. MERWIN 9.654

722 *Julianus Sees the Chair of the Sophist Craterus*

     I'm a fortunate tree. Once I stood
     drinking wind and bird-song, in the wood,
     until the axe brought me better luck.
     Now I suck the stream of elegant
     speech from Craterus the eloquent.

LEE T. PEARCY 9.661

723   *Julianus Sees a Magistrate's Axe*

For guilty men an axe is what I am;
the innocent see just my silver gleam.

                    LEE T. PEARCY 9.763

724 *Julianus Sees a Bronze Statue of Icarus in a Public Bath*

Icarus, by *cire* you were *perdu* –
but by *cire perdu* the bronzesmith brought you
back to life – don't beat your wings! You'll fall
to the water again, and we'll have to call
   this the Icarian Bath.

                    LEE T. PEARCY 16.107

7

OTHER POETS UNDER THE EMPIRE

APOLLINARIUS

725

> If you insult me in my absence
>   it doesn't hurt me.
> But if you praise me in my presence
>   it's a positive insult.

PETER JAY 11.421

CAPITO

The name is attached to this single poem. It is quite undatable, but is probably late.

726

> Lacking grace
>   beauty
> gives pleasure but
>   takes no grip –
> like a bait
>   floating
> without a hook.

PETER JAY 5.67

CEREALIUS

Undatable: perhaps first or second century A.D.

727

> A poet went to the Isthmian games.
> At the sight of the other poets
>   he said he had asthma.

317

He's planning now to go to the Pythian games.
(If he finds poets there
                    he can't get away with *pathma*.)

PETER JAY 11.129

CYRILLUS

728

A two-line epigram is perfect. Step
past three, and it's no epigram, but epic.

PETER JAY 9.369

DIOPHANES OF MYRINA

729

A thief, and triply so!
I speak of Love,
Who, daring, comes by night,
And strips us bare.

EDWARD LUCIE-SMITH 5.309*

EUODOS

730

Echo:
      mimic,
last sip
of the heard wine,
word's tip.

ROBIN SKELTON 16.155*

GAURADAS

731

Dear Echo, do me a favour; it's
   somewhat . . .
                          Some what?
I love a girl, but I don't think she loves . . .   *She loves.*
But time's against me, I've had no good luck . . . *Good luck.*
Tell her I love her, tell her that I will . . .   *I will.*
Give her this pledge, some cash, please hand
   it over . . .
                         Hand it over.
Echo, what else is there, except success?   *Success!*

PETER JAY 16.152*

GLYKON

732

Everything's laughter
     everything dust
          everything nothing.
Out of unreason comes
     everything that exists.

PETER JAY 10.124

HERODIKOS

Herodikos was from Babylon; his date is unknown.

733

Out of Hellas if you please, Aristarchean
pedants. Over the 'broad back of the sea'!
Timider than a bunch of cowering antelopes,

you bombastic bumblers in huddles, busily
picking at particles. Do you mind? Keep those enclitics
to yourselves. Herodikos would contemplate
Hellas & Babylon the divine for ever.

PETER JAY 16.19a

KILLAKTOR

Nine poems are ascribed to Killaktor, if he is the same as the
'Kallikter' of some references. He is probably post-Philip.

734

'Sweet is the fruit,' say
All who taste. Yet sour,
Not plucked, but paid for.

EDWARD LUCIE-SMITH 5.29

735

A young lady may increase her stock
not by her public, but her private parts.

WILLIAM MOEBIUS 5.45

736

Married life for a poor man
is one long dogfight: noise,
arguments, blows, bloody noses,
threats and lawsuits, one after another.

BARRISS MILLS 11.6

PLATO

The philosopher's namesake, known as Plato 'the younger', is perhaps of the first or second century A.D. – possibly later. The second poem here echoes a phrase from Vergil's ninth Eclogue: 'omnia fert aetas.' Four epigrams are attached to his name.

737   *A Satyr by Diodorus*

> This silver was not carved but mesmerized.
> Don't touch the beast or it will be surprised.

G. R. H. WRIGHT 16.248

738

> Life brings everything, time's length can turn
> Names, shapes, natures, and even fortune.

PETER JAY 9.51

SATYROS

739

> Echo, tongueless, sings her sweet
> and mimic song in sheep-strewn meadows,
> taking up the words of birds
> and making her own songs their shadows.

ROBIN SKELTON 16.153

THYILLOS

740

Already swallows build their homes of mud,
   and clinging sails cup the Zephyr's
infancy; already flowers have gilded
   the meadows' leaf of green, and now
the sea has stopped his savage muttering.
   Cast off your moorings, mariners,
and stow your anchors; give the wind full sail:
   the harbour god gives this advice.

ADRIAN WRIGHT 10.5

TRYPHON

741   *Terpander*

Terpês died among the Spartans, playing
   his lyre exquisitely at a feast,
struck not by sword nor hurled weapon
   but a fig that stuck in his lips. Alas!
Death's at no loss for occasions.

PETER JAY 9.488

ANONYMOUS EPIGRAMS

The following anonymous poems are undatable. Nothing in
their subject-matter, style or context in the Anthology
enables any safe conclusions to be drawn. It is probable that
the majority of them belong somewhere in the first five
centuries A.D., but a few may be earlier. Nos. 743 to 752 are
probably contemporary with Rufinus.

742   *Sthenelais*

All night the expensive Sthenelais I laid,
Whose throat roars gold, whose technique
Has set whole towns on fire to have her.
Naked I had her, and free, till dawn
And the end of my dream. Never again
Shall I go on my knees to her barbarous beauty,
Nor burn alone, since I have found
Such liberal pleasure in delicious sleep.

                              GUY DAVENPORT 5.2

743

        Love-goddess, saviour
        Of the sea-wrecked, save me,
        Shipwrecked upon dry land.

        EDWARD LUCIE-SMITH 5.11

744

        The inky gloss of your mane
            or the blonde sheen
                on your regal coiffure –
        The same grace shines from both
            and Eros shall dwell at the last
                in your plain grey hair.

                    W. G. SHEPHERD 5.26

745

    I fell in love. I kissed her.
    Luck was with me. I got what I wanted.
    She loves me. But who she is,
    or who I am, or how
    it happened, Kypris only knows.

                    BARRISS MILLS 5.51

746

Imperious bath-maid, O why
do you chafe me so briskly, so hot?
Before I am stripped, I feel the flame.

W. G. SHEPHERD 5.82

747

I wish I were the wind, and you,
walking along the seashore,
would uncover your breasts and let me
touch them as I blow.

BARRISS MILLS 5.83

748

Could I but become a crimson rose,
I might then hope you would pluck me
and acquaint me with your snowy breasts.

W. G. SHEPHERD 5.84

749   *A Gift*

To you this fragrant oil, sweets to the sweet,
I bring, like brimming wine to the drunken god.

GUY DAVENPORT 5.90

750   *'Not of Itself, But Thee'*

Perfume sweet I send you,
                    gracing not you but the perfume:
You are yourself the perfume of the perfume.

                              DUDLEY FITTS 5.91

751

There are four Graces, two Aphrodites, ten Muses –
Derkylis is one of each,
                    a Muse, Aphrodite and Grace.

                              PETER JAY 5.95

752

            Standing beside you, fiddler
            while you are fiddling away
            I'd like to work it up to a high pitch
            – then loosen your G-string.

                              PETER JAY 5.99

753

                  A tumult in the street!
                  Listen, Cypris, your boy's
                  In trouble! All those with
                  Hearts afire now try to
                  Seize him, as he goes by.

EDWARD LUCIE-SMITH 5.303

754   *Brief Autumnal*

Green grape, and you refused me.
      Ripe grape, and you sent me packing.
      Must you deny me a bite of your raisin?

                              DUDLEY FITTS 5.304

755

Holy is the moon and our own Selene;
  The young men of Alexandria
Conjure her down to do the splits
  And pleasure them in the ethereal night.

PETER PORTER II.262

DEDICATORY POEMS

756 *To Priapos*

His green garden's twytined digging fork,
The curved sickle that pruned and weeded,
The comfortable old coat he wore in the rain
And his raw oxhide waterproof boots,
The stick with which he set the cabbage sprouts
In long straight rows in rich black loam,
The hoe that chopped the runnels that kept
The garden green all the dry summer long,
For you, Gardener Priapos, the gardener Potamon,
Whom you favoured, places on your altar.

GUY DAVENPORT 6.21

757 *To Astarte*

On the temple porch of Syrian Astarte
Heliodoros hangs his luckless net.
It is clean, no fish has touched it,
But seaweed only, which lies in heaps
On the inlet beach.

GUY DAVENPORT 6.24

758   *Epitaph of a Nicene Actor*

Philistion of Nikaia lies here, whose laughter
Lightened the heavy lives of his fellow men;
And with him all life lies,

                            who died
Often, indeed, but never quite in this fashion.

                            DUDLEY FITTS 7.155*

759

          I'm Callicratia
          who bore
          29 children,
          saw none die,
          lived 105
          years & never once
          used walking sticks.

     TONY HARRISON 7.224

760

     At sixty I, Dionysios of Tarsos, lie here –
     not having married

                    and wishing my father hadn't.

                            PETER JAY 7.309

761

Dear earth, take old Amyntichus to your heart,
Remembering how he toiled upon you once:
Fixing in olive-stocks, and slips of vine,
And corn, and channels where the water runs.
He made you rich with herbs and fruit: in turn
Lie soft on his grey head; and bloom for him.

                            ALISTAIR ELLIOT 7.321

762

Under this plaque I lie, the famous woman
Who took her clothes off only for one man.

PETER JAY 7.324

763   *A Gravestone at Corinth*

The only record of our great affection,
my dear Sabinus, is this little stone.
I'll miss you always. When you come to Lethe,
don't drink, I pray, forgetfulness of me.

PETER JAY 7.346

764

Sailor, ask not whose this tomb:
May you fare on seas more calm.

PETER JAY 7.350

THE FAMOUS DEAD

765   *Sophocles*

Aged Sophocles, the light of life has dimmed –
Bloom of poets, rimmed
                    with Bacchus' dark-wine cluster.

LEE T. PEARCY 7.20

766

– Eagle of the tomb, whose tomb is this? Why
    Forever gaze towards the gods' starred home?
– *I am Plato's Image: My soul is there;*
    Here, my Attic crust lies in Attic loam.

PETER WHIGHAM 7.62

767

Here's Dog Diogenes, you ferryman –
The one who saw how much of life's a sham.

EDWARD LUCIE-SMITH 7.63

768   *On Epiktetos the Stoic*

I Epiktetos was born deformed, a slave,
Poor as Homer's beggar: and dear to the gods.

PETER JAY 7.676

769   *The Nine Lyric Poets*

Holy mouthpiece of the Muses PINDAR,
BAKCHYLIDES, talkative Siren,
                Aiolian graces of SAPPHO,
ANAKREON's writing,
                STESICHOROS who drew
from Homer's stream in your works,
SIMONIDES' delectable pages,
IBYKOS who gathered the sweet
                bloom of Seduction and boyhood,
sword of ALKAIOS which often
                drew the blood of tyrants
defending his country's rights,
and ALKMAN's nightingales singing soprano –

Be gracious to me, you who established
the canon of lyric song.

PETER JAY 9.184

GNOMIC POEMS

770

Grey Time moves silently, and creeping on
Steals the voices of articulate humans,
Obscure himself, he hides illustrious men
And brings to light men who have been obscure.
O unforeseeable finish of men's lives,
Who daily always advance towards the dark.

PETER JAY 9.499

771

Wine & bath-house sensualities
steepen the downward slope.

TONY HARRISON 10.112

772

How was I born? Where from? Why did I come
Here? To leave? How can I learn anything,
Knowing nothing? I was born as nothing,
Shall be again as I was; a nought,
Nothing is humanity. Pour out
The pleasurable flow of wine, the drug
That's antidote to evil.

PETER JAY 10.118

773

Inscribed on a Statue of Hermes

I was not
            was born
was
    don't exist
that's all
            anything else
is a lie
        I shall not be

PETER JAY *K*1117a

774

The only rule is enjoy yourself,
   since all things march away with time:
May's spritely kid that rushes
   to a freshet is October's stinking
goat trampling down the ford.

                PETER PORTER 11.51

775

       Don't cry
   over the happy dead
   but weep for those who dread
      to die.

            PETER PORTER 11.282

SATIRICAL POEMS

776

A man once married who hunts wife once more –
A shipwrecked man sails back to his lee shore.

           ALISTAIR ELLIOT 9.133

777   *On a Worthless Politician*

Fortune did not mean to give you promotion
Except to prove that her omnipotence
Stretches as low as you.

              PETER JAY 9.530

778

'There's not a husband whom storms don't benight'
– they all say, and get married, knowing it.

             PETER JAY 10.116*

779

Crateas the doctor and Damon the sexton
have carried economy to such lengths
it passes for ecology. Damon steals
their grave clothes from the dead
and gives them to his partner
to use as bandages. In return, the doctor
sends him all his patients to inter.

PETER PORTER II.125

780

'Rufinianus' was once just Rufus.
Two syllables; but he extended
his name, as also his crimes.
But the two syllables of Justice
were not deceived, and his name
will be pared down again,
Rufus the crook, the criminal, as before.

PETER JAY II.358*

781

Bakchos the wine-god
                    dissolver of limbs
and Aphrodite of love
                    dissolver of limbs
have a daughter, also
                    dissolver of limbs
– the gout.

PETER JAY II.414

782

I think this is something you should get clear,
Placianus: every
Moneyed old woman is a very rich coffin.

PETER JAY II.425

332

783

Borrow to your heart's content.
Leave to the bankers
the cramp they get in their fingers
counting it up.

PETER JAY 16.18

784

'May Grace be with you all' said the bishop,
making his entrance. But how
can Grace be with us, when the bishop
has her inside, on his own?

PETER JAY 16.19

785   *Portrait of a Stupid Teacher of Rhetoric*

Who painted you, the non-speaker,
Professor of Rhetoric?
You're silent, you don't talk.
Utterly life-like.

PETER JAY 16.318

786

Greetings! you seven pupils of Professor Aristides –
Four walls, and three benches.

PETER JAY *M*10.33

787

Keep away from asps and toads,
Vipers and Laodiceans.
Keep well away from rabid dogs,
And also Laodiceans.

ALISTAIR ELLIOT *M*10.40

333

788

Spring garlands the earth with leaves
stars garland the sky
as this land garlands Hellas
and these men, their country.

PETER JAY 9.65

789

On a Statue of Pan

Come sit beneath my pine
that melodiously whispers
to the mild west wind:
Consider my mellifluous brook
where my piping binds
a spell of quiet sleep.

W. G. SHEPHERD 16.12

790

The needles of the lofty pine
murmur sibilant in the steady west wind:
Recline by my fluent stream
and let the syrinx charm you to sleep.

W. G. SHEPHERD 16.13

791

Niobe

From a woman, the gods turned me into stone.
From stone, Praxiteles gave me life again.

PETER JAY 16.129

792

Seeing the *Aphrodite* of Knidos, the Cyprian
goddess said 'Help! When did Praxiteles see me naked?'

PETER JAY 16.162

793

Come with clean hands,
True mind and tongue,
Pure not through baths
But in yourself.
For some, one drop
Of water serves,
Yet others find
The sea not broad
Enough, nor deep.

EDWARD LUCIE-SMITH *M*5.16

8

THE EARLY BYZANTINE PERIOD

c. A.D. 500–600

MARIANOS

A Byzantine legal official ('*scholastikos*') at the Imperial Court,
Marianos was active in the reign of Anastasius I (491–518).
He rewrote Theokritos and Apollonios of Rhodes in iambics
– an exercise somewhat similar to that of the gentleman who
put Milton's *Paradise Lost* into rhymed couplets. Six epigrams
survive. Marianos' chief distinction is that Shakespeare seems
to have imitated the poem included here in his Sonnet 154:
'The Little Love-God lying once a sleepe . . .'. Sonnet 153 is
another variation.

794

    In this bath Cypris once was bathed by Love, her son,
    who warmed its heavenly waters with his torch.
    The beads of sweat which ran into its pure, clear depths
    from her rich flesh – ah, how they smelt of spring!
    Since then, perpetual rosy vapours bubble forth,
    as if the golden one still lingered here.

ANTHONY HOLDEN 9.627

ERATOSTHENES

Like Marianos, a '*scholastikos*'; nothing else is known of this
poet who is probably contemporary with Agathias.

795

        Bacchus, receive my offering, not
        unkindly, as it's all I've got:
        an empty, from your loyal son,
        ever-thirsty Xenophon.

ALISTAIR ELLIOT 6.77

796   *Meditation, Followed by Excellent Advice*

How delectable are the attributes of Virginity!
Nevertheless it is clear
That general virginity would annihilate the Race.

Marriage, therefore, would seem the more practical plan:
Marry, and contrive a man
Who, when you have ceased to exist, will take your place.

Eschew, nevertheless, lechery.

DUDLEY FITTS 9.444

PAULOS

A close friend and contemporary of Agathias, Paulos was a man of high birth and wealth. About A.D. 560 he held the post of '*silentiarius*' at the court of Justinian. There are about eighty epigrams by Paulos, who also wrote a long hexameter poem, the 'Description of the Church of Hagia Sophia' (one of Justinian's great monuments). Opinions on the merit of this long work vary greatly, but there is no disagreement about the elegance of his epigrams, particularly the erotic pieces. He is the liveliest poet of the period: by comparison Agathias is tiresomely verbose. Agathias published his friend's poems in his anthology.

797

> Our kisses
> Rhodope
> let us steal,
> and slip
> with furtive ease
> like burglars
> into bed.
>
> To cheat the eyes
> of stern
> leering prudes
> adds honey to
> love's cup.

ANDREW MILLER 5.219

798

> She lay all night beside me,
> delectable, and wept,
> blaming the stars that rose
> for the star-set of dawn.
>
> I wept too. Lovers
> require Arctic nights.

ANDREW MILLER 5.283

799

> Gold cut the knot of otherwise
> infrangible virginity
> when Zeus, eluding brazen bars,
> rained upon royal Danaë.
>
> Interpreted? Gold masters bronze,
> rampart or chain; gold disallows

all locks & garters, smoothes away
disdainful lines from haughty brows:

gold undid Danaë. Take note,
lovers whom Beauty's ways abash:
worship Her not with hollow words
but full & faithful hearts. And cash.

ANDREW MILLER 5.217

800

A man (they say)
whom a mad dog
has bitten, sees,
stooping to drink,
that dog's image
upon the water.

Did Love, rabid,
fasten his teeth
within my flesh?
Your eyes glance
and smile in
the sea, the stream's
slow eddies,
the wine-cup.

ANDREW MILLER 5.266

801

Kissing Hippomenes, I crave
Leander's touch;
while clinging to Leander's lips
my fancy dwells as much

on Xanthus; locked in his embrace
my heart strays back,

342

restless, toward Hippomenes.
   Yearning for what I lack,

shrinking in turn from those I hold
   in shifting arms,
contentedly I taste the wealth
   of Cytherea's charms.

May she who lifts opprobrious brows
   to censure me
lie cursed between the stale sheets of
   paupered monogamy.

              ANDREW MILLER 5.232

802

        She has not come.
             The lamp
      dims again and
      gutters out:
             the flame
      within – the lust,
      the longing – burns
      bright and hard.
      I cannot sleep.

      That she would come
            she swore
      and swore again
      in Love's name:
      her perjured tongue
            spares
      man nor god.

ANDREW MILLER 5.279

803

Soft are Sappho's kisses,
soft, under silken skin,
those snowy arms – but hard
as stone what lies within.

She opens honeyed lips
to speak what Love himself,
brazen, would blush to hear.
She opens nothing else.

He who endures long nights
beside those limbs of snow
learns to envy the thirst
of Tantalus below.

ANDREW MILLER 5.246

804

Giving her mother's
zealous eye
the slip, she thrusts
into my hands
two rosy apples,
and is gone.

Gone: yet by Love's
black art
her touch lingers
and burns in
th' ensorcelled fruit
with slow flame.
Craving her breasts
my hands clutch
mere rosy apples.

ANDREW MILLER 5.290

805   *On a Bath-House in which Both Men and Women Bathe*

> Close is lust's
> expectation –
>   the act,
> impossible.
> Behind that door
> of frail wood
> Cypris, goddess
> august & bold,
> is pent. Yet
> it is better so:
> Love's *cuisine*
> offers no dish
>   to rival
> those untasted.

ANDREW MILLER 9.620

806

> These wreaths, Lais,
> torn in a thousand
> fragments, these
> shattered cups
> and clipped locks
> drenched with myrrh
> are yours – lying
> here deep in dust,
> the spoils of poor
>   ANAXAGORAS
> outdone by Love.
>
> Many a night
> he wasted by
> your door, rapt

in patient vigil.
And his reward?
No word, no promise
sweetly breathed,
not even a rude
retort to spice
amorous hope.
And now, gaunt,
shadow-eyed,
abandoning this
flotsam of wrecked
festivity
he curses your
inflexible grace.

ANDREW MILLER 6.71

807

She plucked one thread
of her glinting hair
and caught my hands
within that snare.

Laughing, I tried
to shake them free:
the hair, like steel,
imprisoned me.

A shackled slave,
I rue my laughter:
now, where she leads
I stumble after.

ANDREW MILLER 5.230

808

For whom now will you comb your hair
in lover's fashion?
For whose soft skin smooth your hands?
Why edge that cloak
with sea-crimson when Rhodope
has gone? Gone:
cheated of Rhodope, my eyes
gaze with blank
indifference at lucid day
dawning in gold.

ANDREW MILLER 5.228

809

Choicer than all
flush of youth
is your wrinkled prime,
Philinna:
my hands long for
the mellow fruit,
heavy, that fills
them full – not
for a girl's breasts,
unripe. Know,
love, your autumnal
wealth outdoes
another's spring,
your frost
her summer's heat.

ANDREW MILLER 5.258

810

Slip off that gown,
    let limb
lie locked in naked limb:
    the sheerest weave
seems thick as the wall of Babylon
    when we embrace.
Come, let us join breast to breast,
    link lip with lip,
and . . . no! I'll say no more:
    I hate
an idle tongue.

ANDREW MILLER 5.252

811

Goodbye: I bite the word back,
and stay.
        Hell's long night
is less dark than leave-taking:
mere day dawns in silence,
but your sunlit sheen
bears me the voice, the charmed words
my heart hangs on.

ANDREW MILLER 5.241

812

I saw them, caught them in the act.
    They could not slake, though lip
was fixed on feverish lip in fury,
    their tyrannous thirst. They longed
each to invade the other's heart:
    exchanging clothes, they eased
the ache of impossibility.
    So he like young Achilles

348

among the girls of Skyros, she,
   bare-kneed, a counterfeit
of Artemis at hunt, fell to,
   love-ravened, hunger-racked.
Simpler to separate two vines
   plaited in ancient growth
than them, intent in their embrace.
   Thrice blest the man, my love,
who in such chains is snared & locked
   while *we* burn apart.

ANDREW MILLER 5.255

813

Set foot once beyond Nilotic
   Meroë: Love
will snatch me there on wings. Journey
   into the dawn
that glows no rosier than yourself,
   and I, step
by step, will follow. Accept, lady,
   this pearl, prize
from the still sea. She of the Foam,
   the Sea-born,
sends it, token of her defeat:
   she has despaired,
glimpsing you, of her ancient, bold,
   limpid splendour.

ANDREW MILLER 5.301

814

Epitaph: Atticus

He knew how death hunts
at distance:
      dug

349

his own grave
with bold hands and heart
scornful of mortal childishness.

May the sun
of such wisdom
shine long
beneath the sun.

ANDREW MILLER 7.609

815   *Epitaph: Chryseomallus the Mime*

Of gold then
but now locked in brass,
no more to lend breath
    to old tales,
your silence does not charm:
it chills, it weighs down
    our cold hearts.

ANDREW MILLER 7.563

816

Mild, of sweet
countenance,
who wore liberty
as his cloak
and left a son
in old age
to praise him:
                    here
lies THEODORUS
in labors happy
happy in death.

ANDREW MILLER 7.606

817 *Epitaph*

> *Here I –*
>> What does
> the name matter?
> *from –*
>> Who cares?
> *of good family –*
> Oh? Then scum –
> *and decent habits –*
> or the profligate
> meet with worse?
> *am laid in earth:*
>> this stone
> *tells my story.*

> And who listens?

ANDREW MILLER 7.307

818 *On a High House in Byzantium*

> On three sides
>> the sea's
> broad, blue back
> shot with light –
>> the sun
> that dawn scattered
> against wide windows
> clings there
>> till dusk.

ANDREW MILLER 9.651

AGATHIAS

Agathias (536–82) was born at Myrina in Aiolis. He studied law in Alexandria and Constantinople, where he practised as a lawyer and became a '*scholastikos*'. He married the daughter of his friend, the poet Paulos. He was an all-round man of letters; his unfinished history of the reign of Justinian from 553 to 558 is a sequel to that of Prokopios; he edited a collection of contemporary poems (the *Kyklos*, 'Cycle'), and was a voluminous poet himself: his *Daphniaka* ran to nine books. Nearly a hundred of his poems are in the Anthology; they are often rather long and verbose descriptive elegies, letters in verse, etc. His work has been the subject of a recent study: *Agathias* by Averil Cameron (1970).

819

> Restless and discontent
> I lie awake all night long.
> And as I drowse in the dawn,
> The swallows stir in the eaves,
> And wake me weeping again.
> I press my eyes close tight, but
> Your face rises before me.
> O birds, be quiet with
> Your tittering accusations.
> I did not cut that dead girl's tongue.
> Go weep for her nephew in the hills,
> Cry by the hoopoe's nest in the rocks.
> Let me sleep for a while, and dream
> I lie once more in my girl's arms.

KENNETH REXROTH 5.237

820

It is not wine that makes me reel
    Not juice of grape I crave,
Only to drink where you have drunk
    A wine no grape e'er gave.

Let but your lip the wine-cup lip
    Touch – how can I flee
Or wine, or sweet cup-bearer, for
    The kiss it bears of thee?

PETER WHIGHAM 5.261

821 *Manifesto*

Let Aphrodite herself,
            let all the company of Love
Curse me, shrivel my sick heart with their hate, if ever
I turn to the love of boys.
            O Goddess,
From sliding error and perversion guard me!
To sin with girls is sin enough:
Pittalakos may have the rest.

DUDLEY FITTS 5.278

822 *Kallirrhoê: a Dedication*

To Aphrodite these wreaths
To Athene this lock of my hair
To Artemis my girdle:

I Kallirrhoê
Brought to my virgin bed a valiant husband
And bore him men.

DUDLEY FITTS 6.59

353

823 *Partridge*

Never, my partridge, O patient heart,
Were you to see your hills again.
And never now will you wake up
In your elegant wicker coop,
Shake as the fat-eyed day comes on,
And freckle your wings with the dawn.
The greedy cat has got your head,
I've taken what's left from her teeth
And hidden you well from her claws.
Small bodies should not lie so deep.
May the dust be light on your grave.

GUY DAVENPORT 7.204

824

You expect, Puss-in-Boots
        to go on treating my house
as your house
        after treating my pet partridge
as a comestible?

        No, pet partridge!
Over the bones of his treat
        the cat shall be slain,
& you honoured in blood rite:
        As Pyrrhus, recall,
(rightfully) slew
        Polyxena
over the corpse of Achilles.

PETER WHIGHAM 7.205

AGATHIAS

825   *On Lot's Wife Turned to Salt*

This is a tomb, no corpse within;
This is a corpse, no tomb without:
Corpse-shell self-tombed, self in self.

DUDLEY FITTS 7.311*

826   *Troy*

Whither, O city, are your profits and your gilded shrines,
And your barbecues of great oxen,
And the tall women walking your streets, in gilt clothes,
With their perfumes in little alabaster boxes?
Where is the work of your home-born sculptors?

Time's tooth is into the lot, and war's and fate's too.
Envy has taken your all,
Save your douth and your story.

EZRA POUND *after* 9.153

827   *A Bridge on the Sangarios*

With tall-necked Hesperia and the Medes,
With all the nomad armies of the barbarians,
You also, Sangarios, wear Justinian's chains.
Once unconquerable and free of traffic,
Now you lie bound with a collar of stone.

GUY DAVENPORT 9.641

828   *A Latrine in a Suburb of Smyrna*

Here the savoury roast and pungent sauce
Have lost their beauty, changed to filth.
Pheasant, herbs ground with the pestle, fish,
Ox-and-garlic hash, with pickled eels,
Are so much dung. In at the mouth,
Out from the belly! Silly enterprise,
To have spent gold for all this dirt.

GUY DAVENPORT 9.642

829   *A House in Byzantium*

Mousōnios built this solid, windproof mansion, and
    built it well.
It wasn't easy, or cheap. But now he's gone to a
    poky cell
And strangers live in his pride and joy, while he
    beds down in hell.

FLEUR ADCOCK 9.677

830   *The Astrologer*

Farmer Kalligenes sowed his wheat,
Went off to the astrologer Aristophanes
And asked if the summer were auspicious,
If his wheatears would be full, unstunted.
The astrologer cast his stones across the board,
Studied them, wiggled his fingers, and said:
'If, Kalligenes, there is rain enough
On enough of your land, and if the weeds
Don't take over, nor frost wreck the lot,

356

If a hailstorm doesn't knock it all flat,
If the deer don't nibble, if no calamity
Up from the earth nor down from the sky
Occurs, the signs show a good harvest.
Unless there's a plague of grasshoppers.'

GUY DAVENPORT 11.365

ISIDOROS

The single poem by Isidoros 'scholastikos' is included amongst
poems by Paulos and Agathias, and he is doubtless their
contemporary.

831

Now Endymion dedicates
his cold bed's failure to the moon,
for grey hair frosts his ageing head
and all his beauty is long gone.

ROBIN SKELTON 6.58

LEONTIOS

Leontios, author of twenty-four epigrams, is probably the
'referendarius' of the same name who is mentioned by
Prokopios. He lived in the time of Justinian.

832

Touch, cup
        the lips
that drip
        honey
lick while you have them

I am not envious, but
wish that I had your luck

PETER JAY 5.295

833

Orpheus, dying, not all Music died,
As, Plato, with your death, the Lyre is stilled:

In your spirit, under your fingers, sounded still
Echoes, for us, of that primordial Music.

PETER WHIGHAM 7.571

MACEDONIUS

Author of forty-four poems in the Anthology, Macedonius
was consul – then an honorary title – during the reign of
Justinian.

834

Be patient, Morning Star, with Love; though close
to Mars, don't let your heart grow hard.
You've seen the Sun beneath a woman's roof,
and slowed your westward journey down
before; then crown my unforeseen delight
with darkness long as Arctic night.

ADRIAN WRIGHT 5.223

835

Every year men harvest grapes, not seeing
faded locks in severed tendrils.
But I reap love, and hold you, fruit of my
devotion, in the gentle knot
of twining arms; nor could I reap elsewhere,

so rich in charms are you. I wish
you young forever; yet, though wrinkles come
like creepers, I will love you still.

ADRIAN WRIGHT 5.227

836

Beauty kissed your mouth, and gave the petals
for your cheeks; your eyes make play with
love, and from your fingertips the music
springs. Your gaze holds fast men's eyes; with
song you charm their ears: from near or far
you trap the hearts of rash young men.

ADRIAN WRIGHT 5.231

837

You say 'Tomorrow'; a tomorrow which
I never see; you pile delay
upon delay, unending overture.
With this you grace my love, but give
to others better offerings than this
unfaithfulness. 'This evening, then,'
you say; but what is woman's evening?
Age, composed of countless wrinkles.

ADRIAN WRIGHT 5.233

838

You're here! I hadn't dared to hope. Surprise
has cleared my mind's imaginings.
But still a deep disturbance shakes my heart;
love's surges suffocate my soul.
Then save me, who am shipwrecked near to land,
and welcome me within your harbour.

ADRIAN WRIGHT 5.235

839

You ask me, girl, why I withdraw my sword
    from out the sheath. I don't intend,
I swear, to turn my back on love, but just
    to show you that the keenest blade
may softly be outflanked. See here, the guide
    of my desire, the shadow of
myself! But stand by me, or else this sword
    shall plunge to rest between my ribs.

ADRIAN WRIGHT 5.238

840

I dreamt I held the laughter-loving girl
    encircled in my arms. She made
no protest, firing me with manifold
    desires, until the jealous god
of love, who lay in ambush through the night,
    leapt up, put sleep to flight and loosed
my fond embrace, thus even grudging me
    a benefit derived from dreams.

ADRIAN WRIGHT 5.243

841

You neigh and whinny, seeming to invite
    a mate; you quietly nod to me.
But all your provocations are in vain:
    I've sworn my eyes shall never give
a tease a gentle look. Go play elsewhere,
    and blow your futile kisses by
yourself; those lips you're always loosening up
    have never seen the action!
But I've a better course and better guides,
    who know where love's rewards are found.

ADRIAN WRIGHT 5.245

842

She who shook and swayed among the chorus
   girls, the teaser with the golden
castanets, is gripped by age and failing
   health. Lovers who once ran to greet
her shrink away. This waning moon, once proud,
   no longer bears the imprint of a man.

                    ADRIAN WRIGHT 5.271

843   *A Dedication*

Anchored now to Neptune's temple floor, this
   ship once sailed the seas with Crantas.
She heeds the winds no more, and Crantas too
   is stretched in peaceful sleep ashore.

                    ADRIAN WRIGHT 6.69

844

      Earth and Goddess of Birth,
        Who cover and uncover,
      Goodbye to you both: I have done
        The race from one to the other.
      I go on, not knowing where,
        Knowing I never knew
      Whose or what I am
        Or how I came to you.

                    ALISTAIR ELLIOT 7.566

845

      Praise memory and forgetfulness!
      Memory for the good things,
      forgetfulness for the bad.

                    BARRISS MILLS 10.67

JOHANNES BARBUKOLLAS

Author of eleven epigrams, three of them on the destruction
of Berytos (Beirut) by earthquake in A.D. 551. Mackail con-
jectures that he studied at the school of civil law there. An
ancient commentator says 'Barbukalé is a town on the Ebro';
Johannes is therefore probably Spanish.

846

> Don't halt your voyage, sailor, nor drop sail
> Because of me; the dry harbour's in view.
> I am a single tomb. Some other place
> Griefless should hear oars beating your arrival.
> Poseidon and the hospitable gods wish this;
> Adieu, travellers on sea and land, adieu!

PETER JAY 9.427

DAMASKIOS

Damaskios' philosophical works (all now lost) were highly
regarded, according to the polymath ninth-century Byzantine
scholar Photios. They included a history of philosophy and a
life of Isidoros. He was head of the Neo-Platonic school of
Athens when it was closed by Justinian in 529, and went into
exile in Persia, but later returned under an amnesty.

847

> Zosimé was a slave in body only.
> Now she has found freedom for that too.

PETER JAY 7.553

IRENAIOS

Three poems appear in a context which places Irenaios as a contemporary of Paulos and Agathias. He was an official ('*referendarius*') at Justinian's court.

848

O supercilious delicious Rhodope
your flesh (at last) pricked
by Love's piquant edge
                    your pride
thawed to compliancy,
you hold me cradled in your arms.
I lie in chains
with no will toward liberty,
for thus do soul and soul,
body and languorous body meet,
on currents of desire
to drift and mingle.

ANDREW MILLER 5.249

849

Eyes filled with speaking fire,
pouting painted lips,
giggles, a toss of glamorous curls,
coy hands outstretched in invitation –
for all that, your heart's unbent:
wasting, you still scorn woman's softness.

ANDREW MILLER 5.251

Why is the floor, Chrysilla,
  honoured thus
    by your lowered gaze?
Please don't fidget
  with your girdle-ends
    like that.
Kypris has no truck with shame.
If silence is imperative
  could not a little nod
    signify that you have
      submitted
        to the Paphian?

        W. G. SHEPHERD 5.253

THEAITETOS

A Byzantine 'scholastikos' contemporary with Paulos and
Agathias.

851
Already the field, fair with leaves, in her fruitful bringing
  to birth,
Flowers with roses, as they break forth from their buds.
Already on the poising cypress boughs, the cicada,
Muse-crazed, soothes him who binds the sheaves.
A careful parent, the martin has built her house under the eaves,
Sheltering her brood within her mud-formed chambers.
Now the sea drowses, through fair days warming into
  Zephyr-delighting
Calm its ship-bearing broad expanse;
No longer rushing down on the vessels' high-built poops,
Or throwing up spume upon the line of breakers.

DAMOCHARIS

Sailor, to Priapus, lord of the sea and bringer to port,
Sacrifice a marbled collop of squid or mullet,
Or a cuckoo-wrasse, with fire upon his altars –
Fare forth, untrembling, to the Ionian bounds.

JOHN HEATH-STUBBS and CAROL A. WHITESIDE 10.16

DAMOCHARIS

Four poems by Damocharis, a scholar ('*grammatikos*') are
extant. He was probably the Damocharis of Kos who was a
pupil of Agathias; Paulos wrote an epitaph on him (*AP* 7.588).

852
A lead disc composed of black stuff for marking,
A ruler, the officer who kept the lines straight,
The holder of the stream of black writing ink,
His well-cut pens split at the top,
An abrasive stone which regulates the worn-down pens,
To give definition to the characters when they are rough,
His penknife, a broad pointed metal spear –
These things, the tools of his trade, dedicates
Menedemus, on his retirement, his old eyes growing dim,
To Hermes. Take care of your craftsman.

JOHN HEATH-STUBBS and CAROL A. WHITESIDE 6.63

THEOPHANES

Probably of the same period as Paulos and Agathias; Paton puts him later still. Two epigrams survive.

853

> I wish I could be
>> a white-glowing lily
> so you might take me
>> in your hands
> and glut me the more with your flesh.

PETER JAY 15.35

9

ANONYMOUS BYZANTINE
EPIGRAMS

854 *Constantinople (New Rome)*

Rome, queen of all, your fame will never die:
Your *Victory*, being wingless, cannot escape.

PETER JAY 9.647

855 *On a Small Bath*

Do not ridicule the small.
Little things can charm us all.
Eros was not big at all.

ROBIN SKELTON 9.784

856 *Christ*

Trumpet call and grand white stars,
And a shudder through the world,
Yet with what silent stealth you came
Into the labouring virgin's womb.

GUY DAVENPORT 1.37

857

This cattle shed is Heaven now,
or greater far than Heaven, for
the whole of Heaven was the work
of this child huddled in the straw.

ROBIN SKELTON 1.38

858   *Harmony*

Shepherds and angels sing in unison:
What wonder, now that God and man are one?

WILLIAM J. PHILBIN I.39

859   *Nile the Hermit*

As tree and wheat rise green
From the black silt of the flooding Nile,
So grow the hearts that hear
The preaching Nile.

GUY DAVENPORT I.100*

10

THE LATER BYZANTINES

KOMETAS

Kometas was '*chartoularios*' (Keeper of the Records) under Constantine VII (911–59). He seems to have been a contemporary of Kephalas. He edited a revised text of Homer, on which he also wrote three epigrams.

860

'Who, tell me, shepherd, owns these rows of plants?'
'Pallas the olives, Bromius the vines.'
'And who the corn?' 'Demeter.' 'Who the flowers?
What gods?' 'Hera, and rosy Paphia.'
'Stay here, friend Pan, and put your pipe to your lips,
for you'll find Echo on these sunny slopes.'

ANTHONY HOLDEN 9.586

KEPHALAS

It is appropriate that this collection of poems should end with a piece by the man to whom we owe the preservation of nearly all the Greek epigrams. Konstantinos Kephalas of Byzantium compiled what is now known as The Palatine Anthology in the tenth century, when so many remnants of the Greek tradition were saved by the Byzantines. He introduced the book of erotic poems with these lines.

861

To light young poets' hearts
the first of my words is Love,
for He ignites young lives.

W. G. SHEPHERD 5.1*

The Proems

Book Four of The Palatine Anthology contains the proems written by Meleager, Philip and Agathias to their respective anthologies. Meleager's and Philip's are written in elegiacs, Agathias' in hexameters. I give them here in literal prose translation, omitting the irrelevancies from Agathias' long piece. Line references are to the Greek texts.

MELEAGER

Introduction to his Garland

Dear Muse, to whom are you bringing these varied fruits of song; who was it made this garland of poets? – It was Meleager's doing; he worked at this, to present it as a memento to the excellent Diokles.

5 He inwove many of Anyte's lilies, and many by Moiro; few by Sappho, but they are roses; narcissi pregnant with the clear songs of Melanippides, and a fresh shoot of Simonides' vine-blossom; to mix with them he twined the spice-scented flowering iris of Nossis, on whose writing-tablets Love melted the wax. And with her, marjoram from sweet-breathing Rhianos, and Erinna's delicious crocus, with a girl's complexion; the hyacinth, which is vocal to poets, of Alkaios; and a dark-leaved branch of the bay-tree of Samios.

15 He inwove too Leonidas' [of Tarentum] fresh ivy-berries, and the sharp needles of Mnasalkes' pine; he gathered from the twisted tendrils of Pamphilos' vine, woven together with Pankrates' hazelnuts; the fine-leaved white poplar of Tymnes, the green mint of Nikias, the spurge of Euphemos that grows on the sand; Damagetos, the dark violet, too, and Kallimachos' sweet myrtle,

always full of astringent honey; Euphorion's rose-campion, and
the cyclamen skilled in poetry whose name comes from the
sons of Zeus [Dioskouroi: i.e. the poet is Dioskorides].

25 With them he inwove Hegesippos, an intoxicating bunch of
grapes; the scented ginger-grass of Perses which he had cut, with a
quince from the boughs of Diotimos, and the first pomegranate-
flowers of Menekrates; twigs of Nikainetos' myrrh, the terebinth
of Phaënnos, and the tall wild pear-tree of Simias. From the fine
meadow he took and distributed in small batches the flowers of
Parthenis, celery; and yellow ears from Bakchylides' corn-stalks,
fruitful gleanings from his honey-dropping Muse.

35 And Anakreon, whose sweet lyric song is of nectar, but a bloom
which cannot be transplanted into elegiacs; a curly-leaved thistle-
blossom from Archilochos' fodder – a few drops from the ocean.
With them Alexander's [of Aitolia] young olive-shoots, and the
crimson bean-plant of Polykleitos. He put marjoram, the flower
of Polystratos' songs, with them, and fresh Phoenician henna from
Antipater [of Sidon]; he added Syrian spikenard, the poet we sing
of as 'the gift of Hermes' [i.e. Hermodoros]; and the wild flowers
of the corn-field, Poseidippos and Hedylos, and the anemones of
Sikelidas [i.e. Asklepiades].

48 Yes, and the golden branch of the ever-divine Plato, everywhere
bright with his skill; together with Aratos who knew the stars,
cutting the first-grown branches from his heaven-high palm-tree.
And Chairemon's finely-petalled lotus, mixed with the wall-
flower of Phaidimos, and Antagoras' finely turning ox-eyes,
Theodoridas' sprouting, wine-loving thyme, and Phanias' corn-
flowers; and many recently written buds of others, together with
these early snowdrops of his own Muse. I bring the gift to my
friends, but the Muses' garland of sweet words is the common
property of all the initiated.

4.1

PHILIP

Introduction to his Garland

Picking for you flowers of Helikon, and cutting the first blossoms from the famous woods of Pieria, reaping the harvest of recent pages, I in my turn have woven a garland like Meleager's. My good Camillus, you know the fame of the older poets; appreciate now these short poems by younger poets. Antipater [of Thessalonika] will adorn the garland like a corn-ear, Krinagoras like ivy-berries; Antiphilos will shine like a bunch of grapes, Tullius [probably Tullius Geminus] like clover, Philodemos like marjoram, Parmenion like myrtle, Antiphanes like a rose. Automedon is ivy, Zonas lilies, Bianor the oak-leaf, Antigonos the olive and Diodoros a violet. Weave in bay for Euenos, and compare the others to whatever newly-grown flowers you like.

4.2

AGATHIAS

From his Introduction to the Cycle

Agathias' proem is preceded by a prefatory note in the manuscripts: 'A collection of new epigrams presented in Constantinople to Theodoros the Decurion, son of Kosmas. The proems were spoken after the frequent poetry readings held at that time.' The first forty lines of Agathias' proem compare his anthology to a feast of different courses, designed to whet even the most jaded literary appetites. He says, 'I introduce a small portion from each poet, enough to taste; if you want to try all the rest, and take your fill, you must find it in the market.' This is followed by some sixty lines in praise of the Emperor Justinian. The proem concludes:

98   So, now that everything is full of beloved peace, now that the
hopes of revolutionaries at home and abroad have been shattered

by our Emperor, come, blessed Theodoros, let us start a poetry competition, with the festivities of song and dance. I have performed this task for you; for you I prepared this literary work, collecting in one book the merchandise of the far-ranging bee; gathering such a widespread collection of flowers of elegiac poetry, I fitted them into a wreath of poetic eloquence for you – as if I were offering beech-leaves to Zeus, ships to Poseidon the Earth-shaker, a breast-plate to Ares, a quiver to Apollo, a lyre to Hermes and grapes to Dionysos. For I know that the name of Theodoros will establish eternal fame for this work I have laboured at.

113 First I would choose for you, competing with earlier poets, all that the fathers of the new poetry wrote and dedicated to the old gods. It was fitting to adhere to the fine model of ancient literature.

117 Then comes a more ambitious collection of all that our pens wrote either for particular places, or for well-made statues, or for other widely distributed works of painstaking art.

121 The third starting-point of the new book is occupied, as far as is right, by what God allowed us to write in verse for tombs, while adhering to the truth.

124 For what we wrote on the devious paths of life, and the fluctuating scales of inconstant Fortune, see the fourth part of the book.

127 And perhaps you will enjoy the charm of a fifth contest, where we abusively wrote scurrilous verse. Kytherea may steal the sixth book and turn our journey aside for elegiac discourse and sweet eroticism. In a seventh honeycomb you will find the pleasures of Bakchos, drunken dancing, wine, cups and rich banquets.

4.3, lines 98–133

A Poem by Palladas (11.381)

Πᾶσα γυνὴ χόλος ἐστίν· ἔχει δ'ἀγαθὰς δύω ὥρας,
τὴν μίαν ἐν θαλάμῳ, τὴν μίαν ἐν θανάτῳ.

$$\underset{\times}{} \quad - \quad \times \quad - \quad \times \quad - \quad \times \quad - \quad \underset{\times}{} \quad \underset{\times}{}$$

Pasa gyné cholos estin: echei d'agathas du(o) horas,

$$- \quad \times \quad - \quad \times \quad - \quad - \quad \times \quad - \quad \times \quad -$$

tén mian en thalamo, | tén mian en thanato.

× = syllables naturally stressed in speech
— = syllables long in quantity

Every woman $\left. {\text{a-gall} \atop \text{cause-of-anger}} \right\}$ is: she-has, though, good two seasons,
the one in bedroom, the one in death.

This neatly constructed epigram, with its emphatic near-rhyme, must be one of the most translated of poems from The Greek Anthology. I present here, without comment, a number of modern versions for comparison, to illustrate the various possibilities which even such a short and simple Greek poem affords. Tony Harrison's version is included in the main text (no. 665).

> Woman? Oh, woman is a consummate rage,
> but dead, or asleep, she pleases.
> Take her. She has two excellent seasons.
> EZRA POUND (pub. 1915, Lustra)

> *Praise of Women*
>
> Only twice is womankind
> Anything but an affliction:
> [1] in bride-bed
> &
> [2] in the grave.
> DUDLEY FITTS (pub. 1938)

Her Glorious Hour

A woman will gnaw at your bile
Yet she has two fine seasons:
    one, in her bridal bed;
    two, when she is dead.
WILLIS BARNSTONE (pub. 1962)

Every woman is annoying,
Yet twice she's ripe and red:
The first time when she's marrying,
The second when she's dead.
ANDREW SINCLAIR (pub. 1967)

Women are a curse:
    they may be good in bed
    they are much better dead.
ANDRÉ LEFEVERE (pub. 1970)

A woman is a maddening creature
and gives pleasure twice at most,
once when she gives up her virtue,
once when she gives up the ghost.
ROBIN SKELTON (pub. 1971)

A wife will always anger you, but brings
two gifts: her first love and last gasp.
ADRIAN WRIGHT 1970

Notes

Poem

5 The Greek is in hexameters.

7 Also in hexameters.

10 Two versions of this epitaph were current in antiquity: the one ending *rhēmasi peithomenoi* is translated here. *peithomenoi nomimois* ('obeying their laws') is the less well-attested alternative, and is translated by Cicero:

> Dic hospes Spartae nos te hic vidisse iacentes
> dum sanctis patriae legibus obsequimur.

17 *Hospitable Seas* is perhaps an over-translation of 'Euxine Sea', but that is what the name means; the irony is surely intended.

23 According to Athenaios, this piece was by Aischylos himself. The anonymous 'Life of Aischylos' says that the people of Gela had it inscribed on his tomb.

29 An interesting discussion on the authenticity of this and the other poems ascribed to Plato appears in Chapter 8 of C. M. Bowra's *Problems in Greek Poetry* (1953).

38 A Lerian version of the poem by Phokylides (no. 6), removing the slur on the Lerians.

41–4 are all inscriptions of the sixth century B.C., from Attica.

46 About 410 B.C. The Greek is an elegiac couplet plus a hexameter. The stele, headed *Amphareté* (the dead woman's name), can be seen in the Keramikos Museum in Athens.

48 An inscription of the fourth century B.C.

50 According to the Byzantine historian Olympiodoros, this couplet was inscribed on Plato's tomb. He died in 347 B.C. Diogenes Laertios used the couplet in his four-line poem on Plato.

66 *Zeus:* the reference is to the god's visitation of Danaé (see Glossary). 'The god who was your lord' is, of course, Eros. The opening lines are given point by Zeus' traditional role as god of the weather.

67 The disappointed lover leaves the garland he had brought to the party hanging at his boy-friend's door.

69 *tiny lusts:* the Erōtes.

381

76 Arkheanassa was reputed to have been Plato's mistress. An alternative version of the poem, ascribed to Plato himself, was also in circulation:

> Arkheanassa of Kolophon is my mistress,
> Even her wrinkles are set with love's bitterness.
> You who encountered her beauty's maiden voyage,
> Men in distress – through what a furnace you passed!

> (Plato, *E5*; tr. Peter Jay)

78 *Cleopatra:* the sister of Alexander the Great. She married Alexander of Epiros, and ruled Epiros after his death in 330, but later returned to Macedon. Her brother died in 323; she was murdered in Sardis in 308, having spent her last years there.

82 *Deathless Ones:* the Muses and Graces, who are named in the Greek.

87 The shrine of Arsinoë-Aphrodite at Zephyrion was probably built before her death in 270.

88 The text of this satirical mock-epitaph is corrupt and very obscure; the version is based on explanations offered by Gow and Page in their commentary.

89 On a monument at Naukratis to Doricha, mistress of Sappho's brother Charaxos. Sappho fr. 15b is about her.

92 *lesbion:* a kind of drinking-cup.

93 Ktesibios was a famous mechanical engineer, and inventor of the hydraulic organ. His Bes-shaped *rhyton* (wine-jar), which produced a note when poured from, was dedicated in the shrine of Arsinoë.

95 A rather enigmatic compliment to a heavy-drinking poet. No poet by the name of Sokles is known.
   our man from Sicily: Sikelides, i.e. Asklepiades.
   more solid is he: his poetry is weightier in style (?)

96 The fourth of the Greek's six lines is lacking.
   Proteus: the precise point of the reference is obscure, but the sense is that Agis' ingenuity in getting at food is unstoppable; he would do anything. There was a famous fish-cook from Rhodes called Agis, who may be the victim of this epigram.

107 *The Ripper:* this serves both as a literal translation, and to parallel

the reference in the Greek *Sinis* to the name of an Isthmian criminal.

110 Goats were sacrificed to Dionysos, though bulls were the god's more usual fare. The poem describes some work of art in which the connection between god and goat would have been clear.

123 The Greek is in alternate iambic trimeters and hendecasyllables.

124 The metre of the even-numbered lines of the Greek is Pherecratean, with trochaic tetrameters in lines 1, 5 and 9, and iambic trimeters in 3 and 7.

142 *Lysanias . . . :* these lines may well be a later addition; there is a complete epigram without them.

144 The Megarians became proverbial for hardly being on the map when they asked the Delphic Oracle the question, 'Who will become more powerful?' The Oracle ended its catalogue of the merits of various cities with the crushing comment, 'But you Megarians will be neither third, fourth nor even twelfth in reputation or rank.'

147 The quotation from Isaiah is remarkably close to Kallimachos' phrase.

148 The Greek is in iambic tetrameters.

151 The version of the last line paraphrases the most probable explanation of a disputed phrase.

152 *Nightingales:* the title of a collection of poems by Herakleitos.

158 *On the Soul:* Plato's *Phaido.*

160 Theaitetos is probably the poet of no. 141. The exact point of the first line is unclear: *katharēn* might mean not 'virgin' but 'unobstructed', in the sense that he took to non-competitive writing. The poem was probably written after some failure by Theaitetos in a Dionysiac poetry competition.

163 Ritual hair-cutting marked the transition from boyhood to young manhood.

Acharnian ivy: the prayer is that the boy will be a successful dramatic poet. The winner's crown at Dionysiac festivals was made of ivy, which was supposed to have first grown at Acharnai.

164 *Icarian:* the Icarian sea is that between Ikaros (Doliche being the island's older name) and Mykonos.

Dryopian: may refer to the region near Mt Oita, south of the

Spercheios river; the Dryopes came from those parts.

165 The Greek is in alternate hexameters and iambic trimeters.

167 The Greek is in iambic trimeters.

171 *Doros:* here probably the eponymous hero of the Dorians, the pre-classical race who settled in the Peloponnese. 'Daughters of Doros' would then mean 'Dorian nymphs'.

180 *Muse of Glut:* literally 'Pimpleian Muses'. Robert Graves sees the etymology of Pimpla, a mountain near Olympos, as connected with the verb *pimplēmi* (to fill).

191 *mid-Lybian waters:* the southern stretch of the Mediterranean.

193 There was a well-known cult in Sparta of an armed Aphrodite. The river Eurotas here symbolizes Sparta through which it flows.

209 The scene is Samos, whose Heraion (temple of Hera) was the largest Greek temple known to Herodotos in the fifth century B.C.

211 *Malta:* dogs from 'Melite' were very popular, but whether they were from the modern Malta or an island of the same name off Epiros is unknown.

218 The last two lines read literally : 'But why am I pointing out bones to dogs? Midas' reeds testify to what befalls tale-tellers' (Paton tr.). The phrase is reminiscent of Plato's in poem 30. The story is that Midas, who was given ass's ears because he preferred Pan's piping to Apollo's lyre-playing, concealed his ears from everyone except his barber – who entrusted the secret to a hole in the ground. The reeds which later covered the place revealed the secret when they were shaken by the wind. (The story is told by Ovid, *Metamorphoses* 11.180.) Here the point is that a secret, once disclosed – however privately – is bound to come out. The version follows Reitzenstein's suggestion that Dioskorides is also thinking of the *kalamos* (reed-pen) with which he writes.

220 Dedication of a fan to Aphrodite – probably in the temple at Zephyrion (cf. poem 93 above). The last couplet is corrupt in the Greek.

222 *Silenis:* the name is meant to suggest 'Silenos', the Falstaffian demi-god who was an attendant of Bakchos.

223 *Him Whom we speak well of:* Hades. The allusion is to Orpheus' persuasion of the god to allow him to bring his dead wife,

Eurydike, back from the underworld.

224 *Aeolian Thebes:* probably refers to Thebes in Phthiotis, a district of south-east Thessaly.

227 *Wine destroyed the Centaur:* refers to the proverbial story of the Centaurs' defeat by the Lapiths (cf. *Odyssey* 21.295). Philip here is 'one-eyed' – another Homeric allusion, this time to the Cyclops, Polyphemos, as a symbol of bestiality.

228 *Titus:* T. Quinctius Flamininus, victor over Philip V of Macedon at Kynoskephalai in 197 B.C.

247 Corinth was sacked by the Roman general L. Mummius in 146 B.C. *halcyons:* literally, 'halcyons of your sorrows', i.e. mourners of them – the halcyon being noted for its plaintive song.

249 *halcyon of Lysis:* i.e. a fine singer in the manner of Lysis. He was the first person to set obscene songs to music for public performance. Male 'Lysiode' singers appeared in cabaret in drag.

252 *maelids:* nymphs invented by Ezra Pound (cf. his poem based on Ibykos, 'The Spring), embodying the spirits of the apple-tree.

281 *Welsh shepherds:* literally, 'goat-mounting shepherds'.

292 Herodotos (1.82) tells the story of the battle between the Argives and Spartans for the town of Thyreai, *c.* 547 B.C. The two armies agreed to leave the fighting to 300 men of each side; all were killed except two Argives and one Spartan. A dispute followed over who had won; this led to a full battle, in which the Argives were defeated.

301 The Greek is in the form of a dialogue between Pan and a passer-by – though the passer-by only speaks five words.

302 *Violettas:* an anachronistic reference to Verdi's heroine.

303 The daughters of Pandion were Philomela and Prokne, who became a swallow (see n. 819).

306 Peter Porter writes, 'The parallel between the poet's idea of Epicureanism and today's varieties of Zen and Hare Krishna seems legitimate. . . . *Epicurus' Garden* is curiously like the name of a modern Underground magazine or club.'

310 Falsely ascribed to Plato.

311 Falsely ascribed to Anakreon.

316 188 B.C. is a likely date for this event: but see Gow and Page for alternative possibilities.

317 Falsely ascribed to Plato.

318 *Enobarbus* is from Shakespeare's *Antony and Cleopatra*, not from the Greek original of this poem.

332 *Naias:* here a girl's name, not the nymph.

333 Philodemos makes an etymological pun on his name: 'Philo-demos', 'lover of Demo'.

337 *Urges:* the Erōtes.

341 *Penchants:* the Pothoi, another name for the Erōtes.
    Xantho, Xantharia: both are diminutive forms of the name Xanthippé.

342 *Passions:* the Pothoi, see previous note.

347 *Piso:* L. Calpurnius Piso Caesoninus.
    Phaiacian fare: i.e. conversation more entertaining than the tales of his adventures which Odysseus told to the Phaiacians, when he was a guest of King Alkinoos.

348 *five talents:* equals 6,000 drachmas.

356 *Zeus the Finisher:* one of the god's most common cult-titles.

357 Written about 25 B.C.

358 *Eartha:* the Greek name, Gē, is the word for 'earth'.
    Inachos: the name is rare except in legend, where Inachos was the son of Okeanos and Tethys, and founder of Argos.

359 Written about 26–25 B.C. Seleukos was evidently a member of the diplomatic mission on which the poet served.

360 This must be one of his latest poems, written not before about A.D. 11.

361 The poem is possibly by Philip rather than Krinagoras.

362 Written about 27–25 B.C.

363 *Demeter's festival:* the Eleusinian Mysteries, in which Krinagoras had perhaps been initiated.
    the greater company: the common Greek euphemism for the dead.

364 Written in iambic trimeters; its companion-piece, 365, is in elegiacs. 'The practice of inscribing iambic and elegiac epitaphs on the two faces of a gravestone was quite common' (Gow and Page). These are, of course, parodies of the genre.

373 On an Athenian woman taken from Athens, perhaps in 86 B.C., when Sulla sacked the city.

374 *the priest of Rhea:* a *gallos*, or priest of Kybele.

375 *ivy:* see n. 163 above.

honey . . . wax tablets: the idea is that the wax will provide writing-tablets on which Sophokles' plays will be written.

379 The last line of the Greek is corrupt; the version is conjectural.

382 The dispute over Alkman's origins is still unresolved. The last line refers to the similar dispute over Homer's birthplace – cf. Antipater's poem (*AP* 16.296), one of several on the subject.

385 Pompeia here may be the daughter of Sextus Pompeius, wife of M. Licinius Crassus and mother-in-law of Antipater's patron, Piso. The slave-girl seems to have been freed by her mistress.

387 *both Dianas:* i.e. Diana (Artemis) in both her roles – as goddess of hunting and childbirth.

388 *Deserted islands:* these may be the Sporades, or some of the Cyclades.

390 *Pleiades setting:* late October or early November – the beginning of the season of winter storms at sea.

394 Amphipolis remained a Macedonian town for about 200 years after its capture by Philip in 358 B.C. It cannot have been wholly in ruins by this time, though it had lost much of its importance with the decline of the nearby gold and silver mines at Pangaios.

Hellespont: here used rather loosely – the Strymon runs out into the Thracian Sea.

Edonian: the Edōnes were a local people.

Phyllis: the legendary heroine of the district.

great prize of the Aegeidae: Kleon of Athens failed to capture the town from the Spartan general Brasidas during the Peloponnesian War, in 422 B.C.

396 The references are all to metamorphoses adopted by the gods for sexual purposes.

made of brass: exactly translates the unusual Greek idiom; 'brass' being northern slang for money.

397 *Europa:* here a personal name. Antipater makes his point by alluding to the story of Zeus' seduction of the legendary Europa, in the guise of a bull.

398 *Sharpies:* the 'Sharp Islands' (*Oxeiai*) are off the southern point of Akarnania.

408 *ivy:* see n. 163 above.

from his deme: from Acharnai. Aristophanes wrote a play called *The Acharnians.*

410 The Greek is in iambic trimeters.

421 Oil-lamps, the confidants of lovers, were said to 'sneeze' when they sputtered; the third sneeze was a good omen.

429 *Lyre, Crown:* i.e. the constellations Lyra and Corona Borealis. Ariadne was said to have been given a crown of seven stars by Bakchos, who was in love with her, after Theseus deserted her.

437 The Greek is in iambic trimeters.

448 The allusions are to three of Zeus' more spectacular sexual exploits – the rapes of Danaé, Europa and Leda.

450 *Sun's horses:* the Sun was supposed to be drawn through the sky in a chariot drawn by a team of horses with gold bridles.

454 Amphion built the walls of Thebes with his brother, Zethos. The stones rose into place to the sound of his lyre.

fell with the flute: alludes to the story that when Alexander the Great had Thebes destroyed in 335 B.C. he made the musician Ismenias play the flute. He is reputed to have spared only the house in which the poet Pindar was born.

458 Kallimachos and Aristarchos were regarded as prototypes of the pedantic textual critic. Erinna's poetry was generally admired at this time – the gibe is rather at the learned commentators on her work.

461 The Greek is in iambic trimeters, as also are poems 462, 464, 469 and 471.

469 *straight metres in lame bursts:* Hipponax specialized in choliambics, 'limping iambics' in which the iambic trimeter's last foot is a spondee (– –), producing a heavy, dragging effect.

470 Reviving trees with wine was a practice recorded by Pliny the Elder in his *Natural History* (12.8).

474 cf. n. 458 above.

acanthologizing: the Greek *akanthologoi* means, literally, 'thorn-gathering'. Lines 3–4 attack those poets and critics who indulged in pseudo-scientific and genealogical speculation.

490 *Ambrosia:* the food of the gods.

505 *the God of Cock:* Priapos.

506 In literal crib-form, the poem runs: 'The letter "Y" stands for
400; you, tender Lais, have twice that many years, crow-Hekabé,
grandmother of Sisyphos and sister of Deukalion. But dye your
white hair and say "papa" to everyone.' Crows and Hekabé were
proverbial for their longevity; Sisyphos and Deukalion symbolize
the prehistoric past. The point, if any, of the opening phrase is
obscure.

508 The rhyme echoes the Greek assonance: 'pleiona gar *dounai* tou
Dios ou *dynamai*'.

510 The Greek is a complex play on words: transliterated, it reads –

Hoi koris achri korou koresanto m(ou) – all' ekoresthen

achri korou k'autos | tous koris ekkorisas.

511 *The man:* Xerxes, who bridged the Hellespont with ships in 480
B.C. to transport his army for the invasion of Greece.

512 Pheidias or his pupil, Agorakritos, sculpted this statue from a
block of marble which the Persians brought with them. They had
intended to carve a trophy from it after defeating the Greeks.

514 I print the poem as an epitaph on an unknown seafarer. It could be
read, with Gow and Page, as an imaginary address by a passer-by
to the relic; they believe that the last two lines must be spoken in
the person of the skull, and suggest this dialogue for the first two
lines:

– 'Whose skull is this?' – 'A hard-working man's.' – 'Either
a merchant, or a fisher in the sea's confusion.'

I do not find the imperative 'Tell' absurd in my context, where
its metaphorical sense is clear enough.

516 *gold:* the Pactolos, which flowed through Sardis, was said to
contain gold-dust.

521 'These four lines are engraved above a portrait in relief with a
cithara of eleven strings on one side and a lyre of four strings on
the other. Below the portrait is another epigram of eight lines, and
under it the name PETRONIAE MUSAE.' (Mackail)

522 This inscription was found near Florence.

531 The Spartan military martyr Leonidas rejects an honour offered by

his Persian enemy. Herodotos' account (9.78) is rather different: 'When Leonidas was killed at Thermopylai, Xerxes and Mardonios had him beheaded and crucified.'

533 An expanded version of Lucilius' eight-line Greek poem.

539 *armed hoplites' race:* a race in which the runners wore the heavy armour of the hoplites (foot-soldiers).

547 'No excuse, but wantonness, for the quotations from Cotton and Rochester.' (Peter Porter)

550 Some of Odysseus' companions were drowned in punishment for having eaten the Oxen of the Sun on the island Trinacria (sometimes identified with Sicily).

556 *A halfpenny stuck . . . :* the fare, one obol, for transport by Charon across the Styx, was placed in the dead man's mouth before burial.

558 The Greek poem reads literally, 'Eutychides stole the god himself, by whom he was about to make an oath, saying "I can't swear by you."'

559 *The God of Thieves:* Hermes, who had winged feet.

563 The point is that Deukalion survived a devastating flood, and Phaëton was burned by a thunderbolt.

570 The Greek is in hexameters.

580 *five new pence:* ('the smallest coin today which is acceptable as a symbol of total meanness' – Peter Porter) here stands for the Greek 'six coppers'; there were eight to the obol.

583 The reader searching for a pun lost in the translation can be assured that nothing of the kind is lacking.

598 *and answer back:* the phrase is Homer's standard formula, 'addressing him' or 'answering him'.

599 Adding up the letters of the words *proktos* and *chrysos* as numerals produces a total of 1,570. The Greeks used the alphabet for numbers.

623 *the Deep-Sea-Lord:* Poseidon.

630 *Acindynus:* the name means 'taking no risks'.

640 The Greek is in iambic trimeters, as is poem 642.

651 The Greek play on *onos* (donkey) in *onon, ponon, oknon, oneiron* (a donkey, a labour, a delay, a dream) is irreproducible.

652 *alabarch:* official title of the Controller of Customs in Egypt.

659 The Greek is in iambic trimeters.

669 As 659.

671 Palladas is parodying the accent – and ignorance, since he gets the god's name wrong – of a Goth soldier.

672 The Christians melted down many statues from pagan temples.

673 Literally, 'Having lived a pound of years with toilsome grammar, I am sent to Hades as Senator of the Dead.' This means his age is seventy-two – a pound of gold was then coined in seventy-two pieces.

member for Necropolis: Bowra suggests that he belonged to some council of pagan affairs.

675 Literally, 'It is better to endure even a state of affairs [*tyche*] which is growing more slender, than the arrogance of those who get rich.'

677 The Greek is in iambic trimeters.

683 Naucratius appears to have died while fishing, by getting himself caught up while trying to extricate his net from a rock.

686 The play on Ceres/Cereal is in place of the Greek Bromos/Bromios.

687 The Greek is in hexameters.

688 *dolphins shall pasture . . . :* i.e. his reversal is as unexpected as this is improbable.

Black Forest: literally 'the forests of Erymanthos', a mountain in Arkadia.

698 *Lusts:* the Erōtes.

699 The Greek ladies have the names of different kinds of small boat.

704 A parody of the Judgement of Paris; the 'three famous seraphs' were Aphrodite, Athene and Hera. Paris was bribed to choose Aphrodite as the most beautiful of them, with the promise that he could then have the most beautiful woman in the world. He took Helen, wife of Menelaus of Sparta; his abduction of Helen on his return to Troy was the legendary cause of the Trojan War.

Melite: the lines on her are added by Alan Marshfield – the Greek text lacks a couplet here.

705 The Greek is in hexameters.

707 *against two:* i.e. Bakchos and Eros, symbolizing drink and lust.

724 *By cire you were perdu:* i.e. when the wax melted from his wings as he flew too near the sun.

729 The Greek is in hendecasyllables.

730 The Greek is a single hexameter.

731 The Greek is in iambic trimeters.

733 *broad back of the sea:* the phrase is a formula used by Homer.

758 The Greek is in iambic trimeters.

763 An inscription of the fifth century A.D.

767 'Dog' (*kyon*) was Diogenes' nickname; his philosophy came to be called Cynic from the adjective *kynikos*. The ferryman is Charon.

768 *Homer's beggar:* Iros, a beggar in the *Odyssey*.

769 The Nine Lyric Poets formed the Alexandrian canon of major lyric poets. *Siren* here probably means 'Muse', its sense in early lyric poetry. Alkman's nightingales are said to be *singing soprano*, because his choral lyric hymns were written for performance by girl-choirs.

778 The Greek is in iambic trimeters, as is poem 780.

781 Falsely ascribed to Hedylos.
    dissolver of limbs: the adjective *lysimelēs* which this translates is Sappho's favourite to describe sexual desire.

786 'Quoted in an anonymous argument to the Panathenaic oration of Aristides of Smyrna, the pupil of Herodes Atticus and friend of Marcus Aurelius, as having, however, been made not on him, but on a later rhetorician of the same name.' (Mackail)

792 Praxiteles' statue of Aphrodite at Knidos had a reputation as great as that of Michelangelo's David.

793 In the ms. copy in the Laurentian Library at Florence, the poem is headed 'An Oracle of Sarapis [given] to Timainetos'. The poem is very similar to *AP* 14.71, which is supposedly a Pythian oracle.

801 *of Cytherea's charms:* i.e. of all the charms of lovers which Aphrodite allows one to enjoy.

812 *the girls of Skyros:* Lykomedes, king of the island, was entrusted with the baby Achilles by his mother Thetis, who hoped, by hiding him away, to prevent him from going to the Trojan War, where she knew he was destined to be killed. Achilles lived on Skyros disguised as a young girl among the king's daughters, one of whom, Deidameia, later bore him a son, Neoptolemos.

813 *She of the Foam:* Aphrodite.

815 *Chryseomallus:* the name means 'golden-fleeced'.

819 *I did not cut that dead girl's tongue:* the Thracian king Tereus, husband of Prokne, cut out the tongue of his sister-in-law, Philomela, to prevent her accusing him of having raped her. Prokne's revenge was to murder her young son by Tereus, Itylos, and to serve him to Tereus for dinner. Further disasters were averted by the gods, who intervened to turn Philomela into a nightingale, Prokne into a swallow, Itylos into a sandpiper and Tereus into a hoopoe.

825 The Greek is in iambic trimeters.

833 Nothing is known of this Plato, unless he is by chance the author of poems 737 and 738.

846 *hospitable gods:* the gods of hospitality, notably Zeus.

847 *Zosimé:* the name means 'likely to survive'.

856–9 The poems collected in Book 1 of The Palatine Anthology are mainly copies of inscriptions in Byzantine churches.

859 The Greek is in hexameters.

861 The Greek is in iambic trimeters.

Meleager's Proem, *lines 5–14* The wax on Nossis' writing-tablets is seen as specially softened by Love's fire, since she wrote erotic poems.

hyacinth, which is vocal . . .: 'Meleager perhaps means that the markings on the petals had no significance until poets fitted a word to them and made the flower vocal.' (Gow and Page)

Anakreon: Meleager regrets that most of Anakreon's verse, being in lyric not elegiac metre, is disqualified from representation in the *Garland.*

Glossary

Information on the poets included in this book is given in the prefaces to their poems. The Glossary does not include names or places adequately explained where they occur in the text; nor personal names on which there is no information to be given.

All names are given in the form found in the text. Where names appear in both Greek and Latin spellings, the Greek form is given first in the Glossary, with cross-references where necessary. Further information to be found in the Notes is indicated by 'see n. 00'.

ABDERA A coastal town in Thrace.

ACHARNAI The largest Attic *deme* (administrative district). See n. 163.

ACHERON A river in Epiros, adopted in myth through Homer as one of the rivers of the underworld, which it often represents.

ACHILLES Son of Peleus and Thetis, the bravest and most famous of the Greeks in the Trojan War. He killed Hektor. See n. 812.

ACTIUM Town on the northern promontory of Akarnania, and scene of the naval battle of 31 B.C. in which Augustus defeated Antony and Cleopatra.

AEGEIDAE Literally 'the sons of Aegeus', king of Athens; hence 'Athenians'. See n. 394.

AEOLIA See Aiolis.

AGATHON Athenian tragic poet and friend of Plato, in whose *Symposion* he plays a part. Sokrates was said to have been in love with him.

AIGAI Macedonian town on the south-eastern coast of the Pallene peninsula; burial place of the Macedonian kings. There are also towns of the same name in Achaia and Euboia.

AIOLIS The territory of the northern group of Greek colonies in Asia Minor, from the Hellespont to the bay of Hermos. The Aiolians came from Boiotia and Thessaly *c.* 1000 B.C.

AITOLIA (AETOLIA) District east of Akarnania, north of the Gulf of Corinth.

AJAX Son of Telamon, and one of the leading Greek warriors in the Trojan War.

AKANTHOS Most probably the town in Chalkidike, though there are four other places with the same name.

AKARNANIA District on the south-western corner of northern Greece.

AKRAGAS Town in south-western Sicily, originally founded in 582 B.C. by the people of Gela. Now Agrigento.

ALEXANDRIA Founded by Alexander the Great after his conquest of Egypt in 331 B.C., it only became Egypt's capital some years later when Ptolemy I transferred the seat of government from Memphis. Under the Ptolemies in the third century it grew rapidly as a commercial, industrial and cultural centre with the greatest library of the ancient world.

ALKAIOS Lyric poet contemporary with Sappho, born about 620 B.C. in Mytilene, Lesbos. He was a bitter opponent of the Lesbian tyrannies of Myrsilos and Pittakos; many of the fragments of his verse deal with his hatred of them.

ALKIDES A patronymic of Herakles, q.v.

ALKMAN (ALCMAN) Choral lyric poet of the seventh century B.C., whose working life was spent at Sparta. It is disputed whether he was a Lydian from Sardis, or a Lakonian from Messoa. His poetry is written in a Doric vernacular.

ALPHEUS Largest river in the Peloponnese, it rises in south Arkadia and flows past Olympia to the Ionian Sea.

ALYATTES Lydian king, c. 610–560 B.C. A descendant of Gyges and father of Croesus.

AMARYNTHUS Village on the west coast of Euboia, and site of the temple of Artemis Amarynthia.

AMMON God of the city of Thebes in Egypt. His oracle at Siwa was well-known to the Greeks, who identified Ammon with Zeus. There was a legend that Alexander the Great was begotten by Ammon in the form of a snake.

AMPHION Son of Antiope and Zeus, abandoned by his mother and brought up by a shepherd. He was given a lyre by Hermes and became a musician with extraordinary powers. See n. 454.

AMPHIPOLIS Chief city on the north Aegean coast, situated on the river Strymon to the east of the Chalkidikean promontories. See n. 394.

ANDROMACHE Wife of Hektor of Troy. When Troy fell she was taken to Epiros by Neoptolemos as his slave.

ANDROMEDA Rescued by Perseus, whom she later married, from a sea-monster to which she was exposed, chained to a rock, in expiation of her mother's boast that she, Cassiopeia, was more beautiful than the Nereids. She became a constellation.

ANDROS Northernmost island of the Cyclades.

ANTAGORAS A Rhodian poet of the third century B.C., author of two extant epigrams. He was included in Meleager's *Garland*.

ANTIGONOS Poet from Karystos, author of one extant epigram. He was included in Philip's *Garland*.

ANTIGONOS GONATAS Lived *c*. 320–239 B.C. Son of Demetrios, he was conqueror and king of Macedon. His long reign re-established the country as a nation. He was a notable patron of the arts.

ANTIMACHOS Kolophonian poet and scholar, born *c*. 444 B.C. He was reputedly long-winded and involved, but as the originator of the narrative elegy was an important influence on the Alexandrian poets.

ANTIOCH Capital of Syria in the reign of Seleukos and his family, the Seleukids. Founded in 300 B.C. by Seleukos I.

ANTIOCHOS THE GREAT Antiochos III (241–187 B.C.) succeeded in 223 to a divided Seleukid Asian empire. His victorious eastern campaigns in 212–206 earned him the title 'the Great'. He made a secret alliance with Philip V of Macedon, but was defeated by the Romans when he invaded Greece.

APELLES Fourth-century B.C. painter, from Kolophon or Ephesos. He died in Kos in the early third century.

APHRODITE Goddess of love, beauty and fertility, born from the foam of the sea. In Homer she is the daughter of Zeus and Dione, and wife of the lame smith-god Hephaistos. Cults of Aphrodite at Paphos in Cyprus and at Kythera were especially important; hence her names 'Paphia', 'Kypris' and 'Kytherea'.

APOLLO God of music, poetry and prophecy. In art he represents an ideal type of youthful male beauty. His oracular shrine at Delphi was the centre of his most important cult.

APOLLONIOS OF RHODES Epic poet, *c*. 295–240 B.C., author of the

Argonautika. He was Head Librarian at Alexandria *c.* 260–247. See preface to Kallimachos.

APOLLONIS Wife of Attalos (see entry on Pergamon), mother of Attalos II and Eumenes, who erected a monument at Kyzikos to her. This monument was inscribed with the epigrams which form Book 3 of The Greek Anthology.

ARATOS (ARATUS) Poet from Soloi, *c.* 315–240 B.C., patronized by Antigonos Gonatas. His *Phainomena* is extant; it was highly influential and popular, and was translated by four Roman poets including Cicero. Two epigrams are extant; he was included in Meleager's *Garland.*

ARCTURUS Star near the tail of the Great Bear. Its rising and setting were regarded as portents of storms.

ARES God of war; son of Zeus and Hera. He loved Aphrodite.

ARGOLIAN Adjective of the region, the Argolis, which surrounds Argos in the Peloponnese.

ARIADNE See n. 429.

ARISTARCHOS Scholar and textual critic from Samothrace, *c.* 217–145 B.C. Became Head of the Alexandrian library *c.* 153 B.C. See n. 458.

ARISTOPHANES The famous Athenian comic poet, *c.* 450–385 B.C. Eleven of his plays are extant, and remain as popular as ever. They were banned by the military regime which took power in Greece in 1967.

ARKADIA Mountainous area of the central and west-central Peloponnese.

ARKHEANASSA See n. 10.

ARSINOË Arsinoë II, *c.* 316–270, daughter of Ptolemy I and Bereniké I, was sister and wife of Ptolemy Philadelphos. She married him after fleeing to Egypt in about 276; it was her third marriage. After her death she was worshipped as Arsinoë-Aphrodite and had a shrine at Zephyrion. See n. 87.

ARTEMIS Goddess of hunting and childbirth.

ASCRA Boiotian town at the foot of Mount Helikon; birthplace of Hesiod.

ASKALON Syrian town on the Mediterranean coast, west of Jerusalem.

ASKLEPIOS (ASCLEPIUS) God of healing and medicine.

ASTARTE Syrian goddess, often identified by the Greeks with Aphrodite.

ATHENAIOS Author of the *Deipnosophistae* ('Doctors at Dinner'), a long miscellany, still extant, in the form of a symposium. He completed it in about A.D. 192; he lived at Naukratis in Egypt.

ATHENE (ATHENA) Virgin goddess, patron of Athens. She was the goddess of arts and crafts, and women's work in general.

ATLAS In mythology he was a Titan; in Homer, the guardian of the pillars of heaven, and later the propper-up of the sky. He became identified with the mountain-range of the same name in north-west Africa.

ATTICA The easternmost part of central Greece, Attica is the promontory west of southern Euboia. It is separated from Boiotia by Mt Parnes.

ATTICUS, T. POMPONIUS Wealthy friend and correspondent of Cicero, whose letters to him are extant.

BABYLON Town on the Euphrates; ancient capital of the southern kingdom of Mesopotamia. It was conquered by the Persians under Cyrus in 538 B.C. and was visited and described by Herodotos. Alexander the Great died there in 323 B.C.

BAKCHOS (BACCHUS) Another name for Dionysos, q.v.

BAKCHYLIDES Lyric poet of the fifth century B.C., nephew of Simonides. Some of his odes and dithyrambs were rediscovered in 1896. Two of his epigrams are extant; he was included in Meleager's *Garland*.

BASIL Christian writer, *c.* A.D. 330–79, who lived at Caesarea in Cappadocia.

BATHYLLUS A Samian boy, loved by Polykrates and Anakreon.

BATTIADES Kallimachos' patronymic, meaning 'son of Battos'.

BERENIKÉ Bereniké II, born *c.* 273 B.C., married Ptolemy III in 247. He named a star 'Bereniké's Lock' after her; Kallimachos wrote a long poem on the subject, which was imitated by Catullus. She was murdered by her eldest son and joint ruler Ptolemy IV in 221, after her husband's death.

BERYTOS Phoenician town, now Beirut. It was famous for its law school which opened in the third century A.D.

BES A pot-bellied dwarf-like Egyptian god, often pictured dancing.

BITHYNIA Country of north Asia Minor, on the coast of the Black Sea.

BOIOTIA District of central Greece, bordering on Attica.

BOÖTES Constellation near Ursa Major.

BOURA Achaian town, once destroyed by an earthquake.

BRASIDAS Spartan general during the Peloponnesian War, who died in 422 B.C. from wounds received in his victorious battle against the Athenians under Kleon at Amphipolis.

BROMIUS Dionysos.

BUPALUS Sculptor from Klazomenai. Together with his brother he made a caricature statue of the poet Hipponax. The story is that they were driven to suicide by the poet's resultant lampoons – some fragments of which remain.

BYZANTIUM Founded by Megarians in 667 B.C. in a strategic position at the entrance to the Black Sea, Byzantium was captured by the Persians in Darius' time, and was successively under Athenian, Macedonian and Roman jurisdiction. In A.D. 330 it was officially refounded by Constantine as the Christian capital of the Eastern Empire. He named it 'New Rome', but it was known as Constantinople – Constantine's city. With the decline of the Western Empire, the city grew in importance as the centre of a civilization which preserved a great deal of the Greek heritage.

CALLICRATES A Samian admiral, who dedicated statues of Ptolemy Philadelphos and Arsinoë at Olympia. He was himself honoured together with them at Samos.

CALLIOPE One of the nine Muses, she presided over heroic and epic poetry.

CAMILLUS The dedicatee of Philip's *Garland*; for a discussion of his identity, see Gow and Page, *The Garland of Philip*.

CAPPADOCIA At one time the whole area from the Black Sea south to Cilicia. Its northern part later became Pontus.

CARIA See Karia.

CATULLUS See Introduction, p. 14.

CATULUS, Q. LUTATIUS Consul in 102 B.C. and colleague of Marius in the defence of Italy against the Cimbri; he committed suicide in 87 after being proscribed by the Marians. He wrote Latin epigrams, two of which survive.

CENTAURS Mythical tribe of lustful creatures, half man and half horse, given to excessive drinking. Their famous fight with the Lapiths began when one of them, Eurytion, drunkenly attempted to rape a Lapith woman. The Centaurs were routed.

CERBERUS Three-headed dog who guarded the entrance to the under-world.

CHALKIDIKE The southern peninsula of Macedonia, ending in the three promontories of Pallene, Sithonia and Akte.

CHALKIS Euboia's most important town.

CHARAXUS Brother of the poet Sappho; he loved the courtesan Doricha. Herodotos tells the story of this affair (2.135); a few of Sappho's fragments allude to it.

CHARON The old ferryman who for an obol took the dead across the rivers of the underworld.

CHRYSOSTOM Greek Christian writer, c. A.D. 350–407.

CICERO, MARCUS TULLIUS Roman lawyer, orator and statesman (106–43 B.C.). Many letters, speeches and other prose works are extant; he also translated Greek poetry and himself wrote poems. See n. 10.

CILICIA District of south Asia Minor, on the Mediterranean coast opposite Cyprus.

CLEANTHES Stoic philosopher (331–232 B.C.) and disciple of Zeno. His *Hymn to Zeus* is extant.

CLEOPATRA See n. 78.

CLEOPATRA-SELENE Daughter of Antony and Cleopatra, born c. 40 B.C. She married Juba, King of Mauretania (a country of north-west Africa), and seems to have divorced and remarried him. She died in about A.D. 11.

CONSTANTINOPLE See Byzantium.

CORCYRA Now Corfu, an island off the coast of Epiros.

CORINTH City on the isthmus between the Peloponnese and central Greece. See n. 247.

COS See Kos.

CRATERUS A sophist – professor of rhetoric.

CROESUS Son of Alyattes, and the last king of Lydia; he reigned c. 560–546 B.C. He was defeated by Cyrus and the Persians, who captured Sardis. His wealth was proverbial.

CROWN, THE See n. 429.

CUPID, CUPIDS See Eros, Erōtes.

CYCLADES The chain of islands clustered round Delos, which run in a south-easterly line from the Attic peninsula.

CYLLENE A mountain in Arkadia.

CYPRIS Aphrodite.

CYRENE See Kyrene.

CYTHEREA Aphrodite.

DANAÉ Daughter of Akrisios, king of Argos. She was locked away in a bronze cell by her father, who had learnt from an oracle that his daughter's son would kill him. Zeus managed to effect her impregnation, having penetrated the cell in the form of a golden shower. Danaé duly had a son, Perseus, who returned from exile to fulfil the oracle accidentally, by hitting Akrisios with a misthrown discus.

DAPHNIS A mythological Sicilian shepherd, son of Hermes. There are two stories: (1) that he was loved by a nymph who required total fidelity, and who blinded him after he succumbed to a combination of an amorous princess and a quantity of wine. He invented pastoral music, which he played to console himself. (2) Theokritos' version is that he was determined to love no one; Aphrodite punished him by making him fall in love. He defied her to the end and died of unsatisfied longing; everyone, including Aphrodite, mourned him. Pan had taught him to sing and play the pipe.

DARIUS THE GREAT Darius I was King of Persia from 521–486 B.C. His attempted invasion of Greece was halted at Marathon in 490 B.C.

DELOS Small but influential island, regarded as the centre of the Cyclades; birthplace of Apollo and Artemis. During the Persian wars Delos was the administrative centre of a confederacy of Greek states. It was under Athenian jurisdiction until 314 B.C.

DELPHI On the slopes of Parnassos, Delphi was Greece's most important religious centre, famous for its temple of Apollo and the oracle. The Pythian Games were held there.

DEMETER Corn-goddess; in mythology the mother-in-law of Hades or Pluto, who married Koré, or Persephone. The Eleusinian Mysteries with which Demeter was associated are connected with the return to earth of Koré, i.e. the death and rebirth of crops.

DEUCALION Son of Prometheus. A Greek Noah, who survived Zeus' prehistoric floods by building an ark. See n. 563.

DIANA Italian goddess equivalent to Artemis.

DIOGENES Founder of the Cynic movement, he lived in poverty at Athens *c.* 400–325 B.C. He preached self-sufficiency, self-discipline and lack of shame – what is natural cannot be dishonourable – as the path to happiness. See n. 767.

DION Friend of Plato, a relative and minister of Dionysios I of Syracuse. Born *c.* 408, he left Syracuse for Athens in 366, but later returned to capture it with a small army. His attempt at introducing a Platonic constitution failed, and he became a tyrant in spite of himself. He was assassinated in 354 B.C.

DIONYSOS (DIONYSUS) God of an ecstatic religion, whose cult was widespread (cf. Euripides' *Bakchai*). Also a god of fruit, and hence wine.

DIS A god of the Gauls, equivalent to Pluto.

DOLICHE Aegean island, also called Ikaros. See n. 164.

DOMITIAN Son of Vespasian, he lived A.D. 51–96 and was Roman Emperor from 81. In the last years of his reign he abandoned firm rule for outright terrorism.

DORICHA Mistress of Sappho's brother Charaxos. See. n. 89.

DOROS See n. 171.

DRAKANOS The mountain where Zeus delivered Bakchos from his thigh.

DRYADS Nymphs who were tree-spirits.

ECBATANA Persian town; the summer capital of the Achaimenid empire of Cyrus and Darius. Captured by Alexander the Great in 330 B.C.

EËTION A sculptor, perhaps the same person as the artist who painted the wedding of Alexander the Great and Roxana in 327 B.C.

EILEITHYIA Goddess of birth, sometimes identified with Hera or Artemis.

ELAIA An Aiolian coastal town.

ELEUSIS Town in Attica, home of the mysteries in honour of Demeter and Persephone.

ELEUTHERNE Town in Crete, near the centre of the north coast.

ELEUTHO Eileithyia, q.v.

EMATHIA Old name for Macedonia and Thessaly.

ENDYMION A beautiful youth, loved by the Moon. At his request Zeus granted him eternal youth and everlasting sleep.

ENYALIOS Ares, q.v.

EPAMINONDAS Theban statesman and general, who defeated the Spartans at Leuktra and in 370 B.C. helped the Arkadians against the Spartans. He died in 362.

EPHESOS City of Asia Minor famous for its temple of Artemis. *Acts* XIX describes the Ephesos of the mid-first century A.D.

EPICHARMUS Sicilian writer of comedy, *c.* 530–440 B.C.

EPICURUS Athenian philosopher (341–271 B.C.) who founded a school known as 'The Garden'. His influential philosophy is expounded in Lucretius' poem *De Rerum Natura*, and – through Philodemos – influenced Roman writers such as Horace.

EPIKTETOS Stoic philosopher, *c.* A.D. 55–135, from Phrygia. He taught in Rome until Domitian banished the philosophers in 89, when he went to Nikopolis in Epiros.

EPIROS A large country of north-western Greece.

ERETRIA City in Euboia, an important trade centre.

EROS, ERŌTES Eros is the god of physical love: he is young and playful. In Hellenistic poetry he has a bow and arrows, and sometimes appears not as a single god, but a plurality.

EUBOIA (EUBOEA) The long island stretching along the east coast of mainland Greece, facing Attica, Boiotia and Lokris.

EURIPIDES Athenian playwright and poet, *c.* 485–406 B.C. Nineteen of his plays are extant.

EUROPA Daughter of a Tyrian king, she was loved by Zeus who, in the guise of a bull, enticed the young girl onto his back, and then carried her over the sea to Crete.

EUROTAS The river which flows through Sparta.

EURYPYLE A girl loved by Anakreon.

EUXINE SEA The Black Sea. See n. 17.

FURIES Latin equivalent of the Erinyes, the avenging spirits who punished wrongs done to kindred – especially murders.

GLOSSARY

GADARA There were two Syrian towns of this name, one near the coast by Askalon, the other just south-east of the Sea of Galilee. The latter, a culturally Greek town, is the birthplace of Meleager and Philodemos (despite Strabo's testimony: see H. Ouvré, *Méléagre de Gadara*, Chapter I).

GAIUS Born A.D. 12, he was Roman Emperor from 37 until his assassination in 41. Nicknamed Caligula (Little Boots) when, as a baby, he was taken on a campaign by his father Germanicus Caesar. As Emperor he was cruel and autocratic.

GALLUS, CORNELIUS Roman lyric poet, *c.* 69–26 B.C. He became governor of Egypt after helping Octavian to defeat Antony and Cleopatra. He was a friend of Vergil, whose tenth Eclogue is dedicated to him. None of the works of this outstanding love-elegist has survived.

GANYMEDE A lad carried off by an eagle to be Zeus' cup-bearer.

GEA The earth personified.

GELA A town founded by Cretans and Rhodians in southern Sicily.

GEMINUS, TULLIUS Author of nine epigrams in The Greek Anthology – not represented here.

GERMANICUS JULIUS CAESAR Roman general, 15 B.C.–A.D. 19. He was a poet and translator of considerable reputation. His brother was the emperor Claudius, and he was adopted by Tiberius as his heir. A popular though none too successful army commander, he was recalled from his German campaign and posted to Asia; he died at Antioch under mysterious circumstances, probably having been poisoned by Cn. Piso, Tiberius' governor of Syria.

GLAUKOS Ovid (*Metamorphoses* 13.920 ff.) gives one of several versions of how Glaukos became immortal by a magic herb, and then became a sea-god after leaping into the sea.

GLYKON A famous pankratiast (all-in-wrestler), mentioned also by Horace, *Epodes* 1.1.30.

GORTYN An important town in the southern central plain of Crete.

GRACES Goddesses personifying charm, grace, and beauty, both physical and intellectual. They are daughters of Zeus.

GYGES King of Lydia, *c.* 685–657 B.C. He was the first ruler to be called 'tyrant'. Coinage was invented in Lydia during his reign.

HADES Son of Kronos, lord of the underworld; his name means 'the unseen'. He is a person, not a place – the dead go 'to Hades' [residence]'. Though a grim god, he is not satanic or evil. See also Pluto.

HALIKARNASSOS Karian town which had many Greek settlers. Home of Herodotos and site of the once-famous Mausoleum.

HEKABÉ In her Latin form, Hecuba. Wife of Priam of Troy, and mother of Hektor and Paris. Euripides' play tells the story of her last days.

HEKALÉ Lost mythological narrative poem, about 1,000 lines long, by Kallimachos.

HEKTOR (HECTOR) Eldest son of Priam and Hekabé, and the leading Trojan warrior against the Greeks.

HELIADS Daughters of the Sun (Helios), changed into poplars by the gods.

HELIKE An Achaian town on the bay of Corinth.

HELIKON (HELICON) The largest Boiotian mountain, nearly 6,000 feet, sacred to the Muses. There was a sanctuary of the Muses near the summit.

HELLAS Greece, in the sense of the culturally Greek world.

HELLESPONT The Dardanelles – the straits dividing Europe from Asia and the Aegean from the Propontis (Marmara) and the Black Sea.

HERA Goddess of marriage and the sexual life of women. Child of Kronos and Rhea, she is the wife of Zeus and mother of Ares, Eileithyia and Hephaistos, among others.

HERAKLES (HERACLES, HERCULES) The most popular of Greek heroes (not a god). He accomplished the twelve labours set by Eurystheus, and was proverbial for physical strength.

HERCULANEUM The town near Naples buried by the eruption of Vesuvius in A.D. 79.

HERMES A young god with winged feet, son of Zeus and Maia (or Maias). Messenger of the gods. Among his various minor functions he is the god of merchants and others who use roads, and god of thieves. The probable etymology of his name suggests that he was originally the spirit of stones set up by roadsides for magic purposes.

HERMIONE Daughter of Menelaus and Helen. Though engaged secretly to Orestes, she was forced to marry Pyrrhos, Achilles' son.

HERMODOROS Poet named in the Proem to Meleager's *Garland*. He has a dubious claim to one epigram not included here.

HERODOTOS Historian from Halikarnassos, *c.* 484–20 B.C., whose *History* relates the events leading up to Greece's war with Persia. It reflects his wide travels and great interests in the history and customs of the near-eastern world.

HESIOD Greek poet of the eighth century B.C., who lived at Askra near Mt Helikon. He wrote the *Works and Days* and *Theogony*, both extant.

HESPERIA Greek name for Italy, because it was a western land.

HESPERIS African town west of Kyrene, on the site of Bengazi.

HESPEROS The Evening Star, depicted in art as a boy carrying a torch.

HIERON Tyrant of Syracuse from 478 till his death in 466. Patron of philosophers and poets, including Pindar who wrote odes in honour of his victories in the Greek games.

HIPPARCHOS Younger son of Peisistratos, and co-tyrant of Athens with his brother Hippias. Patron of Anakreon and Simonides. He was assassinated in 514 B.C. by Harmodios and Aristogeiton.

HIPPOLYTUS Loved by Phaidra, he refused to comply with her advances. She committed suicide and accused him in her suicide note; her returning husband, Theseus, banished Hippolytus, who was killed while driving away in his chariot before Theseus learned the truth of his innocence.

HIPPONAX Poet from Ephesos who wrote satirical, colloquial verse in iambics. He lived in the late sixth century B.C. See n. 469.

HOMER Author of the *Iliad* and *Odyssey*; probably a bard of the ninth or eighth century B.C., who gave final shape to these oral heroic poems, many elements of which were traditional.

HORACE Q. Horatius Flaccus, 65–8 B.C., was the Roman poet who wrote the *Epodes* (iambic poems), two books of *Satires* (hexameter poems), four books of *Odes* (lyric poems), the *Carmen Saeculare* (a choral lyric hymn) and the *Epistles* (hexameter poems, mostly on philosophical, but some such as the *Ars Poetica* on literary themes).

HORUS Egyptian god, son of Isis and Sarapis.

HOURS, THE The *Hōrai*, goddesses of the Seasons.

HYMEN God of marriage; the wedding-chant 'O Hymen Hymenaie' was thought to invoke a god, Hymen or Hymenaios.

HYMETTOS Mountain near Athens, still famous for its bees and honey.

IBYKOS Erotic lyric poet of the sixth century B.C. from Rhegion. He left Italy for the court of Polykrates at Samos. He was said to have been killed by robbers.

ICARUS Son of Daidalos. With his father he escaped from King Minos' Crete by flying with wings built by Daidalos. He flew too near the sun, which melted the wax from his wings, and he drowned in the Aegean.

IKAROS An Aegean island, also called Doliche. See n. 164.

ILIAD, THE Homer's epic poem of the Trojan War.

ILION (ILIUM) Troy, q.v.

INACHOS See n. 358.

INO A daughter of Kadmos, she became a sea-goddess when with Melikertes, her son, she leapt into the sea to escape her husband, who had murdered her other son.

IONIA The central part of the west coast of Asia Minor, colonized by the Greeks.

IRENE Peace personified.

ISIS Egyptian goddess, wife of Osiris. Herodotos identified her with Demeter, but in the Hellenistic age she was identified with Aphrodite, Arsinoë (q.v.) and later Ptolemaic queens. She was addressed as a 'goddess of countless names'.

ISMAROS Mountain in Thrace; 'Ismarian' means Thracian.

ISTHMIAN GAMES International games held every other year at Corinth, in honour of Poseidon.

ISTHMOS, THE The isthmus which joins the Peloponnese to the rest of Greece.

ITYLOS See n. 819.

JUSTINIAN Roman Emperor of the East, A.D. 527–65. The West was recaptured by his generals, Belisarius and Narses. He codified the laws and built the great church of Santa Sophia at Constantinople, but his administration was reckless and oppressive.

KALLINOS Elegiac poet of the seventh century B.C., from Ephesos.

KARIA Country of Asia Minor, south of Ionia. Its main town was Halikarnassos.

KARYSTOS Town on the southern coast of Euboia.

KEOS An island in the Cyclades.

KLAZOMENAI Ionian coastal town west of Smyrna.

KNIDOS A Greek colony on the tip of the Karian promontory south of Kos.

KOKYTOS A river in Epiros, the etymology (*kokyein*, 'to lament') and proximity of which to Acheron made it one of the rivers of the underworld.

KORESSOS A hill near Ephesos.

KOS Island north-west of Rhodes, facing Halikarnassos and the Karian coast.

KRANTOR Philosopher from Soloi, *c.* 335–275 B.C. He wrote a commentary on Plato's *Timaios* and a book *On Grief.*

KRONOS Son of Heaven and Earth, leader of the Titans, his brothers. He was father of many of the Greek gods, and is thought to have been a god of the pre-Hellenic peoples of Greece.

KTESIBIOS See n. 93.

KYNOSKEPHALAI Thessalian town, where Philip V of Macedon was defeated by the Romans under Flamininus in 197 B.C.

KYPRIS Aphrodite.

KYRENE Port in north Africa, founded *c.* 630 B.C. by Greeks from the islands of Thera and Crete. Birthplace of Kallimachos.

KYZIKOS Town on the island of Arktonnesos in the Propontis.

LAKEDAIMON Official name of the township of Sparta.

LAKONIA District of the south-eastern Peloponnese. Its capital was Sparta.

LAMPSAKOS Coastal town facing the Chersonese at the entrance to the Propontis. Priapos was the chief local god.

LAPITHE Thessalian town, the site of which is not known.

LENAEAN GAMES Part of the Dionysiac festival of the Lenaia, celebrated in Athens early in the new year. It was mainly a dramatic festival.

LEONIDAS Spartan general. See under Thermopylai, and n. 531.

LEROS Island between Samos and Kos, off the Karian coast.

LESBOS Largest of the islands off the Aiolian coast; home of the lyric poets Sappho and Alkaios.

LETHE One of the rivers of the underworld, the waters of which were drunk by the dead, inducing forgetfulness (the word means 'oblivion').

LINDOS Chief town on the eastern coast of Rhodes.

LOKROI Dorian city in the toe of Italy, founded *c.* 700 B.C.

LUCAN Roman poet, A.D. 39–65, who wrote the unfinished epic poem *Bellum Civile* (or *Pharsalia*). At first patronized, then ostracized by Nero, he was forced to commit suicide when his complicity in Piso's plot against the emperor was discovered.

LUCINA Minor Roman goddess of childbirth, equivalent to Eileithyia.

LYDE A long mythological narrative poem in elegiac metre by Antimachos, q.v.

LYDIA A country of western Asia Minor, independent until Croesus' defeat by the Persians, when it became a Persian satrapy. Sardis was its capital.

LYKAIAN Descriptive of Pan, who had a shrine on the Arkadian mountain Lykaion.

LYKAMBES See preface to Archilochos.

LYRE, THE See n. 429.

LYRKOS Title of a miniature epic poem by Nikainetos, dealing with the adventures of the Karian king, Lyrkos.

LYSIS See n. 249.

MACEDON (MACEDONIA) Country linking the Balkans to the Greek peninsula. It became a great power under Philip II and Alexander the Great in the fourth century B.C., and was conquered by the Romans in 167 B.C.

MAIA (MAIAS) Daughter of Atlas and mother of Hermes by Zeus.

MALEIA Name of the south-eastern promontory of Lakonia; also of a promontory in Lesbos, and various places in Lakonia. In poem 299 it is probably a place in Arkadia near Psophis.

MALTA See n. 211.

MANES A Phrygian slave-name.

MARATHON A small town on the north-east Attic coast; scene of the first Greek victory over the Persians, in 490 B.C.

MARCELLUS, M. CLAUDIUS Lived 42–23 B.C. Son of Gaius Claudius Marcellus and Octavia, Augustus' sister, he was a possible successor to Augustus, whose daughter Julia he married in 25 B.C. The

Cantabria campaign, led by Augustus, was his first military service. His death inspired Propertius' elegy (3.18).

MARS Roman equivalent of Ares, the god of war.

MARSUS, DOMITIUS Latin epigrammatist, *c.* 54–4 B.C. A poem on the death of Tibullus has survived.

MARTIAL Roman epigrammatist, *c.* A.D. 40–104, from Bilbilis in Spain. Twelve books of his poems are still extant.

MAUSOLUS Ruler of Karia from 377–353 B.C. It was then under Persian control, but he managed to remain practically independent. The Mausoleum which he planned was completed at Halikarnassos after his death by his widow and sister Artemisia; it was destroyed by an earthquake, probably in the fifteenth century.

MEDES The Persians.

MEGALOPOLIS Arkadian town, founded *c.* 370–362 B.C. by Epaminondas.

MELANNIPIDES Poet named in the Proem to Meleager's *Garland*; none of his work survives.

MELIKERTES Son of Ino, q.v.

MEMNON Mythical Ethiopian king, son of Eōs (Dawn) and Tithonos. He went to help his uncle Priam in the defence of Troy, but was killed by Achilles, and then made immortal by Zeus.

MEMPHIS Main town of Lower Egypt.

MENEKRATES Poet included in Meleager's *Garland*, three of whose epigrams survive.

MENIPPUS Gadarene writer of the third century B.C., who wrote mainly on philosophical subjects in a light, popularizing manner. He wrote in a mixture of prose and verse, a form adopted by Meleager, Lucian and Varro.

MENIPPOS Greek geographer of the late first century B.C., from Pergamon. He wrote a geography of the Mediterranean in three books.

MEROË A city on the Nile, at the extremity of the then explored territory – about halfway down the Nile towards Lake Victoria.

MEROPIAN Of Kos: Merops was a legendary early king of the island.

MESSENE Town founded as the capital of Messenia, a district of the south-western Peloponnese, in 369 B.C.

MIDAS Legendary Phrygian king. See n. 218.

MILETOS Southernmost of the major Ionian cities of Asia Minor.

MIMNERMOS Seventh-century B.C. elegiac poet-musician from Kolophon. He wrote short reflective poems as well as historical and mythological verse.

MINOS Legendary early Cretan king and legislator, who became the judge of the underworld.

MITHRIDATES VI Known as 'the Great', king of Pontus. He was involved in three wars (the Mithridatic Wars) with the Romans over his expansionist policies in Asia. He died in 68 B.C.

MUMMIUS, L. Consul in 146 B.C., he led the Roman attack on the Greek Achaian League and destroyed Corinth.

MYCENAE Town in the Argive plain, at its greatest from c. 1400–1150 B.C., when the walls with the Lion Gate, the palace, and the vast beehive tombs were built. This early Mycenae, the legendary home of the family of Atreus, was destroyed by fire. There were towns on the site during the Greek and Hellenistic periods, but it never again achieved prominence, and was deserted by the time of Pausanias.

MYRINA An Aiolian coastal town.

MYRON Sculptor in bronze, active c. 480–445, some of whose work survives in later copies. His statue of a cow which stood in the agora at Athens occasioned no less than thirty-six epigrams in The Palatine Anthology.

MYSIA A country of north-western Asia Minor.

MYTILENE The capital of Lesbos.

NAIADS Water-nymphs, presiding over rivers and springs.

NAUKRATIS (NAUCRATIS) Town and trade centre on the Nile near Alexandria.

NAUPLIUS One of the Argonauts. To avenge the death of his son during the Trojan War, he lit beacons which drew the returning Greek fleet onto rocks off the Euboian coast, and shipwrecked them.

NAXOS Largest island of the Cyclades.

NAZIANZUS A town in south-west Cappadocia.

NEMEAN GAMES A festival held every other year at the sanctuary of Nemean Zeus in the valley near Kleonai, just south of Corinth.

NEMESIS Goddess of retribution.

NEOBOULÉ See preface to Archilochos.

NEOKLES Name of two distinct persons, one the father of Themistokles, the other of Epicurus.

NEOPTOLEMOS AIAKIDES In poem 168 not the son of Achilles, but a member of the Aiakid family of Epiros, who claimed descent from Aiakos, a son of Zeus.

NEOPTOLEMOS OF PARION Poet, scholar and critic of the third century B.C. His *Poetics* propounded the theory that the aim of poetry was 'to delight and to edify'; this treatise was the basis of Horace's *Ars Poetica*.

NEPTUNE Roman name for Poseidon, god of the sea.

NEREIDS Sea-nymphs, daughters of the sea-god Nereus.

NERO Roman Emperor A.D. 54–68, infamous for his extravagance and ruthlessness, yet genuinely devoted to the arts.

NESSUS One of the Centaurs, killed by Herakles after he attempted to rape Deianeira, Herakles' wife. The poisoned shirt Nessus gave her killed Herakles.

NESSUS, STRAITS OF The crossing between Thasos and the coast of Thrace, named after a Thracian river.

NESTOR An old man always giving advice or reminiscing, who appears in the *Iliad*. He kept his mental agility well into a proverbially long old age.

NICETES This may be the Greek rhetorician mentioned by Seneca the Elder.

NIKAIA Bithynian town (now Iznik) on the eastern shore of lake Askania in west Bithynia.

NIKOPOLIS Name of several towns throughout the Hellenistic world, one of which was a suburb to the east of Alexandria, where Octavian defeated Antony.

NIOBE The daughter of Tantalos who, according to Homer, had twelve children. She incurred the wrath of Apollo and Artemis by boasting about her fecundity.

NISYRUS Small island south of Kos; its volcanic rock was used for millstones.

NYMPHS General name for the female spirits of nature. Though daughters of Zeus, they are mortal. They represent the powers of mountains, waters, woods and trees, and are benevolent to men – with the exception of unresponsive lovers, such as Daphnis.

ODYSSEUS The Greek warrior and king of Ithaka, hero of the *Odyssey*.

ODYSSEY, THE Homer's epic poem which recounts the adventures of Odysseus and his companions on their return from Troy to Ithaka.

OLYMPUS The highest mountain in Greece, on the borders of Macedonia and Thessaly. It was the home of the gods.

ORCHOMENUS A Boiotian town, the burial-place of the poet Hesiod.

ORION A giant hunter, identified with the constellation of the same name.

ORPHEUS Legendary early lyric poet and musician, who could charm animals and stones with his song. He rescued his wife Eurydike from the underworld, but lost her by disobeying the condition that he should not look back before he had brought her up to earth's surface.

OSSA Mountain in Magnesia, the eastern coastal strip of Thessaly.

OVID Prolific Roman poet, 43 B.C.–*c.* A.D. 17, author of elegiac poems (*Amores, Heroides, Ars Amatoria,* etc.) and the great *Metamorphoses.* He died in exile at Tomis on the Black Sea.

PACTOLOS (PACTOLUS) Lydian river flowing from Mt Tmolos into the river Hermos, via Sardis. See n. 516.

PALLAS A title of Athene.

PAN Arkadian shepherd-god, half goat in form. Son of Hermes. He haunts mountains, caves, etc. – wherever flocks go; and plays the pipe.

PANDION King of Athens, father of Prokne and Philomela. See n. 819.

PANKRATES Poet named in the Proem to Meleager's *Garland*, author of three extant epigrams.

PAPHIA Aphrodite.

PAPHOS Town in Cyprus, notable for its great temple of Aphrodite.

PARIS Son of Priam and Hekabé, who had to judge which of the three goddesses, Hera, Athene and Aphrodite, was the most beautiful. He was bribed by Aphrodite, and his judgement was the legendary cause of the Trojan War. See n. 704.

PAROS Second largest island of the Cyclades; an important trade centre, famous for its marble. Home of Archilochos.

PARTHENIOS Greek novelist and poet from Nikaia, friend of Cornelius Gallus and Vergil. He wrote elegiac poems in the manner of Kallimachos.

PARTHENIS An unknown poet mentioned in the Proem to Meleager's *Garland* – but the reading of the text is doubtful and this name may be incorrect.

PAUSANIAS Writer and traveller of the second century A.D., author of the *Guide to Greece*.

PEDO Latin epigrammatist and friend of Ovid.

PEISISTRATIDS, THE Hipparchos and Hippias, the sons of Peisistratos. Hippias' rule became harsher after his brother's murder in 514 B.C.; he fled Athens when it was occupied by the Spartans, and went to the court of Darius. He was with the Persian forces at Marathon.

PEISISTRATOS Athenian statesman and tyrant of Athens from 560–527 B.C. He reformed the constitution of Solon.

PELIAS Usurping king of Iolchos who died when his daughters, impressed by Medea's magic which restored an old ram to a lamb when she cut it up and boiled it, tried the same treatment on their father. To avenge the wrongs done to her husband Jason by Pelias, Medea forgot her magic on this occasion.

PELLA Capital of Macedonia from *c.* 400–167 B.C. It stood by the lake of the Lydias river, by which the sea could be reached.

PELOPONNESE Literally, 'the island of Pelops': the southern part of Greece joined to central Greece by the Isthmos.

PERGAMON (PERGAMUM) Town about fifteen miles inland from the Aiolian coast, opposite Lesbos. It became very powerful under Attalos I (269–197 B.C.), who opposed Philip V of Macedon, and his successors.

PERIKLES Great Athenian statesman, *c.* 495–429 B.C.

PERSEPHONE A pre-Hellenic goddess, identified by the Greeks with the virgin daughter, Koré, of their corn-goddess Demeter. She was the wife of Hades, and spent half the year in the underworld. See also under Demeter.

PERSEUS Legendary hero, son of Zeus and Danaé (q.v.). He killed the Medusa, rescued and married Andromeda (q.v.), killed his father accidentally in Argos, and became king of Tiryns.

PERSIUS Roman Stoic poet, A.D. 34–62, author of six *Satires*.

PETRONIUS Author of the fragmentary novel *Satyricon* and a collection of poems. He committed suicide in A.D. 66.

PHAËNNOS Two epigrams by this third-century B.C. poet are extant. He was included in Meleager's *Garland*.

PHAËTON Son of Helios (the Sun). He died when he was allowed to drive the Sun's chariot, but could not control the team of horses; Zeus had to kill him with a thunderbolt to save the earth from destruction by fire. See n. 563.

PHAIDIMOS Elegiac poet of the third century B.C. He was included in Meleager's *Garland*, and four of his epigrams are extant. He also wrote a long poem, the *Herakleia*.

PHAIACIA See n. 347.

PHEIDIAS Athenian sculptor, *c.* 490–417, commissioned by Perikles to design the Parthenon sculpture.

PHILIP II King of Macedon 359–336 B.C., who laid the foundations of Macedon's power. His great political opponent at Athens was the orator Demosthenes.

PHILIP V See preface to Alkaios (p.119), and poem 233.

PHILOMELA See n. 819.

PHOEBUS A name of Apollo (it means 'the bright one').

PHRYGIA Country of Asia Minor, conquered by the Lydians and subject in turn to the Persians, Seleukids and Attalids of Pergamon.

PHYLLIS See n. 394.

PHYROMACHUS Playwright who lived in the second half of the fourth century B.C.

PINDAR Choral lyric poet, 518–438 B.C., from Kynoskephalai. His *Victory Odes* have survived complete, but a great deal of his poetry has been lost: there were seventeen books, of which the *Odes* form four.

PIRAEUS Promontory four miles from Athens, serving as its port.

PISO CAESONINUS, L. CALPURNIUS Patron of Philodemos, consul in 58 B.C. He was Julius Caesar's father-in-law.

PISO FRUGI, L. CALPURNIUS Son of Piso Caesoninus, he was patron of Antipater of Thessalonika. See preface to this Antipater.

PITANA A town on the Aiolian coast, about ten miles west of Elaia.

PITTALAKOS 'A notorious bad character at Athens, mentioned by Aeschines.' (W. R. Paton)

PLATAIA Town in south Boiotia between Mt Kithairon and the river Asopos. It was the scene of the Greek victory over the Persians led by Mardonios in 479 B.C.

PLAUTUS Roman comic poet-playwright, *c.* 254–184 B.C. Twenty-one of his plays survive.

PLEIADES The seven daughters of Atlas and Pleione, who became the constellation after their deaths.

PLUTO A name of Hades, meaning 'the rich one' – a god of earth's wealth.

POLYKLEITOS Poet named in the Proem to Meleager's *Garland*. None of his verse survives.

POLYKLEITOS Argive sculptor, contemporary with Pheidias and Myron; his work covers the period 450–400 B.C. He specialized in statues of Olympic victors, mainly in bronze.

POLYKRATES Became tyrant of Samos *c.* 540 B.C., and made it a great naval power. He organized many public works, and patronized poets and artists, but his political opportunism in attempting to preserve Samos' independence led to his assassination in about 522.

POLYSTRATOS Poet, contemporary with Antipater of Sidon. Two epigrams are extant; he was included in Meleager's *Garland*.

POLYXENA Daughter of Priam and Hekabé in mythology, though not in Homer. In some stories she is buried by Pyrrhos after being wounded at the fall of Troy; in others, she is sacrificed by him to the spirit of Achilles.

POMPEIA See n. 385.

PONTUS Large country of north-east Asia Minor, east of Bithynia on the coast of the Black Sea. See under Mithridates.

POSEIDON Greek god of earthquakes and water, especially the sea.

PRAXITELES Athenian sculptor of the mid fourth century B.C., famous for his much-copied Aphrodite at Knidos.

PRIAM King of Troy at the time of the Trojan War. Married Hekabé; Hektor and Paris were his sons, and Polyxena was his daughter.

PRIAPOS (PRIAPUS) Fertility god whose cult at Lampsakos spread to Greece and Italy. His symbol was the phallos; figures of him with a detachable phallos (ready for use as a truncheon against trespassers) were kept in gardens, where he combined the functions of a scarecrow and garden-god. As the Latin Priapean poems show, he was not taken too seriously. He was also a god of sailors.

PROKNE See n. 819.

PROKOPIOS Secretary to Justinian's general Belisarius, he wrote a *History of the Wars of Justinian*, and the *Secret History*, an attack on Justinian full of scandalous information.

PROMETHEUS An immortal demi-god and master-craftsman, who stole fire from the gods. Zeus punished him by chaining him to a rock where an eagle pecked at his liver daily. Herakles released him.

PROPERTIUS, SEXTUS Roman elegiac poet from Umbria, *c.* 50–16 B.C. Four books of his erotic and mythological elegies survive.

PROTEUS A sea-god who had, in Homer, the power of changing shape.

PSOPHIS Arkadian town near mount Erymanthos.

PSYCHE The soul personified, often represented as a butterfly. Being the seat of the emotions, she was tormented by Eros.

PTOLEMY EUERGETES A Macedonian king of Egypt, *c.* 182–116 B.C.

PTOLEMY PHILADELPHOS The second Macedonian king of Egypt, he lived *c.* 308–246 B.C. Son of Ptolemy I and Bereniké, he married Arsinoë I and later Arsinoë II. He built the Alexandrian Museum and Library.

PYGMALION Legendary king of Tyre, brother of Dido; or a king of Cyprus, who fell in love with a woman's statue, which was then given life by Aphrodite.

PYRRHO Founder of the Sceptic school of philosophy, he lived at Elis, *c.* 360–270 B.C.

PYRRHOS Son of Achilles and Deidameia, also called Neoptolemos. He either buried or killed Polyxena (q.v.). He was allotted Andromache when the Trojan prisoners were divided, and took her home as his mistress. He married Hermione (q.v.), who failed in an attempt to murder Andromache while Pyrrhos was at Delphi, where he was killed.

QUINTILIAN Roman teacher of rhetoric, born *c.* A.D. 35/40. His *Institutio Oratoria* ('Education of an Orator') survives; Book 10 is a survey of Greek and Latin literature.

RHAMNUS Town in Attica; the statue of Nemesis there was sculpted by Pheidias.

RHEA In poem 374 stands for Kybele, the Lydian earth-mother goddess.

RHEGION A Greek colony in the toe of Italy, now Reggio.

RHINTHON Third-century B.C. writer of burlesques, especially of Euripides.

RHODES Large and prosperous island off the Karian coast.

SALAMIS Island in the Saronic gulf between Attica and Megara. The Persian fleet was destroyed off its east coast in 480 B.C.

SAMIOS Author of two extant epigrams, he was included in Meleager's *Garland*. An opponent of Philip V of Macedon, who had him executed.

SAMOS Island off the coast of Asia Minor, just south-west of Ephesos, colonized by Ionians. Home of notable artists and poets in the time of Polykrates.

SAMOSATA Syrian city on the Euphrates.

SAMOTHRACE Mountainous Aegean island off the coast of Thrace; its Greek population came originally from Samos. Centre of a cult of the twin gods who protected sailors, the Cabiri.

SANGARIOS (SANGARIUS) River which runs through Bithynia into the Black Sea.

SAPPHO Lyric poet of the late seventh and early sixth centuries, from Lesbos. Substantial fragments of her poems remain.

SARAPIS Egyptian god whose cult originated at Memphis, and was well established at Alexandria. A miracle-worker and healer, he was supposed to speak to his devotees in dreams.

SARDIS Chief Lydian city, capital of the kingdom of Croesus, captured by Darius. It was under Macedonian rule in the Hellenistic period.

SATYRS, THE Spirits of wild life in the woods and hills, usually young and, like Pan, half goat.

SCARPHEA Town near Thermopylai.

SELENE The moon-goddess, identified with Hekaté (Artemis).

SELEUKOS Name of the Syrian kings of the Seleukid dynasty, founded in 312 B.C. by Seleukos Nikator, ending with Seleukos VI in the nineties B.C.

SENECA THE ELDER Father of Seneca the philosopher and poet, the elder Seneca lived *c.* 55 B.C.–A.D. 40. He was a rhetorician; parts of his prose works on rhetoric survive.

SERAPIS See Sarapis.

SERIPHUS An island in the Cyclades.

SIDON Phoenician coastal town.

SIKYON Town west of Corinth, two miles from the sea.

SILENOS See n. 222.

SIPHNOS An island in the Cyclades.

SIRON With Philodemos, one of the leaders of the Epicurean school of philosophy at Naples.

SISYPHEAN Corinthian; Sisyphos was the legendary founder of Corinth.

SKYROS Aegean island, east of Euboia. See n. 812.

SMERDIES A boy loved by Polykrates of Samos, who had the boy's hair cut off in punishment for becoming too involved with Anakreon.

SMYRNA City on the Aiolian coast, in the bay of Hermos.

SOKRATES Athenian philosopher, 469–399 B.C.; the central character of Plato's dialogues. He married Xanthippé.

SOLOI Cilician coastal town, a little west of Tarsos.

SOPHOKLES Athenian tragic poet, *c.* 496–406 B.C. Seven of his tragedies are extant.

SPARTA Important town in the southern Peloponnese, on the river Eurotas.

SPERCHEIOS River in Thessaly, a little north of Thermopylai.

STESICHOROS Early sixth-century B.C. narrative and lyric poet. A few fragments of his verse remain.

STRABO Greek historian and geographer, *c.* 64 B.C.–A.D. 21, author of an extant *Geography* in seventeen books.

STRYMON Macedonian river flowing into the Aegean through Amphipolis.

STYX Arkadian mountain river, thought to be one of the nine rivers of the underworld.

SUDA, THE Name of a lexicon compiled in the tenth century A.D.

SUSA Town north of the Persian Gulf. Capital of the Persian Empire under Darius.

SYRIA A Persian satrapy until conquered by Alexander the Great.

Syria was partitioned into north and south Syria and divided between the Seleukids and the Ptolemies, until 201 B.C. when Antiochos III, a Seleukid, reunited it.

TANAGRA Boiotian town, famous for its fighting-cocks.

TANTALUS An immortal who stole the food of the gods; his punishment was to be 'tantalized' by standing in water, with fruit hanging over him, both perpetually evading his reach. Pindar's version gives him the punishment of perpetual fear – a huge stone is poised over his head.

TARENTUM Leading south Italian city, colonized c. 700 B.C. by Spartans. Now Taranto.

TARSOS Capital of the Cilician kings and the Persian satraps. Centre of a school of philosophy in the first century B.C.

TEGEA Town in south-east Arkadia.

TELLEN Comic poet and flute-player of the fourth century B.C.

TELOS A small island near Rhodes.

TEOS Ionian coastal town, between Smyrna and Ephesos.

TERENCE Roman comic playwright, c. 195–159 B.C., author of six plays based on the Greek 'New Comedy' of Menander.

TEREUS See n. 819.

TERPANDER Seventh-century B.C. poet and musician from Lesbos. He worked in Sparta. A few fragments assigned to him are probably spurious.

TERPÊS Another name for Terpander.

THASOS Northern Aegean island, colonized by Parians c. 680 B.C. Gold was mined there.

THEBE Eponymous legendary heroine of Boiotian Thebes.

THEBES Name of three towns: (1) the main Boiotian town (2) Phthiotid Thebes, a Thessalian town (3) the former capital of Egypt on the Nile, still an important town under the Ptolemies.

THEMIS Goddess originally identified with Gē (the Earth); later, Justice personified.

THEMISTOKLES Athenian statesman, c. 528–462, whose naval policy was largely responsible for the Greek victory in the wars with Persia.

THEODOSIUS Roman Emperor of the East and general who subdued the Goths; he died in A.D. 395. A strict Athanasian who imposed religious orthodoxy on his Empire.

THEOGNIS Megarian gnomic elegiac poet of the sixth century B.C.

THERMON Religious centre of Aitolia, sacked in 218 B.C. by Philip V of Macedon.

THERMOPYLAI The narrow mountain-pass separating Thessaly from Phokis, unsuccessfully defended by Leonidas' three hundred Spartans against Xerxes in 480 B.C. The name ('Hot Gates') derives from the nearby sulphur springs.

THESSALONIKA Macedonian city and port which became capital of the Roman province in 146 B.C.

THESSALY The district of north-eastern Greece with Macedonia to the north and Epiros to the west.

THETIS A Nereid fated to bear a son greater than his father. Zeus and Poseidon therefore let her marry Peleus; their son was Achilles.

THRACE The eastern half of the Balkan peninsula, in the third century B.C. partly under Macedonian rule.

THYNIA See Bithynia.

THYREAI (THYREAE) Chief town of the border district between Lakonia and Argolis. See n. 292.

TIBERIUS He lived 42 B.C.–A.D. 37, succeeding Augustus as Roman Emperor in A.D. 14.

TIMOKREON Rhodian lyric and elegiac poet of the early fifth century B.C., famous as a glutton. Simonides criticized both him and his poetry.

TIMON The famous Athenian misanthrope seems to have lived in the time of Perikles.

TIRYNS Town in the Argive plain, near Nauplia. The surviving ruins are of the thirteenth century B.C.; in classical times it was an unimportant, though independent, town. Herakles was supposed to have lived there.

TITHONOS Loved by Eōs (the Dawn), who requested Zeus to make him immortal, but forgot to ask for eternal youth as well. He grew more and more decrepit, and she kept him locked away in a bedroom.

TITUS See n. 228.

TMOLOS The Lydian mountain which dominates Sardis.

TORONE A port on the west coast of the central promontory of Chalkidike.

TRINACRIA See n. 550.

TROY Several towns were built on the site of Troy, just inland and south of the Aegean entrance to the Hellespont. The seventh of nine clearly defined strata which have been excavated was destroyed by fire, and its date tallies with the traditional date of the Trojan War (about 1190 B.C.).

TYCHON A minor deity, either the god of chance, or a Priapic fertility god.

TYRE Phoenician coastal city, about twenty miles south of Sidon.

TYRRHENIAN SEA The sea between Italy and Sardinia.

TYRTAIOS Spartan elegiac poet and general who led the Spartans in a war against the Messenians. Active in the mid-seventh century B.C.

VENUS The Roman goddess of love, equivalent to Aphrodite.

VERGIL Roman poet from Mantua, 70–19 B.C., author of the *Eclogues*, *Georgics* and the *Aeneid*.

VESPASIAN Born A.D. 9, he was Roman Emperor for the last ten years of his life, A.D. 69–79.

VICTORY The Greek goddess Niké was Victory personified; she was usually represented in sculpture as winged.

XANTHIPPÉ Wife of Sokrates, supposed to have been bad-tempered.

XERXES Son of Darius and king of Persia from 485–465 B.C. Little is known of his career after the naval defeat at Salamis and that on land at Plataia. See n. 511.

ZENO One of several philosophers of the name, Zeno of Sidon, born about 150 B.C., is the Epicurean referred to in poem 432. He was a well-known teacher.

ZEPHYR The west wind.

ZEPHYRION A promontory midway between Alexandria and the western, Canopic mouth of the Nile. There was a shrine of Arsinoë (q.v.) there.

ZEUS 'Father of gods and man' in Homer, Zeus is the weather-god and the protector of law and morals. He is also god of the household, of suppliants and of guest-friends. He remained the pre-eminent civic deity throughout the historical period.

A Select Bibliography

The most convenient general text is the five-volume Loeb edition, *The Greek Anthology*, edited by W. R. Paton (1916), with facing prose versions. The poets of the Hellenistic and Graeco-Roman periods have been comprehensively edited with a detailed commentary, introductions and bibliography by A. S. F. Gow and D. L. Page: *Hellenistic Epigrams* (1965) and *The Garland of Philip* (1968) – both in two volumes, text and commentary. These are indispensable.

J. W. Mackail's *Select Epigrams from the Greek Anthology* (3rd edition, 1911) has been out of print for many years, but has a long and extremely interesting introduction. About 500 poems are given in Greek with prose versions and minimal notes. Mackail includes a number of the best poems from non-literary sources, mostly drawn from G. Kaibel's massive compilation of inscriptions, *Epigrammata Graeca ex lapidibus conlecta* (Berlin, 1878).

CRITICAL AND GENERAL

Apart from Mackail's introduction mentioned above, and comments by Gow and Page *passim* – their introductory notes to the commentary on each poem are often penetrating, occasionally puzzling – there is very little criticism of the epigrammatists in English, although there is no shortage of historical studies. T. B. L. Webster's *Hellenistic Poetry and Art* (1964) can be thoroughly recommended as a fascinating study of that period. Other works of some usefulness are J. A. Symonds' *Studies of the Greek Poets* (3rd edition, 1920) – still readable, despite some wayward critical estimations of poets like Strato; A. Körte's *Hellenistic Poetry* (translated by Jacob Hammer and Moses Hadas, 1929); and A. Couat's *Alexandrian Poetry* (translated by James Loeb, 1921). R. Reitzenstein's *Epigramm und Skolion* (1893) has not been translated into English.

Some essays on individual poets have been mentioned in the headnotes to the poets and in the Notes. C. M. Bowra has a chapter on

Simonides in *Greek Lyric Poetry* (2nd edition, 1961), part of which is devoted to the epigrams. H. Ouvré's *Méléagre de Gadara* (1894) is a full-length study of the poet. C. A. Sainte-Beuve also wrote on some of the epigrammatists – notably 'Méléagre' (1845), collected in *Portraits Contemporains*, vol. V; for an account of his interest in the poets of The Greek Anthology, see R. E. Mulhauser's *Sainte-Beuve and Greco-Roman Antiquity* (1969), pp. 147ff. A recent collection of essays on individual poets, in various languages, is *L'Epigramme Grecque – sept exposés suivis de discussions* (Entretiens sur L'Antiquité Classique, Tome IV, 1967).

TRANSLATIONS

Most slim volumes of 'Poems from the Greek Anthology', and the like, make pretty depressing reading. Anyone interested should consult the long, but incomplete, bibliography of translations made up to 1919 in Sir Edward Cook's *More Literary Recreations* (1919). I am indebted for this information to Mr Thomas Higham, who kindly allowed me to consult his own supplementary list of translations.

Richard Aldington published prose versions of *The Poems of Anyte of Tegea* (1919) and *The Poems of Meleager of Gadara* (1920). Another volume of prose versions is Shane Leslie's *The Greek Anthology* (1929), which includes over a thousand poems.

Distinguished verse translations are few and far between. Dudley Fitts' *Poems from the Greek Anthology* (2nd edition, 1956) still, in my view, holds the field – despite some notable failures. There is nothing in English to equal Salvatore Quasimodo's *Dall'Antologia Palatina*(1968). Willis Barnstone includes a number of epigrammatists in his *Greek Lyric Poetry* (revised edition, 1967). The most recent one-man selections are Kenneth Rexroth's *Poems from the Greek Anthology* (1962) and Robin Skelton's *Two Hundred Poems from the Greek Anthology* (1971), both of which are readable. Rather less so are Andrew Sinclair's *Selections from the Greek Anthology* (1967) and André Lefevere's *Classical Epigrams, love and wit* (1970). The only individual poet to receive recent attention is Meleager – *The Poems of Meleager*, selected and translated by Peter Whigham (1973).

Notes on Contributors and
Index to the Translations

FLEUR ADCOCK A New Zealander living in London, she has published two collections of poems, *Tigers* (1967) and *High Tide in the Garden* (1971).

133, 134, 185–9, 411–21, 423–8, 430–35, 829

WILLIS BARNSTONE Poet and translator, he is Professor of Comparative Literature at Indiana University. His *Greek Lyric Poetry* was first published in 1962.

720, Appendix 2

JOHN PEALE BISHOP American poet (1892–1944). His *Collected Poems* was published in 1948.

497

EDMUND BLUNDEN Born 1896, he has published many volumes of poetry and criticism. He was Professor of Poetry at Oxford from 1967–8.

211

SAM BRADLEY American poet who teaches at St Augustine's College, Raleigh, N.C. His most recent book is *Manspell/Godspell* (1973).

676

ROBERT BRIDGES Poet (Laureate) and essayist (1844–1930).

622

J. V. CUNNINGHAM Professor of English at Brandeis University. *Collected Poems and Epigrams* was published in England in 1971.

634

GUY DAVENPORT Poet and translator of Archilochos (*Carmina Archilochi*, 1964) and Sappho (*Sappho - Poems and Fragments*, 1965). He teaches English at the University of Kentucky, Lexington.

1, 2, 4, 742, 749, 756, 757, 823, 827, 828, 830, 856, 859

ALISTAIR ELLIOT Works as a librarian at the University of Newcastle-on-Tyne. He read Greats at Oxford and has also translated Euripides' *Alcestis* (1965). He has published a pamphlet of poems, *Air in the Wrong Place* (1968).

38, 68, 163, 164, 192, 212–14, 226–8, 232, 296, 300, 314, 322, 323, 325–8, 351–69, 378, 379, 381–9, 393–6, 398, 399, 402, 403, 406–10, 422, 429, 477, 478, 482, 494–6, 512, 546, 548, 564, 572, 595, 761, 776, 787, 795, 844

RICHARD EVANS Read Classics and English at Oxford, and did research on twentieth-century translators at Bristol University. He lives in Wales; his poems have appeared in various magazines.

24, 291, 292, 445, 446

DUDLEY FITTS Poet, classicist and teacher (1903–68), best known for his adaptations of Aristophanes, and other translations of Greek drama. *Poems from the Greek Anthology* first appeared in 1938; the revised edition was published in 1956.

43, 82, 225, 241, 295, 299, 317, 320, 447, 456, 485, 522, 525, 531, 555, 621, 635, 677, 679, 713, 750, 754, 758, 796, 821, 822, 825, Appendix 2

FREDERICK GARBER Teaches Comparative Literature at the State University of New York, Binghamton. He has written a book on Wordsworth, and has translated Ilse Aichinger.

489, 490

TONY HARRISON Born 1937, he read Classics at Leeds University. He lives in Newcastle-on-Tyne. His first book of poems, *The Loiners* (1970), was awarded the Geoffrey Faber Memorial Prize in 1972.

231, 239, 240, 243, 244, 246, 248, 249, 311, 390, 392, 400, 404, 405, 505, 589, 604, 618, 637–75, 759, 771

JOHN HEATH-STUBBS Born 1918, his most recent books are *Selected Poems* (1966) and *Satires and Epigrams* (1968). He has also translated some of Leopardi's poetry. The poems included here were translated with the assistance of Carol A. Whiteside.

97–100, 105, 106, 108, 114, 115, 205, 223–4, 500, 851, 852

TEDDY HOGGE Suburban satirist, author of *Expostulations* (1970).

600, 606, 608, 610, 611, 614–16, 619, 620

ANTHONY HOLDEN Poet and translator of Aeschylus' *Agamemnon* (1970) and *Greek Pastoral Poetry* (1973).

118–30, 234, 794, 860

PETER JAY Editor of this volume.

6–21, 25–33, 35–7, 39, 40, 42, 44, 45, 48, 76, 80, 81, 83, 85, 139, 140, 142–60, 196, 207, 210, 215, 217, 229, 235, 236, 245, 247, 297, 308–10, 312, 313, 315, 316, 319, 377, 448, 454, 481, 484, 491, 501, 504, 507–11,

514, 515, 520, 527, 534, 588, 592–4, 623, 624, 680, 681, 686, 687, 725–8, 731–3, 738, 741, 751, 752, 760, 762–4, 768–70, 772, 773, 777, 778, 780–86, 788, 791, 792, 832, 846, 847, 853, 854

FRANK KUENSTLER New York poet and film-maker.

517, 682

RICHMOND LATTIMORE Classicist and poet, he has translated Homer's *Iliad* and *Odyssey*, several Greek tragedies, the poems of Pindar, Hesiod and a selection of *Greek Lyrics*.

5, 41

ANDRÉ LEFEVERE Translator of *Classical Epigrams* (1970).

Appendix 2

PETER LEVI Teaches at Campion Hall, Oxford. He has published six books of poetry, the most recent being *Life is a Platform* and *Death is a Pulpit* (1971). He has also translated Pausanias' *Guide to Greece* (1971) and a collection of poems by George Pavlopoulos, *The Cellar* (1973).

49, 166–71, 181–4, 193–5, 370–73, 375, 376

CHRISTOPHER LOGUE Poet, playwright and adaptor of Homer (*Patrocleia*, 1962 and *Pax*, 1967). His most recent book of poems was *New Numbers* (1969).

617

EDWARD LUCIE-SMITH Poet, art-critic, editor of several anthologies and translator of French poetry. His most recent book of poems was *Towards Silence* (1968).

65, 75, 86–90, 161, 198–204, 293, 498, 613, 729, 734, 743, 753, 767, 793

ALAN MARSHFIELD Born 1933, he teaches at a school in Edgware. Two collections of poems, *Mistress* and *Dragonfly*, were published in 1972.

51, 57–60, 62–4, 66, 67, 69, 74, 77, 78, 180, 483, 487, 503, 528, 688–712

LENORE MAYHEW Poet and translator. Lives in Oberlin, Ohio. With William McNaughton she has translated *A Gold Orchid: The Tzu Yeh Songs* (1972).

131, 132

W. S. MERWIN American poet, translator of several French and Spanish works, and *The Satires of Persius*. His most recent book of poems is *The Carrier of Ladders* (1970).

84, 488, 492, 523, 524, 526, 529, 532, 715–17, 719, 721

THOMAS MEYER Lives in Yorkshire and is amanuensis to Jonathan Williams, The Jargon Society. He has published *The Bang Book* (1971) and *The Umbrella of Aesculapius* (1972).

70, 230, 304, 321, 439, 518, 519, 596–9, 601, 633

ANDREW MILLER At present working on his doctorate in Comparative Literature at the University of California, Berkeley. Some of his translations of Greek poetry appear in *Greek Readings*, ed. Michael Grant (1972).

397, 797–818, 848, 849

BARRISS MILLS Teaches English at Purdue University, Indiana. He has published translations of Catullus, Theokritos and a selection of Martial's epigrams.

216, 294, 437, 736, 745, 747, 845

WILLIAM MOEBIUS Teaches at the University of Massachusetts, Amherst. His first book of poems, *Elegies and Odes*, appeared in 1969. He has also translated Sophokles' *Oedipus at Colonus*.

92–6, 329–50, 735

EDWIN MORGAN Born 1920 in Glasgow, he is a prolific poet, concrete-poet and translator (*Beowulf*, Montale, Mayakovsky et al.). *The Second Life* (1968) is his largest collection of poems; a selection of his work appears in *Penguin Modern Poets 15*.

22, 23, 162, 165, 233, 438, 451, 453, 455, 457–70, 472–5, 479, 480, 499, 625–32

LEE T. PEARCY JR Fellow in Latin at Bryn Mawr College. He is now translating *The Homeric Hymns*.

73, 513, 530, 718, 722–4, 765

WILLIAM J. PHILBIN Bishop of Down and Connor, he lives in Belfast. He has published translations into Irish of St Patrick's writings, and *To You Simonides*, poems from The Greek Anthology.

50, 858

PETER PORTER An ex-Australian resident in London, he has published four books of poetry. *The Last of England* (1970) includes some of his versions of Martial's epigrams.

301, 302, 305–7, 318, 533, 535–45, 547, 549–54, 556–63, 565–71, 573–84, 755, 774, 775, 779

EZRA POUND (1885–1972) One of the pioneers of modernism in English and American poetry. As well as *Collected Shorter Poems* and

428

The Cantos, his work includes diverse critical and economic writings and a version of Sophokles' *Women of Trachis*. He has translated from many languages, notably Provençal and Chinese.

111, 678, 826, Appendix 2

SALLY PURCELL Born 1944, she has published *The Devil's Dancing Hour* (1968), *Provençal Poems* (1970) and *The Holly Queen* (1972).

101–4, 107, 109, 110, 112, 116, 117, 135–8

KENNETH REXROTH American poet, born 1905. He has translated French, Japanese and Chinese poetry as well as *Poems from the Greek Anthology* (1962). Eric Mottram's *The Rexroth Reader* (1972) is a large selection of his work in prose and verse.

61, 71, 72, 79, 113, 172–8, 190, 237, 242, 391, 819

CLIVE SANSOM Born in London in 1910, he is at present living in Hobart. He has published three collections of poetry as well as two books of poems for children, a novel and an anthology (*The World of Poetry*).

34, 191, 197, 298, 486

DENNIS SCHMITZ Born 1937, he teaches at Sacramento State College, California. He has published two books of poems, *We Weep For Our Strangeness* (1969) and *Double Exposures* (1971).

141, 303, 324, 449, 450

W. G. SHEPHERD Born in 1935, he read English at Cambridge and now works in the electronics industry. He lives in north London. His books of poetry are *Allies* (1968), *Sun, Oak, Almond, I* (1970) and *On Separate Planets* (1973).

179, 206, 290, 380, 436, 493, 502, 516, 602, 603, 605, 607, 609, 612, 744, 746, 748, 789, 790, 850, 861

STUART SILVERMAN Associate editor of *Unicorn*, he lives in Chicago.

3

ANDREW SINCLAIR Novelist, film-maker, publisher and author of *Selections from the Greek Anthology* (1967).

Appendix 2

ROBIN SKELTON English poet and author of several anthologies. He edits *The Malahat Review* and is Professor of English at the University of Victoria, B.C. *Two Hundred Poems from The Greek Anthology* appeared in 1971.

238, 374, 401, 444, 452, 471, 476, 585–7, 590, 591, 636, 683–5, 714, 730, 739, 831, 855, 857, Appendix 2

STEPHEN SPENDER His first book of poems for many years was *The Generous Days* (1971). He is Professor of English at University College, London.

46

PETER WHIGHAM English poet, whose published works include *The Poems of Catullus* (1966), *The Blue Winged Bee* (1969), ASTAPOVO *or What We Are To Do* (1970), *The Crystal Mountain* (1971) and *The Poems of Meleager* (1973).

47, 52–6, 208, 209, 218–22, 250–89, 440–43, 521, 766, 820, 824, 833

ADRIAN WRIGHT Born 1947, he teaches in Middlesbrough. He has published two collections of poems – *Waiting for Helen* (1970) and *The Shrinking Map* (1972).

91, 506, 740, 834–43, Appendix 2

G. R. H. WRIGHT Lives in Beirut, where he works at the Institut Français d'Archéologie as an adviser on the restoration of ancient monuments.

737

Index of Greek Poets

(Numbers refer to the poems as numbered in this book)

Adaios, 476–8
Agathias, 819–30
Aischylos, 22–3
Alexander, 84
Alkaios, 226–32
Alpheios, 479–80
Ammianus, 589–94
Anakreon, 8–9
Anonymous Inscriptions, 41–50
Anonymous, 308–21, 515–22,
   742–93, 854–9
Antimedon, 481
Antipater of Sidon, 236–49
Antipater of Thessalonika,
   378–410
Antiphanes, 455–8
Antiphilos, 523–32
Antistius, 482
Anyte, 97–117
Apollinarius, 725
Apollonides, 440–43
Archias, 483–6
Archilochos, 1–4
Argentarius, Marcus, 411–35
Aristodikos, 216
Ariston, 290
Artemidoros, 234
Asklepiades, 57–78
Asklepiodotos, 595
Automedon, 487–92

Barbukollas, Johannes, 846
Bassus, 448
Bianor, 444–7

Capito, 726
Cerealius, 727
Chairemon, 291–2
Cyrillus, 728

Damagetos, 223–5
Damaskios, 847
Damocharis, 852
'Delphic Oracle, The', 687
Demodokos, 38–9
Diodoros, 493
Diogenes Laertios, 635–6
Dionysios, 293–4
Diophanes of Myrina, 729
Dioskorides, 218–22
Diotimos, 295–6
Douris, 85

Eratosthenes, 795–6
Erinna, 131–2
Erucius, 370–77
Euenos, 494–7
Euodos, 730
Euphorion, 163–4

Flaccus, Statilius, 436–9

Gaetulicus, 498
Gauradas, 731
Glaukos, 297–9
Glykon, 732
Gregory, 683–5

Hedylos, 91–6
Hegemon, 40
Hegesippos, 165
Herakleitos, 162
Hermokreon, 213–14
Herodikos, 733
Honestus, 452–4

Irenaios, 848–50
Isidoros (of Aigai), 499
Isidoros (Scholastikos), 831

Julianus, Flavius Claudius ('the Apostate'), 686
Julianus (ex-prefect of Egypt), 714–24

Kallimachos, 142–61
Karphyllides, 300
Kephalas, 861
Killaktor, 734–6
Kleoboulos, 5
Kometas, 860
Krinagoras, 351–69

Leonidas (of Alexandria), 586–7
Leonidas (of Tarentum), 166–97
Leontios, 832–3
Lucian, 623–32
Lucilius, 533–73

Maccius, 502–4
Macedonius, 834–45
Marianos, 794
Meleager, 250–89
Menander, 51
Mnasalkes, 198–204
Moiro, 133–4
Myrinos, 505–6

Nikainetos, 208–9
Nikarchos (of Meleager's Garland), 301–2
Nikarchos, 574–85
Nikias, 129–30
Nossis, 135–40

Palladas, 637–82, Appendix 2
Pamphilos, 303
Parmenion, 507–12
Parrhasios, 24–5
Paulos, 797–818
Perses, 52–6
Phalaikos, 83
Phanias, 304–7
Philip V (of Macedon), 233
Philip, 459–75
Philitas, 79–80
Philodemos, 329–50
Phokylides, 6–7
Pinytos, 513
Plato, 27–37
Plato ('the younger'), 737–8
Polyaenus, Julius, 500–501
Pompeius, 449–50
Poseidippos, 86–90
Ptolemaeus, Claudius, 621–2

INDEX OF GREEK POETS

Rhianos, 217
Rufinus, 688–712

Satyros, 739
Serapion, 514
Simias, 81–2
Simonides, 10–21
Skythinos, 633–4
Strato, 596–620

Thallos, 451
Theaitetos, 141
Theaitetos (Scholastikos), 851

Theodoridas, 205–7
Theokritos, 118–28
Theon, 713
Theophanes, 853
Thukydides, 26
Thyillos, 740
Thymokles, 215
Trajan, 588
Tryphon, 741
Tymnes, 210–12

Zenodotos, 235
Zonas, Diodoros, 322–8

Index to Poems from The Palatine Anthology

BOOK I		BOOK 5 cont.		BOOK 5 cont.		BOOK 5 cont.	
37 –	856	24	262	80	32	121	335
38	857	26	744	81	293	123	336
39	858	27	712	82	746	124	337
100	859	28	697	83	747	125	448
		29	734	84	748	126	348
BOOK 4		30	379	85	58	129	487
1 –	Append. 1	32	412	87	698	131	338
2	Append. 1	33	507	89	413	132	339
3	Append. 1	34	508	90	749	133	503
		36	704	91	750	136	263
BOOK 5		37	706	92	702	141	264
1 –	861	38	574	93	707	143	265
2	742	39	575	94	701	144	258
3	380	41	710	95	751	145	67
4	329	42	708	96	274	146	146
5	436	44	699	98	483	147	266
6	144	45	735	99	752	152	259
7	65	46	331	102	414	153	59
8	275	48	711	104	415	155	267
9	693	51	745	105	416	156	256
10	229	56	218	107	332	157	268
11	743	57	253	109	397	158	60
12	695	59	484	110	417	162	62
13	330	60	689	111	528	163	269
14	690	64	66	112	344	165	270
15	700	66	694	113	418	166	271
16	411	67	726	114	502	169	57
18	709	69	691	115	333	170	140
19	688	74	703	116	419	171	260
20	453	75	692	118	420	173	257
21	696	77	705	119	351	175	276
23	161	78	31	120	334	177	261

INDEX TO POEMS FROM THE PALATINE ANTHOLOGY

BOOK 5 *cont.*		BOOK 5 *cont.*		BOOK 6 *cont.*		BOOK 6 *cont.*	
179 – 250		257	664	89	504	234	374
182	277	258	809	90	461	236	459
187	273	261	820	92	462	238	440
189	77	266	800	96	370	239	441
194	75	271	842	98	323	242	356
197	255	278	821	100	355	250	523
199	91	279	802	102	463	252	524
200	308	283	798	106	324	254	505
201	309	290	804	107	464	259	466
203	63	295	832	119	133	262	176
206	180	301	813	123	97	263	179
207	64	303	753	125	199	265	135
210	61	304	754	133	4	272	52
212	251	306	340	146	149	274	53
213	86	309	729	148	147	279	163
217	799			153	98	285	302
219	797	BOOK 6		156	205	290	220
223	834	1 – 310		161	357	294	305
227	835	9	198	164	623	298	177
228	808	19	714	177	119	303	290
230	807	21	756	188	169	307	306
231	836	22	322	189	134	309	174
232	801	24	757	196	437	312	109
233	837	32	715	200	173	333	421
235	838	33	716	202	166	334	168
237	819	35	175	204	172	336	118
238	839	36	460	210	79	345	354
241	811	47	242	211	167	352	131
243	840	58	831	222	206	353	136
245	841	59	822	223	243		
246	803	63	852	226	178	BOOK 7	
249	848	69	843	227	352	6 – 236	
251	849	71	806	228	476	8	237
252	810	77	795	229	353	9	223
253	850	85	671	231	465	11	73
255	812	88	455	232	366	16	513

INDEX TO POEMS FROM THE PALATINE ANTHOLOGY

BOOK 7 cont.		BOOK 7 cont.		BOOK 7 cont.		BOOK 7 cont.	
18 –	382	196	252	286	384	424	240
20	765	199	210	292	713	436	40
22	82	202	107	295	190	447	153
30	238	203	81	307	817	449	183
31	221	204	823	308	624	451	154
35	35	205	824	309	760	452	187
36	375	208	105	311	825	453	155
39	383	211	211	317	157	456	222
45	26	215	108	321	761	465	162
51	477	216	386	324	762	469	291
54	204	217	76	346	763	471	158
58	717	219	450	348	20	477	212
62	766	224	759	350	764	478	188
63	767	226	9	353	239	481	80
71	498	232	246	364	426	482	314
72	51	242	200	365	325	486	101
80	152	247	228	368	373	487	54
99	29	249	10	371	358	488	201
100	30	250	15	374	424	490	102
105	21	251	12	375	530	497	225
109	50	253	13	376	359	502	208
112	636	254	19	377	376	510	17
140	485	255	22	380	364	511	18
153	5	256	34	383	468	512	14
155	758	259	33	384	433	524	151
160	8	260	300	395	425	532	499
168	407	263	311	398	400	533	294
170	90	265	312	400	514	534	84
173	295, 296	269	313	401	365	535	288
182	287	270	16	402	401	536	232
185	385	273	191	403	434	537	307
186	467	277	156	405	469	538	117
187	475	278	486	408	186	540	224
189	216	282	207	414	139	553	847
190	116	284	74	415	150	563	815
192	202	285	298	419	289	566	844

INDEX TO POEMS FROM THE PALATINE ANTHOLOGY

BOOK 7 cont.		BOOK 7 cont.		BOOK 9 cont.		BOOK 9 cont.	
571	– 833	730	55	153	826	326	170
576	718	731	192	161	422	327	213
600	719	736	196	165	662	329	171
601	720	743	402	167	663	330	301
606	816	744	635	172	674	332	137
609	814			184	769	334	56
630	525			186	408	337	194
632	493	BOOK 8		205	234	338	126
633	360	158	– 683	220	451	341	299
636	367	227	684	226	326	347	586
639	398	233	685	227	444	350	587
646	103			229	428	368	686
648	182			234	369	369	728
649	104	BOOK 9		237	371	378	670
651	164	7	– 500	241	396	412	345
655	184	8	501	242	529	416	471
657	185	24	195	244	442	418	403
659	120	28	449	245	456	420	395
660	122	43	509	247	470	421	388
661	121	44	438	250	454	423	446
669	27	51	738	251	494	424	85
670	28	57	303	259	445	427	846
676	768	58	404	268	387	432	128
677	11	65	788	270	429	435	125
682	646	74	515	277	526	437	127
692	410	75	495	286	423	439	368
705	394	87	427	292	452	444	796
711	244	97	479	294	531	486	653
712	132	101	480	304	511	488	741
713	245	112	378	305	389	489	681
714	315	113	510	309	339	499	770
715	189	120	625	312	327	506	36
719	181	122	497	313	112	507	159
721	292	133	776	314	113	518	226
723	316	144	111	320	193	530	777
724	100	145	516	323	248	541	393
		151	247				

BOOK 9 *cont.*		BOOK 10 *cont.*		BOOK 11		BOOK 11 *cont.*	
546 –	527	4	430	6 –	736	102	590
554	435	5	740	8	517	104	547
556	328	16	851	12	227	106	548
558	372	18	431	13	589	113	577
559	362	20	478	22	618	120	578
562	361	21	342	23	392	121	579
564	129	23	489	25	443	125	779
565	160	26	626	28	432	129	727
567	249	31	627	29	488	133	549
570	341	45	648	30	349	137	550
572	533	49	660	31	390, 391	138	551
575	472	56	658	34	346	139	552
577	621, 622	57	643	36	473	148	553
586	680	58	644	37	405	158	591
599	123	59	678	41	343	159	554
600	124	60	639	42	363	165	555
604	138	62	638	44	347	169	580
620	805	63	637	46	481	170	581
627	794	65	645, 682	51	774	171	556
641	827	67	845	54	661	172	557
642	828	72	654	55	657	175	558
647	854	77	655	67	506	179	559
651	818	78	666	68	534	185	560
654	721	79	667	71	576	186	582
661	722	81	677	75	535	192	561
677	829	84	649	79	536	204	668
745	110	85	647	80	537	211	562
752	78	93	675	83	538	214	563
763	723	94	642	85	539	215	564
773	672	97	673	88	540	217	565
784	855	98	650	89	541	221	592
823	317	100	457	92	542	224	406
		112	771	93	544	225	619
BOOK 10		116	778	94	543	226	593
1 –	197	118	772	99	545	236	38
2	241	124	732	101	546	237	39

INDEX TO POEMS FROM THE PALATINE ANTHOLOGY

BOOK II cont.		BOOK II cont.		BOOK 12 cont.		BOOK 13	
251 – 583		433	594	107	319	7 – 148	
256	566	414	781	116	320	12	165
257	567	415	409	127	278		
262	755	418	588	133	280	BOOK 15	
264	568	421	725	134	145	35 – 853	
274	628	425	782	135	70		
277	569	429	630	136	321	BOOK 16	
282	775	430	631	139	143	(The Planudean	
287	659			147	272	Appendix)	
289	640	BOOK 12		154	285	11 – 214	
290	641	1 – 596		159	286	12	789
291	669	3	597	161	71	13	790
293	656	4	598	163	72	14	235
295	570	6	599	164	279	18	783
310	571	7	600	166	69	19	784
315	572	12	439	171	219	19a	733
317	651	13	601	172	496	26b	233
322	458	15	602	179	603	107	724
324	490	17	518	185	604	129	791
325	491	19	519	188	605	152	731
327	381	22	633	192	606	153	739
341	679	23	282	205	607	155	730
347	474	29	230	213	608	162	792
355	676	30	231	214	609	188	130
358	780	31	304	216	610	222	512
364	447	32	215	222	611	228	114
365	830	34	492	227	612	231	115
381	665,	41	281	232	634	234	350
	Appendix 2	43	142	237	613	238	632
383	652	44	297	240	614	242	377
384	680	47	254	245	615	243	482
391	573	50	68	246	616	248	737
395	585	59	283	248	617	291	99
406	584	103	318	258	620	318	785
410	629	106	248			333	532

Index to Poems from Other Sources

For abbreviations see page 28

1 Archilochos, *E* 1, *D* 1
2 Archilochos, *E* 2, *D* 2
3 Archilochos, *E* 6, *D* 6
6 Phokylides, *E* 1, *D* 1
7 Phokylides, *E* 4, *D* 3
23 Aischylos, *E* 4, *D* 3, *M* 3.12
24 Parrhasios, *E* 2, *D* 2; Athenaios 12.543C
25 Parrhasios, *E* 3, *D* 3; Athenaios 12.543C
37 Plato, *E* 18, *D* 14
41 Anonymous, *K* 1
42 Anonymous, *K add.* 1a, *E* 5, *M* 3.37
43 Anonymous, *K* 6, E 6
44 Anonymous, *G* 41, *E* 7a
45 Anonymous, *G* 86
46 Anonymous, *P* 1600
47 Anonymous, *K* 373, *M* 3.38
48 Anonymous, *K* 56, *E* 45
49 Anonymous, *E* 33; Pausanias 9.15.5
83 Phalaikos, *HE* 1; Athenaios 10.440D
87 Poseidippos, *HE* 13; Athenaios 7. 313D
88 Poseidippos, *HE* 16; Athenaios 10.414D
89 Poseidippos, *HE* 17; Athenaios 13.596C
92 Hedylos, *HE* 3; Athenaios 11.486A
93 Hedylos, *HE* 4; Athenaios 11.497D
94 Hedylos, *HE* 5; Athenaios 11.472F
95 Hedylos, *HE* 6; Athenaios 11.473A
96 Hedylos, *HE* 8; Athenaios 8.344F
106 Anyte, *HE* 10; Pollux 5.48
141 Theaitetos, *HE* 2, *M* 11.7; Diogenes Laertios 4.25
209 Nikaintos, *HE* 4; Athenaios 15.673B
217 Rhianos, *HE* 9; Athenaios 11.499D

INDEX TO POEMS FROM OTHER SOURCES

520 Anonymous, *M* 12.25; Plutarch *Consolatio ad Apollonium* c. 15
521 Anonymous, *M* 3.45, *CIG* 6261
522 Anonymous, *M* 3.57, *K* 627
595 Asklepiodotos, *M* 9.19, *CIG* 4747
687 'The Delphic Oracle', *OBGV* 627; Cedrenus p. 304a
773 Anonymous, *M* 12.33, *K* 1117a
786 Anonymous, *M* 10.33 (see Note on poem 786)
787 Anonymous, *M* 10.40; Synesius *Epist.* 127
793 Anonymous, *M* 5.16

Maps

Greece, the Aegean Islands
and Asia Minor

0   50   100 Statute
                         Miles

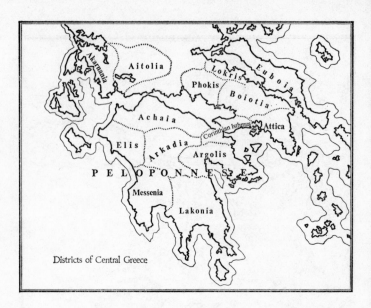

Districts of Central Greece

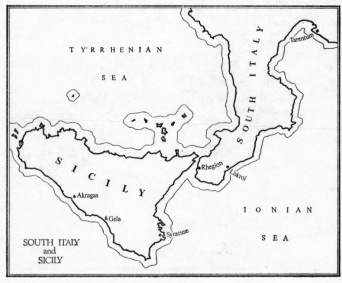

SOUTH ITALY
and
SICILY

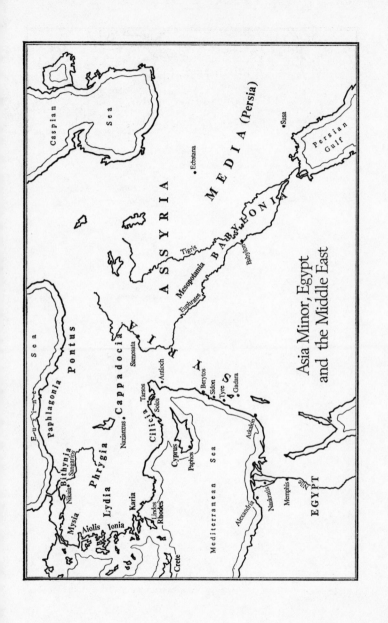

Asia Minor, Egypt and the Middle East